STO

ACPL ITEM
DISCARD

3 1833 00132 3

SO-AUH-555

9.30.77

Nonmetropolitan Urban Housing

Nonmetropolitan Urban Housing:

An Economic Analysis of Problems and Policies

Michael A. Stegman
Howard J. Sumka

Ballinger Publishing Company • Cambridge, Massachusetts
A Subsidiary of J.B. Lippincott Company

All of the material incorporated in this work was developed with the financial support of the National Science Foundation grant number GI-33649. However, any opinions, findings, conclusions or recommendations expressed herein are those of the authors and do not necessarily reflect the views of the National Science Foundation.

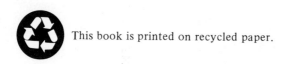 This book is printed on recycled paper.

Copyright © 1976 by The University of North Carolina. All rights reserved. No part of this publication may be reproduced, stored in a retrieval system, or transmitted in any form or by any means, electronic mechanical photocopy, recording or otherwise, without the prior written consent of the publisher.

International Standard Book Number: 0-88410-581-4

Library of Congress Catalog Card Number: 76-17023

Printed in the United States of America

Library of Congress Cataloging in Publication Data

Stegman, Michael A
    Nonmetropolitan urban housing.

    Rental housing—United States. 2. Cities and towns—United States. I. Sumka, Howard J., joint author. II. Title.
HD7293.S673   301.5'4'0973   76-17023
ISBN 0-88410-581-4

Contents

1978325

List of Figures

List of Tables

List of Exhibits

Acknowledgments

We are, of course, grateful to the RANN Division of the National Science Foundation for their financial support of the research upon which this book is based. The completion of the research, however, would have been impossible without the assistance of a staff of highly skilled and motivated people to whom we are deeply indebted. Tamar Savir was primarily responsible for the development of our household interview schedule and for managing the landlord field survey. She was assisted in the latter task by Michael Mandel, who also supervised the collection of tax appraisal data. Kathleen Gallagher's responsibilities included assisting in the field survey and preparing the data for analysis; most importantly, her editing skills were invaluable to the preparation of project working papers and the final manuscript.

In a number of areas, our work relied heavily on background papers prepared by staff assistants. Richard Goodwin examined the historical development and racial segregation patterns of the cities; Jon Heaslet performed the basic analyses of consumer housing demand; John M. Mordecai analyzed housing deprivation patterns and the operating experiences of subsidized housing projects in our study cities; and John R. Ottensmann prepared a census analysis of spatial segregation in the cities. Sylvia Hubbard and James Lott shared computer programming and data processing responsibilities. Margaret Williamson, Patricia Dehner and Donna Nunn typed the many working papers and drafts from which this report was distilled, and a special thanks is due to Norma Wood for her careful and efficient typing of the final manuscript.

In addition to the project staff, we were extremely fortunate to have been involved with a host of local officials and housing professionals who, in numerous ways, greatly facilitated our work in their cities. While many others assisted us in our efforts, we would like to single out for special acknowledgment: William Carstarphen, City Manager, and J.C. Lamm, Assistant Director of the Housing and Redevelopment Authority of Greenville, North Carolina; Don Daniels, Statesville Building Inspector, and Fran Broughton, Assistant Director of the Statesville Housing and Redevelopment Authority; Wade Gibbs, City Engineer of Lexington, North Carolina, and Rogers Nichols, Executive Director of the Lexington Housing Authority; Joseph Taylor, Kinston City Manager, Roland Paylor, Jr., Executive Director of the Kinston Housing Authority and Robert Joyner of his staff.

We would also like to thank Daniel Horvitz of the UNC Department of Biostatistics for his assistance in the design of our sampling plan. Special gratitude is extended to our colleague Hugh Knox whose critical review of our work contributed to a more thoughtful final manuscript. Finally, part of the analysis which appear in Chapter 9 was developed with the support of the U.S. Department of Housing and Urban Development under Work Order: HUD 143-75. The authors must be held accountable, however, for the analyses, their interpretation and whatever errors they may contain.

Nonmetropolitan Urban Housing

✳ *Chapter 1*

Introduction

THE NATIONAL HOUSING POLICY CONTEXT

Perhaps the most important determinant of the short-run utility of applied policy research is the degree of alteration which occurs in the relevant policy environment over the research period. When results become available, are the issues with which the research was designed to deal still dominating the attention of policy makers? While this question is endemic to a wide variety of applied research where the ultimate client is the public policy-maker, it is especially important in the housing sphere, where the macroeconomic environment is subject to substantial short-run instability and the housing policy environment is susceptible to even more abrupt changes in direction. Indeed, it may well be that one measure of the utility of applied housing research is the extent to which the empirical analyses can clarify the implications of policy alternatives which were not of foremost concern during the development of the research design.

Changes in national housing policy can best be illustrated by a review of the major housing issues that preoccupied Congress and the Administration in early 1972 and in the spring of 1975: the endpoints that mark the period of this study of the dynamics of nonmetropolitan, urban rental housing markets. Essentially, two issues dominated the policy scene in 1972, one relating to new construction, and the other to the existing stock. With respect to the former, it will be recalled that new subsidized housing starts exceeded 400,000 for the first time in 1971, and this figure was reached again in 1972 [*Sixth Annual Report on the National Housing Goal*, 1975:26]. Moreover, for the first time since the depression, the timely allocation of housing subsidy funds played a major role in stabilizing a residential construction industry that was severely shocked by the credit crunch of 1969–70. Thus, atop the Administration's housing agenda in 1972 were both a continuation of the high rates of subsidized output necessary to achieve the production levels enshrined in the landmark Housing and Urban Development Act of 1968 and an assurance to the nation's builders that they could count on a continued flow of housing subsidies to bolster their existing overhead and planned expansion of operations.

The second issue, the full implications of which were not clearly visible in early 1972, concerned the rapid erosion of housing quality in our major inner-cities and the virtual collapse of their rental housing markets, as reflected in the abandonment by investors of thousands of potentially useful dwellings which housed low and moderate income families [Sternlieb and Burchell, 1973; Stegman, 1972:63–66]. The interdependence of these two policy issues, which was not fully grasped by program planners then, is that, at an annual federal subsidy cost exceeding $1,500 per assisted dwelling, the central city housing problem could not be solved efficiently through a new production strategy alone [Solomon, 1974:149]. If losses to the stock through abandonment, disinvestment and vandalism were to continue at their then prevailing rates, housing problems would worsen despite the maintenance of unprecedented levels of subsidized new construction. Efforts had to be made to stabilize inner-city markets by developing feasible ways of preserving the existing sound and marginally substandard housing occupied by lower income families.

Over the 36 months of our research period, the nation's economic fortunes declined so substantially that the housing policy environment that existed in 1972 is all but unrecognizable at the end of 1975. Over this relatively brief period, for example, we have become engulfed in a severe inflation, and we concurrently suffer from a severe recession which has produced an unemployment rate exceeding nine percent of the civilian labor force. Accompanying the inflation has been a credit crunch of greater magnitude than those experienced in the volatile 1960s and a consequent decline in new housing starts that likely will endure for a longer period than most of the recent building slumps [Frieden and Atkinson, 1975:19–20]. Overall, public and private acquisition of long-term residential mortgage loans was down more than $11 billion in 1974 from the $91.7 billion level achieved in 1973. With mortgage interest rates hovering in the 9–11 percent range, private housing starts in 1974 were just 1.3 million, some 35 percent below 1973 levels and 43 percent lower than the 2.4 million starts recorded in 1972 [*Housing Affairs Letter*, 1975b:8, 1975e:8]. At year-end 1974, unemployment in the construction industry hit a 13-year high of 15 percent, almost twice the 1973 rate of 8.2 percent

[*Housing Affairs Letter,* 1975g:8]. During this period, too, the cost of new housing continued to increase steeply, with the average sales price of single family dwellings having risen by more than nine percent in 1974, to $38,700 [*Housing Affairs Letter,* 1975c:8].

The combination of a conservative Republican Administration which inherited potentially costly Democratic housing assistance programs and the erosion of the national economy has led to a dramatic shift in housing policy. The Administration has all but abandoned its efforts to achieve the 1968 national housing goals through a strategy of subsidized new construction. In January, 1973, not only was a moratorium placed on all subsidized housing applications, but more than 300 million dollars in already appropriated subsidy funds was impounded [*Housing Affairs Letter,* 1974a:6]. No further funding has been requested by HUD for these programs, and the new leased housing assistance program enacted into law in the Housing and Community Development Act of 1974 is stalled [*Housing Affairs Letter,* 1975a:2–3]. As a result, subsidized starts have plummeted from the 1971–72 record levels of 400,000-plus units to just one-tenth that output in 1974 [*Housing Affairs Letter,* 1975f:4; *Sixth Annual Report on the National Housing Goal,* 1975:28–29].

The Administration's stated intent has been to shift its low income housing policy focus away from new construction and toward a more efficient utilization of the existing stock. Under more favorable economic conditions, the principal component of this new strategy would be a housing allowance program under which eligible families would receive direct cash payments from the federal government which they could use to rent or purchase existing, standard housing [*Sixth Annual Report on the National Housing Goal,* 1975:15]. But even in the absence of any major housing initiatives in the near future, the federal budget deficit will be about 70 billion dollars in fiscal 1975 and at least that much in 1976. This will require a net increase in treasury borrowing in calendar 1975 of some 81 billion dollars, while during the coming fiscal year government borrowing is expected to use 80 percent of the net new money in our capital markets: an economic reality that hardly bodes well for the housing sector [*Housing Affairs Letter,* 1975b:8; 1975d:8].

The policy void resulting from the abandonment of existing subsidy programs has not been filled by market stabilization or rehabilitation programs. Indeed, in calendar year 1974, rehabilitation was begun on about 12,000 urban dwelling units across the country with the aid of federal loans or grants [*Sixth Annual Report on the National Housing Goal,* 1975:27]. Rather, the void is destined, in the short-run at least, to be filled by a reoriented new construction strategy, this one aimed at the growing needs of the middle class and the problems of the home building sector, however, rather than at the housing problems of the poor. Legislation already has been passed which grants substantial tax credits to purchasers of new housing, while Congress is deliberating on a number of bills that would provide cash rebates to new home purchasers and long-term mortgages at below-market interest rates to middle income consumers [*Housing Affairs Letter*, 1975b:2–4]. In short, this research began at a time when there was a reasonably coherent lower income housing policy with an identifiable posture towards the housing problems of metropolitan cities. Three years later, we are a nation with a much less coherent lower income housing policy that suffers from a lack of program options, an unclear definition of high priority client populations and an overall blandness that masks the true magnitude of housing deprivations across the country.

Although any bold new initiatives may be stalled by the low income policy vacuum created by our ongoing economic difficulties, programmatic activities and issues continue to demand attention and resources at all levels of government. In some local communities, for example, code enforcement problems continue to plague city officials; efforts are being made to develop municipally financed rehabilitation programs; urban renewal programs are being phased out in favor of the untested revenue sharing approach to community development; rent control laws are under consideration in some cities as one possible way of stemming the tide of rising housing prices; and in other communities, growth control and environmental protection legislation produces upward pressures on land and development costs. Several state legislatures are considering comprehensive measures which would reform the law governing landlords and tenants [Stegman and Sumka, 1975]. In addition, although state housing finance agencies are becoming increasingly important sources of long-term mortgage capital for lower income housing, the current economic slump, in combination with the federal subsidy moratorium, has caused many of them substantial problems [Stegman, 1974].

At the federal level, a crash effort is being made to work out the guidelines for a newly enacted rental assistance program at the same time the courts are preparing to rule on the legality of the Administration's impounding of appropriated housing program monies. Efforts are also underway in Congress to appropriate additional subsidy funds for programs the Administration has already rejected as unworkable. Costs continue to outstrip revenues for hundreds of local public housing authorities whose needs for operating subsidies and modernization monies continue to grow. Similar problems, including severe management difficulties, burden limited dividend and nonprofit sponsors of lower income housing, with the result that government insured mortgages have been foreclosed recently on multifamily developments covering thousands of subsidized dwellings. At the same time, numerous problems with the government's major subsidized homeownership program have resulted in high rates of housing abandonment and a substantial drain of the FHA insurance fund. National economic conditions notwithstanding, the federal government must respond to these and other housing problems.

HOUSING RESEARCH IN THE NONMETROPOLITAN CITY

In the spring of 1972, the federal policy concern, traditionally metropolitan in orientation, was becoming ever more narrowly focused on central city problems. It was at this time that we began to assess the relevance of current national housing policy concerns to nonmetropolitan communities. One principal element of our work was to determine the extent to which recent market-shattering experiences in such core cities as New York, Baltimore, Newark, Chicago, and Detroit were being felt in a class of smaller urban communities far removed from the sociopolitical forces of metropolitan areas. Underlying this effort was the concern that national housing policy was becoming unduly biased by the weight of research findings and policy feedback from major core city housing markets. When our work began, a meaningful indicator of the policy utility of our research was to be whether we were able to isolate those market forces that at least partially determine the quality and price of investor-owned housing occupied by lower-income families. With this basic understanding of nonmetropolitan rental market dynamics, it would be a relatively straightforward problem to evaluate the validity of emerging metropolitan-based market stabilization and new supply strategies for the smaller city.

This study is based upon the hypothesis that important qualitative differences exist between the structure and operations of core city and nonmetropolitan rental housing markets. From a policy standpoint, important differences would be defined as sets of market conditions which either necessitate the development of distinct intervention strategies for nonmetropolitan markets or suggest the deployment in smaller communities of traditional housing resources which have been tried and found wanting in the inner-city. Despite the applied emphasis of our work, at virtually each stage we were confronted by the fact that most conventional knowledge on housing market dynamics, as well as the supporting empirical literature, is metropolitan and central-city based. The only way of dealing with this institutionalized central-city bias was to develop nonmetropolitan benchmarks which we could then compare with published estimates of important metropolitan market conditions.

Research Design

Our first task, therefore, was to develop a sampling plan from which we could generate the data necessary to provide detailed and systematic analyses of the nonmetropolitan rental housing market. A discussion of the sampling procedures, response rates, and data collection and preparation tasks is presented in Appendix A. Briefly, the data were collected from the 25 North Carolina cities which have populations between 10,000 and 40,000 and which are not subjected to unusual economic influences that might distort the rental market. A two-stage stratified cluster design was employed to assure sampling efficiency. One city was selected from each of four strata which were defined according to census housing indicators; within each city, dwelling units were sampled from six randomly selected enumeration districts. At each stage, sampling probabilities were computed so that the final sample of 589 dwellings is self-weighting.

The rich data-base which was generated for each dwelling unit included information obtained from interviews with the occupant and the landlord, as well as from public records. Detailed characteristics of renter households and their attitudes toward their housing and landlords were collected. Data related to market experiences, modes of operation, and management practices were collected from the owners, as were cash flow and related financial and investment information. Finally, important characteristics of the structures were obtained primarily from tax appraisal records which were acquired for each dwelling. Additional structure-specific information was elicited from landlords, households, and photographs which were taken of each dwelling.

Together these data sets provide us with the capability to perform a broad set of analytic tasks relating to the estimation of important market parameters and to their interpretation within a meaningful theoretical context. Essentially, two statistical models comprise the core of our basic analyses. A rent determination model is used to explore and test specific hypotheses related to pricing patterns across the market (Chapters 5 and 6). An important variable in this model is a statistical measure of housing quality which is developed in Chapter 2 and used in our examination of differences in housing consumption patterns among household groups (Chapter 3). A model of housing demand (Chapter 3) is developed to estimate likely housing expenditure responses to changes in income and to assess the impact on housing consumption of various sociodemographic characteristics of the renter population. Less formal models are employed to assess the relative vitality of the nonmetropolitan rental investment environment (Chapter 7) and to test for important price and quality implications of nonrational behavior by landlords (Chapter 4). The estimates of the market parameters that are generated by these analyses provide the basis for testing our overall hypothesis that smaller city and core markets are characteristically different.

Policy Output

Translating basic research output into useful policy terms is by far the most challenging dimension of an applied research effort. Indeed, because the housing policy environment has changed so dramatically over our work period, the policy translation of our empirical work is made all the more difficult. Nevertheless, a national policy void does not diminish the general policy utility of our work. On the local level, our empirical analyses of housing conditions, consumption patterns, supplier characteristics and motivations, and our evaluations of existing subsidized housing programs remain relevant to such policy areas as: housing assistance or community development planning, the development of locally initiated rehabilitation programs, or improved code enforcement efforts. Similarly, our work should prove useful to state legislators and others who are engaged in the ongoing effort to define a viable state responsibility and role in housing.

With respect to national housing policy problems, we have attempted to respond to the changed environment by focusing our program analyses around specific issues that have either maintained their currency or emerged during our work period. Our applied research into the dynamics of nonmetropolitan urban rental housing markets is useful to national policy for four reasons. First, although the Administration's stance is that current economic conditions dictate that policy be primarily concerned with the macroeconomic impacts of government housing expenditures, we believe a gradual return to economic normalcy will be accompanied by a renewed federal interest in the microcommunity impacts of alternative housing strategies and programs. As we have already indicated, our analyses of nonmetropolitan market structure, landlord behavior, and housing consumption patterns provide a substantial basis for evaluating likely program impacts at the community level.

Second, even before this policy transition is complete, important segments of our empirical analyses may be useful to current policy deliberations. Our investigation of the relative strength of the smaller city rental investment environment includes benchmark cash flow data for various submarkets. For example, our analysis of the operating characteristics of privately owned new multifamily rental developments includes an assessment of the relative capacities of such housing investments to withstand alternative debt service requirements (Chapter 7). On the demand side, our estimates of income elasticities provide some sense of the magnitude of housing consumption responses to increases in income (Chapter 3). These same elasticities can be used to gauge consumption declines that would accompany income losses of primary and/or secondary wage earners; in the short run at least, it may well be that the effects of consumption declines upon housing welfare and the quality of the occupied stock are more policy relevant than the effects of consumption increases.

Third, altered policy environment notwithstanding, the serious welfare implications of severely segregated rental housing markets must be recognized. Since most empirical studies of racial segregation and resulting racially-based price premiums are metropolitan-based, our analysis of this market phenomenon in the smaller city is important to policy-making (Chapter 6).

Finally, while we adhered to our original decision to investigate supply and demand housing programs separately, the altered policy environment did influence somewhat our choices of which programs to consider and the general evaluation approach to adopt. On the demand side, we have limited our effort to a detailed analysis of the likely market impacts of a direct cash assistance program that is modeled after HUD's experimental housing allowance program now being implemented in several metropolitan areas (Chapter 9). Though current economic reversals will delay any decision to expand the experimental program, our estimates of the likely price effects of a housing allowance in nonmetropolitan cities will be useful to national policy.

Because of growing federal concern with the financial stability of existing subsidized housing projects, our supply-side analysis (Chapter 10) includes the operating characteristics of existing nonmetropolitan Section 236 projects and an evaluation of the financial state of the local housing authorities in our study cities. Although we originally intended to investigate these programs as part of our overall inquiry into nonmetropolitan rental housing, recent federal actions to abolish or seriously curtail these programs because of serious performance deficiencies increase the policy importance of our analyses. Essentially, if the difficulties alleged to be the cause of the Administration's withdrawal of program support are not found in nonmetropolitan cities, it would lend credence to the thesis that prevailing program opinion is weighted too heavily by the relatively more accessible metropolitan experiences and data. Important characteristics of the new Section 8 subsidized rental program [Housing and Community Development Act of 1974] that was enacted into law during the latter stages of our research are also investigated in the context of the program's utility as an umbrella program to replace existing efforts.

THE NONMETROPOLITAN CITY IN THE NATIONAL URBAN CONTEXT

To provide the broadest possible context for the empirical work that follows, and to establish prima facie support for the proposition that nonmetropolitan housing markets are qualitatively different from their central city counterparts, in this section we compare recent growth trends in central city, suburban, and nonmetropolitan communities across the nation. Because the use of national averages tends to obscure potentially important differences in growth patterns within cities of similar size, and since our empirical work pertains just to one subset among all nonmetropolitan cities, we also assess the extent to which our sampling of smaller cities in North Carolina deviates in significant ways from the national, nonmetropolitan experience.

Significant differences in the internal operations of nonmetropolitan and core city housing markets cannot be inferred directly from observed distinctions in their respective growth characteristics. Nevertheless, intermarket variations in such variables as population growth and headship rates, race, and income should be related to important differences in market structure and dynamics. Weicher and Simonson [1975:182], for example, have indicated that housing costs vary with the size of the housing market, prices being the highest in the largest metropolitan cities and lowest in communities of less than 50,000 people. In a related vein, de Leeuw et al. [1974:28] suggest that growth rates are positively related both to housing prices and to supply elasticities; that is, prices should be higher and supplier responses to price changes relatively greater in high growth cities. Moreover, because prices in the existing stock are, in part, a function of minimum supply costs for new housing, used housing should also command relatively higher prices in communities characterized by a combination of high minimum supply costs and high growth rates [de Leeuw et al., 1974:7]. Finally, it is widely recognized that a community's racial characteristics and the relative changes in its racial composition over time impact upon local housing market operations. For example, it has been argued that population redistribution along racial lines, such as that which has characterized the recent growth patterns of central cities and their suburbs, creates and reinforces mechanisms of injustice related to the housing market and the distribution of housing services [Morrison, 1972:22].

According to the U.S. Commission on Population Growth and the American Future, "the spatial distribution of the American people changed in important ways during the last decade," creating problems of growth and decline and of racial separation [Morrison, 1972:15]. Overall, the trend toward metropolitan expansion continued unabated, with the result that in 1970 about seven of every ten Americans lived within metropolitan areas. This process, however, was not accompanied by growth in the central core. Quite to the contrary, metropolitan suburbs grew 34 percent during this period while the central city population remained nearly constant [Morrison, 1972:19]. Indeed, as has been widely reported, "an unprecedented number of the nation's central cities have ceased to grow, and are in fact losing population"; one-third of the nation's 292 central cities declined in size over the decade, losing in excess of two million people [Lowry, 1971:3–4]. In contrast, the average nonmetropolitan city grew by a moderate three percent during the past decade, while the mean growth rate in North Carolina was a slightly higher five percent (Table 1–1).

Although differences in relative growth rates may induce different kinds of stresses within local housing markets, the changing characteristics of the resident populations are equally important determinants of intercity variations in housing market operations. Changes in racial composition, income, and the propensity of populations to form households all affect the operation of the housing market. We have already alluded to the fact that the continued growth of the metropolitan population has further widened racial separation. Indeed, by 1970, it was clear that "the city line had become an economic and social boundary between the races" [Morrison, 1972:22]. Between 1960 and 1970, the white central city population actually declined by more than five percent, core population stability being a function of a 33 percent growth rate among blacks (Table 1–1). Though in 1970 there were in excess of one million more blacks in suburbia than ten years earlier, the suburbs drew whites away from the central cities in such record numbers that the black proportion of the total suburban population remained constant at around 4.5 percent.

While it is generally acknowledged that "central cities and suburbs alike have become specialized along racial, ethnic, and class lines" [Morrison, 1972:22], little is known of the racial composition and dynamics of smaller cities, particularly those far removed from the metropolitan orbit. From a relatively small base in 1960, the nation's nonmetropolitan black population grew by less than 70,000 during the decade, a growth rate of five percent (Table 1–1). That blacks constituted nine percent of the total nonmetropolitan population in both 1960 and 1970 implies a stability among both black and white populations that is lacking in the central city. This stability is matched, albeit at expectedly higher base levels, among North Carolina's smaller cities. There, the 1960 black representation of 27 percent remained virtually unchanged in 1970, be-

Table 1-1. Selected Characteristics of Populations in Metropolitan and Nonmetropolitan Cities, 1970, and Changes Between 1960 and 1970

	U.S. Urbanized Areas		U.S. Non-Metro Cities*	N.C. Non-Metro Cities*
	Central City	Urban Fringe		
Total Population, 1970 (in thousands)	63,912	54,527	16,618	651
Increase 1960–70	1.5%	33.5%	2.8%	5.3%
Change in White Population, 1960–70	−5.4%	+32.3%	+1.9%	+10.9%
Change in Black Population, 1960–70	+32.8%	+45.5%	+4.7%	+6.3%
Black Population, 1970	20.5%	4.7%	9.4%	26.9%
Ratio of Household to Population Increase, 1960–70	10.67	1.52	2.57	2.08
Mean Household Size, 1970	2.89	3.26	2.98	3.05
Change 1960–70	−5.3%	−4.4%	−6.0%	−10.0%
Median Household Income, 1970	$7,197	$10,204	$6,038	$5,478
Median Income of Black Households, 1970	$5,297	$5,929	$3,338	NA
All Households Below Poverty, 1970	16.1%	8.1%	17.8%	19.8%
Black Households Below Poverty, 1970	28.7%	23.7%	43.2%	31.4%

* All places of 10,000 to 50,000 population.

Sources: Morrison, 1972:19.
U.S. Bureau of the Census, 1970c; 1970d; 1970e; 1960a; 1960b.

cause the six percent black growth rate was almost matched by identical growth among whites.

In the case of nonmetropolitan, suburban, and central core cities, the trend toward smaller household sizes and higher headship rates is evident. In central cities, the number of households grew at 10 times the rate of the total population, while in the suburbs, the ratio was only 1.5. In nonmetropolitan communities, however, households grew two and a half times as much as total population, and among North Carolina cities the ratio was slightly over two. Thus, despite relatively low population growth rates, the national trend toward the formation of larger numbers of independent housing consumers from a given population pool is also strikingly evident in nonmetropolitan cities. Overall, nonmetropolitan cities experienced slightly greater declines in average household size during the decade than did any other city size class. In 1970, average household size was highest among suburbanites (3.26) and lowest among central city populations (2.89). Nonmetropolitan cities in general, and North Carolina cities in particular, still average slightly larger households than do central cities.

Expectedly, household incomes are highest in the rapidly growing suburbs, where the incidence of poverty among both blacks and whites is the lowest (Table 1-1). Mean household income in central cities is 13 percent higher than in nonmetropolitan communities; furthermore, despite the national attention paid to the economic plight of central city blacks, their nonmetropolitan counterparts across the country are much more seriously deprived. Whereas slightly fewer than 30 percent of all central city black households have incomes at or below the poverty level, the corresponding figure in nonmetropolitan cities is 43 percent. From the standpoint of local housing market conditions, the lower poverty incidence among nonmetropolitan blacks in North Carolina (31%) is offset by the larger black population in these cities.

Throughout the literature on national population problems and policy alternatives, the plight and future of smaller cities are given substantial attention. It is not our purpose to support the proposition that nonmetropolitan cities represent nascent growth centers that can, with appropriate public support, attract industry and population away from overcrowded metropolitan complexes. On the other hand, it is important that the term "nonmetropolitan city" not automatically trigger thoughts of staggering economic decline and high rates of personal despair among resident populations consisting "mostly of remnants left behind after successive waves of departure . . . generally those least able to cope with the unfavorable conditions responsible for depopulation" [Morrison, 1972:23]. Despite the relative income disparities between metropolitan and nonmetropolitan cities, for example, the decline in the proportion of families with incomes under $5,000 has kept pace in the small city with that in central cities or suburbs. Finally, the fact that the median education level achieved by nonmetropolitan adults is virtually identical to the national central city norm of 12 years does not support the contention that the smaller city population is a remnant of a bygone era. The fact is that 15 percent of the nation's population lives in nonmetropolitan cities and that, while population trends have varied and metropolitan growth rates tend to be higher, "the predominant trend is one of growth" [Fuguitt, 1972:124].

This cursory analysis of national growth patterns suggests that recent nonmetropolitan experiences differ in significant ways from those in metropolitan areas. Central city markets must adjust to severe reductions in overall housing demand brought about both by absolute population declines and by the increased concentration of lower income families who live there. In these unstable environments, market processes are distorted by serious negative externalities, and the adjustment of the stock to the reduced demand will occur through downward filtering. In contrast, in rapidly growing suburban markets, short-run prices generally exceed long-term equilibrium levels and the relative quantity of stock per capita is less than the desired quantity. As a result, upward price pressures are generated throughout the stock. Although price rises will be moderated by an absolute expansion of supply, where minimum supply costs are high, stock expansion will not always result in a softened price structure in the lower reaches of the inventory.

At the risk of oversimplifying, we suggest that the population stability which is characteristic of the smaller city is consistent with housing markets which closely approximate conditions of long-run equilibrium. In such markets, the moving forces behind long-run changes in the supply derive from secular increases in real income, changes in headship rates, and the depreciation of dwellings over time. In such stable or slowly growing communities, supply responses to changing prices would be relatively low; racial segregation, relatively high; and racial composition, fairly stable. In addition, in the absence of demand influences which exert upward price pressures throughout the existing stock, we would expect moderate quality housing in the nonmetropolitan city to command prices significantly lower than the costs prevailing for new housing.

RESIDENTIAL SEGREGATION IN THE NONMETROPOLITAN CITY

The aggregated census data presented above indicate important population-related factors which distinguish the nonmetropolitan city from metropolitan areas. In the chapters that follow, we shall present detailed analyses of disaggregated data specific to the nonmetropolitan rental market. Although both of these approaches provide insights into the nature of the nonmetropolitan city, much of what is unique about cities of this size relates to the pattern of their past growth and development. Although it is beyond the scope of this work to delve into the social and economic history of these cities, our market analyses will demonstrate that it is critical to understand at least the dynamics of race in the market. The black minority of these cities accounts for nearly one-third of the population, but its size is not the result of a recent influx of blacks; over the past 50 years, blacks have constituted a relatively constant proportion of the total population (Table 1–2). Since 1920, the rate of growth of the black population has, in fact, been steadily declining, and in each decade, it has been less than that of the white population. Although some of the white growth has occurred as a result of annexation, even if we were to consider the population changes within the existing city boundaries, the population growth and racial change figures for the small city stand in sharp contrast to the experiences of metropolitan cities during the recent past. In the latter, the black population growth rate often exceeded that of the whites even in the 1930s, while the two decades from 1940–60 were characterized by substantial changes in the racial composition of the central cities [Taeuber and Taeuber, 1965:115–119].

The existing pattern of segregation is, in large part, a function of the late nineteenth century industrialization of these cities, which in general distinguishes the nonmetropolitan southern city from its older, metropolitan counterparts. The social and economic infrastructures of the cities were developed during the period from 1870–1915, when evolution of cotton, tobacco, lumber and flour industries provided the basis for a five-fold increase in population. Although it is difficult to trace the origins of the black populations in these cities, it is likely that the major influx of blacks occurred at this time and was accommodated by the development

Table 1–2.   Growth Rate of Population by Race 1920–70

Year	Population Increase Over Decade			Black Population as Percent of Total
	White	Black	Total	
1920	—	—	—	32.0%
1930	45.0%	36.1%	42.1%	30.7
1940	19.7	30.2	22.9	32.5
1950	30.6	27.1	29.4	31.9
1960	34.3	18.1	29.1	29.2
1970	8.9	1.6	6.8	27.7
Change 1920–70	231.4	170.3	211.8	

Source: Adapted from U.S. Bureau of the Census, Census of Population: Population Reports, 1920–70.

of segregated clusters of cheaply built housing. Historically, the open and explicit racial prejudice that persisted for so long affected the spatial location of blacks and whites in a way that is still apparent.

Insofar as race is concerned, the neighborhood change processes and housing allocation systems in these cities are sharply different from those in both southern and nonsouthern metropolitan cities. As we document below, most existing black neighborhoods were present at least as early as the 1920s, and there has been virtually no evidence of substantial neighborhood change. In the remainder of this section we present a more systematic analysis of neighborhood change and existing segregation which will provide the background for our analyses of both housing consumption differences between blacks and whites and price discrimination. From our policy analyses it is clear that race per se may be a critical factor in the achievement of program objectives. In many respects, the current policy significance of race can be attributed to a long history of discrimination not only in housing, but throughout the economic and social structure of these cities.

Neighborhood Change

The racial stability of nonmetropolitan cities suggests that they have not experienced the abrupt social and economic changes that have accompanied racial transition in metropolitan areas. More importantly for our work, it also suggests that the process by which housing is allocated to blacks in these cities has been very different from the frequently observed central city pattern of racial invasion and succession. It does not, however, imply that the nonmetropolitan city is any more or less segregated than the central city. To examine both the segregation and neighborhood change issues, we used city directories to map the locations of black households for three ten-year intervals covering the period 1927–57.[1] By plotting the location of designated black households on a block-by-block basis, we were able to note the pattern of black occupancy during each period. In all cases, each block, defined as one side of the street located between two cross-streets, was either exclusively white- or black-occupied; we can, therefore, assume that segregation is accurately described by the distributional pattern of black-occupied block faces. A black neighborhood is defined as a concentration of contiguous block faces which are occupied by black households, and in virtually every case there are no interior blocks occupied by whites. A comparison of the plots between the ten-year intervals enabled us to trace the movement of the black population throughout the 30-year period. In addition, this mapping procedure provided information which could be used to estimate the extent to which individual dwelling units changed from white to black occupancy.[2]

In 1927, there were nine identifiable concentrations of black house-holds, which apparently were never occupied by white households (Table 1–3). According to 1930 Sanborn maps, these areas were characterized by narrow, often unpaved streets; the houses typically were small, single family, frame structures. It is highly unlikely that these neighborhoods or that these houses, which were capable of satisfying only the most basic shelter needs, were ever occupied by white families. In fact, one of the early street directories identified an area of town as "a colored settle-ment" without listing the names and addresses of the households. Had this been a previously white area, at least the street addresses would have been listed, since city directories are compiled by updating and amending previous editions. Thus, it is reasonable to conclude that the black neighborhoods as they existed at the end of the 1920s were designed and constructed exclusively for blacks.

By 1957, the number of black neighborhoods had increased from nine to thirteen. Of the four additional neighborhoods, three developed be-tween 1927–37, and the fourth during 1947–57. During this period the total number of block faces occupied by blacks increased by about 55 percent, while the black population nearly tripled during the corresponding census period (1930–60). Thus, the bulk of the new housing demand among blacks was satisfied not by outward expansion, but by a "filling-in" of existing black-occupied block faces. Moreover, a substantial por-tion of the areas that became black-occupied during this period were previously undeveloped and did not undergo racial transition. As late as the 1950s, for example, a 15-block development was constructed on a large tract of vacant land adjacent to an existing black area.

Table 1–3. Geographic Distribution of the Black Population 1927–57

Size of Neighborhood (No. Block Faces)	Percentage Distribution of Black-Occupied Block Faces by Size of Neighborhood				Percentage Increase in No. Blocks 1927–57
	Year				
	1927	1937	1947	1957	
125+	19.9%	19.7%	36.1%	62.3%	386.9%
100–124	33.3	42.1	27.4	11.6	−45.9
50– 99	33.5	25.5	23.3	10.8	−49.8
9– 49	10.2	8.7	9.6	12.2	86.4
1– 8	3.2	4.0	3.7	3.2	52.4
Total No. Block Faces	654	778	843	1,016	
Increase During Period	—	19.0%	8.4%	20.5%	55.4%

Most of the expansion of black neighborhoods that did occur took place in already existing and relatively large black neighborhoods. Nearly two-thirds of the block faces that became black-occupied during this 30-year period were contiguous with areas that in the late 1920s already included more than 50 block faces. Within this group of large black neighborhoods, however, growth has been concentrated in the largest areas. Contiguous neighborhoods of 125 or more block faces included about 20 percent of the black housing during 1927–37; by 1957, nearly two-thirds of the black area was included in neighborhoods of this size. In contrast, the more recently developed black areas remain relatively small; ranging in size from 12 to 22 block faces, they accounted for less than seven percent of the area occupied by nonwhites in 1957. The number of scattered blocks in which nonwhites are housed (i.e., clusters of eight or less) has remained virtually constant since 1937 and accounted for only 3.2 percent of the black area in 1957.

This pattern of neighborhood growth suggests that invasion and succession have not been important elements in the racial dynamics of these cities, a proposition which is further supported by additional information available from the city directories. In order to estimate the extent of racial conversion, each address occupied by a black household was compared with the same address in the preceding directory to determine the race of the previous occupant.[3] Of the nearly 2,500 new black households listed by the directories during this period, only 2.7 percent lived in houses previously occupied by whites. Even acknowledging the possibility of substantial undercounts, this small number of conversions leads to the conclusion that, by and large, the demand for black housing was satisfied by new construction within black neighborhoods.

This is consistent with a general trend of direct new construction for blacks in the South which Taeuber and Taeuber [1965:124–5] attribute "to the lesser volume of Negro migration" and to the fact that, in contrast to the situation in the North, segregated black areas in the South "have had considerable land available for new construction." In part, they suggest that the availability of vacant land in black areas may have been the result of informal racial zoning of the cities. The net result is that while in northern cities blacks replace whites in built-up areas adjacent to existing black neighborhoods, "the pressure for Negroes to occupy dwellings formerly occupied by whites is less in southern . . . cities" [Taeuber and Taeuber, 1965:125]. Another explanation of this phenomenon that is relevant at least to the small southern city is the absence of zoning, building, and occupancy codes until the mid-1950s, which made the construction of housing for low income blacks financially feasible.

Although the introduction of housing standards probably removed the profitability of new construction for low income families, the conversion of units from white to black occupancy was probably not an important element in the racial dynamics of these cities even during the 1960s. The number of black-occupied dwellings increased by 10 percent during the last decade to a total of 7,203 for the four cities [U.S. Bureau of the Census, 1970e; 1960c]. During that period, however, more than 730 new public housing units became available for occupancy. These new units are exclusively black-occupied and are located in black neighborhoods or in previously undeveloped areas of the city; they were sufficient in number to accommodate the increase of about 655 new black households.

The Extent of Segregation

It is not possible to estimate for nonmetropolitan cities a measure of racial segregation that is directly comparable to segregation indexes which have been computed for metropolitan areas. Census data are not available on a block basis for small cities, and an index of dissimilarity computed using enumeration district data would understate the level of segregation relative to the figures presented by the Taeubers [1965] for metropolitan cities.[4] However, an intuitive sense of the extent of segregation can be obtained by simply noting the degree to which people occupy neighborhoods which contain primarily members of their own race. More than one-third of the nonmetropolitan rental stock is occupied by black households, and in a completely unsegregated market we would expect the occupants of rental units to be randomly distributed. Ignoring the effects of the socioeconomic correlates of race that may contribute to segregation, and neglecting the problems inherent in defining neighborhood boundaries, we would expect to find each household occupying an area that is approximately one-third black.[5] In the nonmetropolitan city, however, nearly three-quarters of the renter households live in ED's in which black households occupy either fewer than 10 percent or more than 60 percent of the total rental units (Table 1–4).

A better understanding of the importance of segregation can be obtained from the block analysis we discussed earlier. By the end of the 1950s, black households occupied a combined total of over 1,000 block faces in the four cities (Table 1–3). Each city contained two to four identifiable neighborhoods ranging in size from 12 to 198 contiguous block faces. In addition, blacks occupied a small number of scattered locations which included a total of only 32 block faces. Of the 13 black neighborhoods, seven were comprised of 50 or more block faces and contained about 85 percent of the area occupied by blacks. Not only are black households concentrated in large, contiguous neighborhoods, but the neighborhoods themselves are generally proximate to each other. In one city, for example, 95 percent of the black-occupied area in the late 1950s consisted of three neighborhoods adjacent to the central business district

Table 1–4. Spatial Segregation of Rental Households by Enumeration District*

Percent of Rental Units Occupied by Black Households	Percent of Enumeration Districts	Percent of Rental Units
0– .9%	40.9%	28.9%
1.0– 9.9	11.8	16.3
10.0– 19.9	7.5	8.3
20.0– 39.9	7.5	8.3
40.0– 59.9	7.5	9.8
60.0– 79.9	9.7	12.6
80.0–100.0	15.1	15.8
Total	100.0	100.0

* Based on data for 25 cities sampled.
Source: U.S. Bureau of the Census, 1970f, File A.

and separated by natural boundaries and areas of nonresidential uses. In another city virtually all of the black population was contained in two very large neighborhoods, which apparently have been growing together in recent years. Although ED boundaries are not coincident with the boundaries of these neighborhoods, the area between the neighborhoods has been filling in with black households [U.S. Bureau of the Census, 1970f]. Moreover, all the public housing units in this city, with the exception of one elderly project and a few scattered-site units, have been located within or between these neighborhoods. Whether the location of public housing followed, anticipated, or in fact caused this filling-in trend, it is clear that the local government has acted to encourage the further concentration of blacks.

From the standpoint of racial segregation patterns, southern cities can be usefully classified according to whether they developed before or after the Civil War [Taeuber and Taeuber, 1965:190]. A number of writers have noted that blacks tend to be less segregated in older southern cities due to the historical pattern of small settlements of blacks, primarily servants, having been located near the homes of their white employers. Newer southern cities, whose spatial growth has been determined by the economic forces of industrialization, tend to be characterized by large concentrations of blacks.[6] These observations were tested by Schnore and Evenson [1966] who found that, controlling for the size of the city and the percentage which is nonwhite, the older a southern metropolitan city, the less highly segregated it is likely to be. This relationship did not hold for cities outside the South, and it was more discernible for cities located in the South Atlantic subregion than in the South Central.

These historical trends apparently affected southern nonmetropolitan cities as well. In 1880, the four cities had an average population of about

920 persons, and the industrial expansion of the next 30 years stimulated rapid growth that produced an average population of nearly 5,000 persons by 1910. Although the size of these cities was small then and remains modest today, their spatial patterns and physical infrastructures were developed under the economic influence of late nineteenth century forces of industrialization. Their sharply segregated residential living pattern is thus entirely consistent with the observations of urban historians. Although it is not always possible to account for them explicitly, the influences of these historical factors on both the spatial patterns and housing stock characteristics in these cities are reflected throughout our analyses.

NOTES TO CHAPTER 1

1. For each of the four cities included in our study, a directory for each of the periods 1925–28, 1936–39, 1947–49, and 1956–59 was consulted. For one city, a 1951 volume was used since there was not one available for either of the periods around 1948 or 1958, and the data were extrapolated to the missing date. By the end of the 1950s, the racial designation was dropped from the directories [Baldwin Directory Company; Hill Directory Company; Southern Directory Company].

2. A number of errors are, of course, inherent in this work. Particularly in the earlier volumes, the street directories may be incomplete and may contain imprecise designations of areas within the city. It is also likely that the racial designations contain some inaccuracies. These factors may produce some errors in the location of individual black-occupied parcels or block-faces, and they probably result in an understatement of the extent of black occupancy. The maps are, however, good representations of the locational pattern of black residences for each of the years studied, and their accuracy is greatest for the later years.

3. Since the data were collected over ten-year intervals, housing that was built for whites and converted to black occupancy within a decade would be recorded as new construction specifically for blacks, thus understating the extent of conversion. It is likely, however, for two reasons that this would not result in a very large error. First, the growth of black neighborhoods has, as we have seen, been characterized by marginal expansion at the borders; little new construction for whites would have occurred within or even near black areas. Second, new housing built for whites would likely have been beyond the price range blacks could afford. Another potential source of error lies in the incompleteness of the directories, particularly in black neighborhoods in the early years. Many of the addresses which appear for the first time in later directories may have been in existence ten years earlier, but simply were not recorded. This would, of course, inflate the number of new black households for a given interval.

4. For the four cities, the average index is about 76 using the ED as the areal unit. This figure is probably 10 to 20 percent lower than it would be if blocks were used as the areal unit.

5. A more detailed analysis indicated that if renters in these markets were spatially distributed according to income alone, blacks would comprise from 30 to

40 percent of every area. Given that black households constitute 34 percent of the renter population, this suggests that socioeconomic differences account for little of the observed racial segregation [Sumka, 1976:73–7].

6. Schnore and Evenson [1966] present a brief summary of the more relevant observations of those who have studied the urban South.

Chapter 2

The Rental Housing Stock

INTRODUCTION

The housing welfare of a population cannot be gauged solely from an evaluation of the conditions of the housing stock.

Nevertheless, because the nature of the housing stock is relatively fixed in the short run, at any given time the range of available housing opportunities is largely determined by the characteristics of the existing inventory. Thus, being able to differentiate the housing stock in meaningful ways is basic to building an understanding of price and consumption patterns in the rental housing market.

Although we might approach this problem from a number of perspectives, most important to our subsequent analysis is an ability to distinguish that portion of the housing stock that meets or exceeds some minimum standard of acceptable quality from that portion that does not. After we briefly summarize important characteristics of the nonmetropolitan rental stock, we will use these stock attributes to operationalize and measure housing quality concepts that will be employed throughout the remainder of our work. Baseline estimates of housing adequacy are derived from an analysis of the extent to which rental units fail to satisfy the various criteria specified in typical housing occupancy codes. Although these estimates are derived in part from subjective evaluations of dwelling quality, they provide an important perspective on housing conditions in the nonmetropolitan rental market.

A more complete analysis of housing quality variations is then performed in order to develop an indicator that is more objective and better suited to our analytical needs. Utilizing structural and related information obtained from tax appraisal records, we derive a summary measure of housing quality; this statistical construct allows us to reduce a large number of objective dwelling characteristics into a single index of the physical attributes of a dwelling. Not only is the index a useful device for exploring differences in housing consumption across the market, but the development of a continuous variable of housing quality is an essential element of the econometric analyses of market structure and price determination processes which are presented in Chapters 5 and 6. A substantial portion of this chapter thus is devoted to the statistical analysis required to derive the index and validate its utility. This analysis involves, first, an evaluation of the consistency and reliability of the tax appraiser's assessment of building value, which is accomplished by relating the objective characteristics of the unit to the appraisal valuation through multiple regression techniques. The utility and validity of the index are then verified by reference to external criteria related to housing quality. In conjunction with the index, these criteria are employed to develop an operational definition of substandard housing. Finally, an analysis of rehabilitation potential is provided through an examination of the relationship between rent and quality.

HOUSING CONDITIONS IN THE RENTAL MARKET

Characteristics of the Stock

One of the most distinguishing characteristics of the housing stock in the nonmetropolitan southern city is the predominance of single family detached dwellings, which account for about 59 percent of all rental units. Two unit structures (duplexes) represent an additional 22 percent of the stock, and half of the multifamily dwellings are in buildings containing six or fewer units. This structure-type distribution sharply distinguishes the nonmetropolitan southern city from metropolitan inner cities, although it seems likely that the importance of single family structures is as much a function of geography as it is of the city size. In 1970, for example, only 28 percent of the rental stock of all U.S. urban areas was in single family detached structures, but for the urban South, the figure was nearly double the national average [U.S. Bureau of the Census, 1970e]. In any case, these cities are characteristically different from the metropolitan areas that have been the focus of most recent empirical housing research. Our study cities are not dominated by the tenements which characterize central Newark [Sternlieb, 1966] or the complexes of six-story walk-ups and high-rise buildings that mark other major northeastern and midwestern cities.

Theoretically, at least, nonmetropolitan rental market dynamics are influenced by the dominance of the detached single family dwelling. In their seminal work on rental market structure, for example, Blank and Winnick [1953] distinguished the single family stock from the rest of the rental stock. They hypothesized that, in general, rents for single family units would be more responsive to changes in short-run demand because vacancy losses cannot be averaged over a large number of units as they can in the multifamily stock. Since at any point in time a single family dwelling is either fully occupied or 100 percent vacant, during periods of declining demand, the owner is more likely than owners of other types of dwellings to lower rents in a continuing effort to amortize at least some portion of his fixed costs. Moreover, because the tenant is traditionally responsible for routine maintenance chores in single family dwellings, slackened demand is more likely to result in relatively greater rent reductions than in the multifamily stock where continuing occupants expect to receive a constant flow of housing services. Single family dwellings may move relatively freely and at virtually no conversion cost from owner to rental tenure, thus increasing the potential for significantly larger short-run variations in the size of the rental inventories in markets characterized by such housing. Finally, since investment in an individual single family dwelling may not require a great deal of risk capital, there is a higher probability that rental markets dominated by such housing will also be characterized by very small scale, nonprofessional landlords. To the extent that this is the case, this ownership pattern should be reflected in pricing practices, rent-quality relationships, tenant selection processes, and in related management aspects of rental housing operations.

Although the existing stock in the nonmetropolitan city continues to be dominated by the single family house, it is important to recognize that new additions to the supply are weighted more heavily by multifamily structures, probably a consequence of rising land and construction costs. While single family units accounted for over 40 percent of the private rental housing built during 1955–65, only one-quarter of the post-1965 housing is in single family structures. Although this is still a sizable fraction, some of these units may be in the rental stock only temporarily, or they originally may have been intended for owner occupancy. The growing importance of multifamily housing in these markets, however, is indicated by its 40 percent share of the private new construction market during the period 1965–72.

The following analyses deal with the measurement of housing quality, but even the most casual observers of the nonmetropolitan market would conclude that the overall quality of the rental stock is low. In terms of the quality of original construction, for example, nearly 63 percent of all rental units were rated by tax appraisers as being below average or worse.

In comparison, tax appraisers judged one-quarter of the rental stock to be in poor or very poor condition as a result of maintenance deficiencies (Table 2-1). In both cases single family dwellings fare the worst.

The mean 31-year age of the entire inventory is similar to the U.S. urban average for rental housing [U.S. Bureau of the Census, 1970a]. While single-unit structures are slightly older than duplex and apartment buildings, the six- and nine-year differences in average age do not appear to be large enough to explain the respective quality differences. Within the multifamily sector, the 25 year average masks the dichotomy between two distinct housing types. Single family conversions, which account for approximately one-third of the apartment units, were built an average of 48 years ago. All other apartments, most of which are garden apartment structures containing ten or more dwellings, have a mean age of only 15 years.

In terms of the nonshelter services provided by the dwelling unit, the nonmetropolitan rental stock is also seriously deficient (Table 2-1). Only 30 percent of the stock contain central heating systems, and about nine percent have built-in floor or wall furnaces. In the vast majority of the stock, and particularly among single family units, heat is provided by inefficient, tenant-supplied space heaters. The high rate of heating deficiencies implies that much of the stock is not capable of supporting the major expense of installing any form of central heating. Although one might hypothesize that the need for central heat is minimized by the mild southern climate, over two-thirds of the owner-occupied units in these cities do have central heat [U.S. Bureau of the Census, 1970b]. Finally, all the units are served by city water and sewer, but 19 percent do not have complete bathrooms (a separate room containing a sink, tub or shower,

Table 2–1. Selected Characteristics of the Rental Housing Stock

	Single Family Detached	Duplex	Multi-family	Total
Mean Age (yrs.)	34	28	25	31
Mean Dwelling Size (sq. ft.)	1,141	904	805	1,025
Mean Lot Size per Dwelling (sq. ft.)	8,748	4,737	2,559	6,675
Percent with Central Heat	18.5	34.9	63.1	30.1
Percent with Complete Bathroom	77.4	88.5	98.2	83.8
Percent Rated as Below Average Construction*	77.5	55.9	25.9	62.8
Percent Rated as Being in Poor or Very Poor Condition*	82.9	12.9	11.7	25.7

* Tax appraiser rating.

and a commode). In lieu of bathrooms they have toilet rooms and lavatories—many of which are add-on features installed to conform with relatively recently enacted city health standards.

In short, large portions of the nonmetropolitan rental stock are capable of providing only minimal flows of shelter services. Nowhere is this more obviously the case than in the lowest quality market sector, which is dominated by shanties that are appropriately referred to as "shotgun shacks" or "rabbit boxes." This nonmetropolitan analog to the core city tenement and conversion is primarily single family, but includes some duplexes, and accounts for nearly nine percent of the rental stock. These dwellings are small, wood frame structures, which typically have open pier foundations and metal roofs. Two-thirds of these units contain less than 800 square feet of interior space, while one-third are built at a density of 16 dwellings to the acre. None has a landlord-provided heat source, and only 30 percent have a complete bathroom.

Although one would expect to find houses of this type in southern rural areas, their presence in these cities is not an anomaly of the annexation process, since virtually all are located in the central portions of the city. Nor are they holdovers from the distant past; over 60 percent have been built since 1950. Rather, they are a result of direct construction for the poor in a market where minimum building codes and zoning ordinances have only recently arrived. These units were apparently constructed originally for blacks, for whom they remain an important source of housing. Virtually all are black-occupied and, conversely, they house 24 percent of the black population. That they have lasted this long and continue to have high occupancy levels reflects the shortage of housing opportunities for low-income blacks and a lack of vigorous enforcement of minimum health and safety standards by the city.

Housing Codes and Deficiency Rates

Although this brief description of the rental stock indicates a wide range of housing deficiencies, housing adequacy can be measured only with reference to a set of criteria that establish minimum requirements for either the presence or the performance of certain facilities and features. Attempts to operationalize the concept of adequate or standard housing are often undermined by difficulties related to the precise measurement of objective criteria. The task of defining a minimum housing standard is further confounded by the relative nature of the concept of housing adequacy. As the standard of living enjoyed by a particular population increases, its housing expectations also increase. The tendency, therefore, is for the definition of substandard housing to change considerably as general income levels increase. An equally serious problem is that rising standards "permeate society gradually" [Grigsby and Rosenburg,

1975:38]. The definition of "standard," therefore, varies across communities.

The measurement difficulties are illustrated by the experience of the Bureau of the Census, which provided indicators of structural quality for the nation's housing stock from 1940 through 1960. The classification system was changed somewhat for each census until 1970 when it was eliminated entirely. In 1960 a dilapidated structure was defined as one which

> has one or more serious deficiencies or was of inadequate original construction so that it provided inadequate shelter or endangered the safety of the occupants . . . [or] had a combination of minor deficiencies to the extent that it did not provide protection against the elements or was physically unsafe . . . [U.S. Bureau of the Census, 1967:1].

That there are inherent ambiguities in these definitions is eminently clear. Without the ability to define and itemize specific structural defects of inadequate facilities, the subjectivity of the evaluation severely limited its utility as a measure of the housing welfare of the population. An evaluation of the 1960 Census data on housing quality indicated the importance of these ambiguities in quantitative terms. Random error caused the misclassification of over one-third of the dwellings which were rated as dilapidated in 1960, and apparent enumerator bias resulted in a net undercount of over one million occupied dilapidated dwellings [U.S. Bureau of the Census, 1967:11].

One of the pioneering attempts to delineate specific, measurable housing standards was that of the American Public Health Association (APHA), which developed an appraisal method for measuring housing quality using 30 basic housing principles essential to the "physical, social, and mental health" of the occupants [American Public Health Association, 1939]. These principles were operationalized into specific measures of housing adequacy and were then converted into a penalty point scoring system. The score assigned to each of the specific dwelling attributes is intended to penalize dwellings for failing "to meet a reasonable contemporary housing standard" [American Public Health Association, 1945:12]. The definition of substandard can then be based on the total point score or on the presence of one or more of seven basic deficiencies which were identified as being unambiguous indicators of inadequacy (e.g., no indoor plumbing or excessive deterioration) [American Public Health Association, 1946:17].

The APHA standards provide the foundation of a recommended model ordinance for housing occupancy [U.S. Department of Health, Education, and Welfare, 1969]. The general format and most specific elements of this ordinance are embodied in numerous local codes and in the Southern Standard Housing Code [Southern Building Code Congress, 1969], and these same criteria are used to define standard existing housing units under both the Experimental Housing Allowance Program and Section 8 of the 1974 Housing and Community Development Act [U.S. Department of Housing and Urban Development, 1975a, Appendix II; U.S. Department of Housing and Urban Development, 1975b, Appendix 7]. Rather than evaluating and scoring the various dwelling features essential to a healthful living environment, these codes specify minimum acceptibility criteria each unit must meet; those failing to satisfy any one of the specifications are classified as substandard. While we cannot measure all of the dimensions of quality as they are specified by the various codes, it is useful to summarize the basic requirements for standard housing. The following criteria represent, in abbreviated form, the minimum acceptibility criteria as they appear in the administrative regulations for Section 8 of the 1974 Housing Act and in the guidelines for the housing allowance experiment. As such, they at least implicitly reflect a broad-based national housing standard.

1. *Plumbing:* An adequate water supply; a private, indoor flush toilet; wash basin and tub or shower with hot and cold running water.
2. *Kitchen:* Private kitchen area with adequate space for food preparation and waste storage and disposal; sink with hot and cold running water; stove and refrigerator.
3. *Heat:* Safe, operating heating facilities adequate to maintain a healthy environment; unvented fuel-burning heaters and units heated mainly by portable electric room heaters are unacceptable.
4. *Electric:* Approved electric service must be available; generally one or two electric convenience outlets per room.
5. *Ventilation and Light:* One window or skylight per room.
6. *Access:* Safe, direct means of egress; usually two per dwelling.
7. *Sanitation:* Free of vermin and rodent infestation.
8. *Interior Condition:* Wall surfaces free of loose material, holes or other serious damage; no missing parts or holes in floor; no buckling or movement in floor under walking stress.
9. *Structure and Exterior:* Roof structure firm and weathertight; no leaning or buckling of walls; wall surfaces free of serious defects and weathertight.

In general, these specifications are also contained in the Southern Standard Housing Code and in the local ordinances of the nonmetropolitan cities, although there is some variation among the latter. At one end of the spectrum, one of our study cities has no occupancy code per se, but relies on plumbing, sanitation, and electrical codes to enforce at least basic housing standards. The Southern Standard Housing Code provides the foundation for the ordinances of the other cities, although they, too, differ in specifics. One of the more important deviations, for example, is the absence of a hot water requirement in one of the cities.

The Southern Standard Code and the local ordinances are all consistently different from the above nationally-based criteria with respect to the heating requirement. Although they include a performance criterion, they do not require that the dwelling be equipped with heating facilities, but only that chimneys or vents be available for tenant-supplied heating units. This, coupled with the fact that only 40 percent of the nonmetropolitan rental units are equipped with built-in heating facilities, suggests that the heating requirement may be too restrictive given the realities of these rental markets. Accordingly, we do not consider the absence of built-in heat to constitute a code violation, and our estimates of substandard housing are conservative in this regard. Among the occupied units, the 53 percent which are heated by fireplaces, stoves, or portable room heaters would be automatically substandard according to the above criterion. Another eight percent have "built-in" heaters, but we have no information with respect to their adequacy or safety; it is likely that some portion of these would fail to meet a reasonable performance standard.

In the absence of inspection-based dwelling information, we cannot derive a complete estimate of the portion of the rental stock which would fail to meet an APHA-based minimum housing code. We can, however, derive a baseline estimate of the extent to which dwellings in the stock are deficient in terms of basic, service-related facilities and structural soundness. Because the tax appraisal records we employ in the next section lack the necessary detail, this analysis relies on dwelling information obtained from respondent households; therefore, we can estimate deficiency rates only in the occupied stock. The data indicate that 20 percent of the rental stock is substandard by virtue of not containing full plumbing and kitchen facilities (Table 2–2). Virtually all of these dwellings lack either hot water or a private bathroom containing a flush toilet, sink, and tub; the addition of requirements for a kitchen sink, a stove, and a refrigerator increases the total only slightly. This figure represents an objective minimum estimate of substandard occupancy in the nonmetropolitan market. Besides not accounting for heating deficiencies, it does not incorporate a number of other factors, particularly measures of structural quality.

Since we have no inspections data, an estimate of the number of dwellings with serious structural defects, electrical problems, and/or rodent infestation was obtained from household responses. Although the responses are highly subjective, they suggest that measuring substandard

Table 2–2. Incidence of APHA-Based Code Violations in Occupied Rental Stock

Criterion	Percent of All Units Failing Criterion	Cumulative Portion of Occupied Stock Which Is Substandard
Plumbing Hot and cold running water; private flush toilet; sink; tub	18.5%	18.5%
Kitchen a. Private kitchen area with sink	2.0	18.9
b. Stove and refrigerator	1.8	19.6
Vermin	14.1	26.6
Structure Drafts or leaks	34.2	42.5
Interior Condition Falling plaster; weak or broken floors	35.5	52.6
Electric Frequently blown fuses	7.5	54.2

housing using plumbing criteria alone is not sufficient. Depending on the credibility one attaches to these data, up to 54 percent of the rental stock is substandard. Problems with vermin infestation were cited by 14 percent of the households; excluding those dwellings which are substandard due to the plumbing and kitchen criteria, this adds another seven percent of the stock to the substandard inventory. The extent of structural defects across the inventory is indicated by the 35 percent of the renters who complained that their dwelling either leaks or is drafty. Net of the previously defined substandard units, this increases the estimated rate of substandard occupancy from 27 to nearly 43 percent. The seriousness of interior deficiencies is suggested by the 35 percent of the households who complained of weak or broken floors or falling plaster, problems which increase the substandard portion of the stock by a net of 10 percent. Finally, to the extent that household complaints that fuses blow often is a reliable measure of inadequate electrical systems, an additional two percent of the stock is below code.

In sum, the approximately 20 percent of the occupied rental stock which has incomplete plumbing or kitchen facilities represents a minimum estimate of the rate of substandard occupancy in the nonmetropolitan market. The successive addition of less precise and more subjective housing quality criteria increases this estimate to about 54 percent of the stock. The former figure, by ignoring structural quality factors, underestimates the portion of the stock which is below code. The latter figure, on the other hand, is likely to overstate substandard occupancy depending on the extent to which households are likely to express dissatisfaction with minor problems or inconveniences. At the very least, however, these estimates bracket the actual rate of dwelling unit deficiencies in the nonmetropolitan rental market and they indicate that renters suffer extensive quality-related housing deprivations. We might note further that if all dwellings which lack an adequate built-in heating system are considered substandard, 69 percent of the rental stock would be classified as deficient. The heat, plumbing and kitchen requirements alone are not met in over 54 percent of the units.

ANALYSIS OF DWELLING UNIT TAX VALUE

Although the preceding analysis provides important insights into the extent of housing inadequacies using a widely recognized set of quality-related criteria, a simple division of the stock into that which is above and below code is not sufficient for many of our analytical needs. Within each class of dwellings, there are wide variations in quality which would make it difficult for us to identify and examine the reasons for systematic differences in housing prices and levels of consumption across the rental market. Since much of our effort in the following chapters focuses on these tasks, in this section we derive a continuous measure of housing quality which is more suited to the multivariate analyses which follow. The APHA-based estimates of deficiency rates, as well as other criteria, will be used to evaluate the ability of the index to discriminate among quality levels.

The index is derived from dwelling information contained in tax appraisal records, a data set which lacks the detail required for the APHA analysis but which provides a rich array of dwelling-specific information. Since our objective is to reduce these data to a single measure, it is useful to consider two empirical studies which derived similar indicators. The first of these [Morris et al., 1972] was based on a field survey in which each of 26 dwelling characteristics was rated on a separate ordinal scale. Analysis of the data indicated that simply summing the individual item scores produced an index as useful as those generated by principal components factoring. It was also found that the interior and exterior quality indexes were very highly correlated with each other and with the total summed index, from which Morris et al. [1972:386] concluded "that it is not necessary to observe both the interior and exterior of a dwelling to obtain a measure of quality." Finally, they used the sales price of owner-occupied units as an external criterion to measure validity. The high correlation between market value per room and the index further suggested a high degree of reliability in the measure.

Kain and Quigley [1970] utilized factor analysis to reduce 39 dwelling and neighborhood features to a more workable number of quality dimensions. Their five factor solution clustered seven dwelling-specific variables on one factor which they denoted as "dwelling unit quality." Of the remaining variables, those which were related to the structure exterior, the parcel, adjacent structures and the block face formed a single measure which apparently reflected "basic residential quality" [Kain and Quigley, 1970:535]. The underlying structure of the data set suggested by their solution corresponds reasonably well to the way one would expect the market to aggregate housing characteristics. The unambiguous separation of dwelling unit characteristics and neighborhood quality implies that the various components of the physical quality of the unit can be combined usefully into a single index. It is also of interest that the factor solution clustered indicators of parcel quality with those of adjacent structures and the block face. This implies that, at the microlevel, there is a high degree of homogeneity in the exterior upkeep of dwellings and, in turn, that the maintenance of public areas is highly correlated with that of the dwellings in the area. The utility of these indicators was demonstrated by their consistent behavior in hedonic price estimating equations in which they served as independent variables. It is noteworthy that composite indexes constructed by taking the "simple unweighted means of the individual quality measurements" for each category of variables produced results which were consistent with those obtained using the derived factors [Kain and Quigley, 1970:534]. In other words, a linear combination of the structural quality indicators, for example, was analytically equivalent to the factor on which these indicators loaded. This is consistent with the findings of Morris et al. [1972] and supports our use of multiple regression to derive a quality index.

Rather than combining a series of quality indicators into a single measure, as was done in the studies cited above, our quality analysis is designed to verify that an existing summary measure (tax value) may be treated *as if* it were derived by combining several measures of dwelling characteristics. In effect, we use regression analysis to estimate the implicit weights that are assigned to each element in the underlying structure of the index. Since virtually all the building appraisals were obtained from a replacement cost-less-depreciation estimate, the index is essentially a production cost evaluation of worth [Triplett, 1971:8]. That is, we assume that the quality of a dwelling is a direct function of the cost to construct it. The central hypothesis is that the tax appraiser's estimate of the current market value of the structure is determined solely by the physical characteristics of the building. Multiple regression techniques are used to estimate the contribution of each characteristic to value, and the explanatory power and prediction accuracy of the estimator are used to examine the consistency of the building appraisal process.[1] Finally, the correspondence between the index and external housing quality criteria is evaluated to confirm the utility of the index.

The analyses which follow address, at least implicitly, a number of a priori objections to the use of tax value as a housing quality measure. It is useful, however, to consider explicitly the interpretation of values derived from mass appraisals for tax purposes.[2] Since fee appraising is performed in order to establish a fair market price for a particular property, numerous factors specific to the property can alter the appraiser's calculus. Mass appraisals performed for the purpose of estimating tax value, however, require the evaluation of large numbers of properties over a relatively short period of time. The scale of the evaluation task demands that basic rules-of-thumb and general relationships between value and property characteristics be applied. While mass appraisals may not in fact coincide with actual market value, all that is required for our purposes is an overall consistency between appraised value and the objective characteristics of buildings. The existence of this consistency, which should be reflected in a relatively strong correlation between tax value and sales price, is supported by a number of empirical studies. Eisenstadt [1972:115], for example, found that tax value explained 91 percent of the variation in actual transaction price for a sample of rent-controlled apartment buildings in New York City, and Sternlieb [1966:210], in his study of tenement housing in Newark, concluded that "well-kept parcels and poorly-kept parcels show very little difference in assessment/sales ratios." A similar conclusion was reached by Berry and Bednarz [1975], who attempted to isolate systematic variations in assessment-to-price ratios using a hedonic model. They found that, in general, tax assessments are reasonably consistent with market price, and the assessment-to-price ratios are essentially uncorrelated with the characteristics of the house.

Although our analyses are designed to provide a direct test of appraisal consistency, the relationship between market and assessed values was examined by regressing owner estimates of market value against tax value. Since we have no way to test the accuracy of the owner estimates, it is impossible to isolate the source of differences in owner versus appraiser values. In order to minimize the error in the owners' estimates, we restricted the analysis to those units which were sold or constructed within the last five years. Tax value explains 84 percent of the variation in the owner estimates, and the coefficient of variation (C_v) of .25 indicates a reasonable level of prediction accuracy.[3] The estimate suggests that tax valuations are reasonably consistent with actual market values.[4]

Finally, the ability of the appraiser to make unambiguous individual estimates of land and building values may be questioned. Although Turvey [1957:23] argues that, in an equilibrium sense, this separation of total property value is an artificial convenience, Berry and Bednarz [1975] provide evidence that it is in fact meaningful. Once the structural characteristics of 275 single family homes were controlled, the addition of neighborhood, environmental, and locational variables increased the ability of their model to explain the assessed value of improvements from about 47 to 55 percent. In contrast, their ability to explain land assessments nearly doubled with the addition of these same variables.[5] In fact, the only dwelling variable that was significantly related to land value was age, which they attribute to the "historical-locational structure of the city" as it is reflected in the date of development [Berry and Bednarz, 1975:34].

1978325

The Model

The hypothesis that tax value is a function of the objective characteristics of the dwelling unit is tested using multiple regression analysis. In order to standardize for dwelling unit size, the dependent variable is the appraised building value per square foot of living area. Explicit tests for potential biases in tax value are performed by including a number of variables in addition to those measuring the physical attributes of the dwelling. First, dwelling size is entered as an independent variable to test for a nonlinear scale factor in the appraisal estimates. Second, since the sample of dwellings was taken from four different cities in which appraisals were done over a seven-year period, variables to account for price trends over the period are also included.

Since our objective is to determine if building value can be employed as an indicator of dwelling quality, it is critical that we also isolate any environmental factors that influence the appraiser's estimate. This is accomplished by adding a vector of neighborhood characteristics to the set of explanatory variables. Finally, it is important to estimate the influence that subjective appraiser judgments, such as those made on quality, condition, and depreciation, have on the total value. The less this set of variables contributes to the explanatory power of the model once all building characteristics have been controlled, the more confidence we will have in the objectivity of the tax valuation. The regression model can thus be written as:

$$V = a + \sum_i b_i X_i + cS + \sum_j d_j P_j + \sum_k e_k N_k + \sum_m f_m A_m \qquad (2\text{--}1)$$

where: V = assessed building value per square foot;
X_i = a vector of dwelling unit characteristics;

S = dwelling unit size;
P_j = a vector to measure price trends;
N_k = a vector of neighborhood characteristics; and
A_m = a vector of appraiser judgment factors.

With the one exception of the age of the building, all the variables are entered in linear form. There is no theoretical reason to expect important nonlinearities, and, as we demonstrate, both the prediction accuracy and explanatory power of the estimator are very high. The major assumption embodied in the linear model is that the contribution to value of each component in the housing bundle is invariant across the market, irrespective of the total size of the bundle or the neighborhood in which it is located [King, 1973:8].

Independent Variables

Among the five basic structural variables, three simply measure the presence or absence of specific features (Table 2-3). As we have noted,

Table 2-3   Independent Variables in Tax Value Estimating Equation

Characteristics of the Structure

FDN   A dummy variable describing the foundation (single family and duplex equations only).
       1 = completely closed foundation

ROOF   A dummy variable describing the roof construction.
       1 = nonmetal construction

STRUC A dummy variable distinguishing frame and brick structures.
       1 = brick structure

AGELN Natural logarithm of building age.

DUSQFT A continuous variable measuring the square foot size of the dwelling unit.

Interior Construction Features

CONV   A dummy variable for single family conversions (multifamily equation only).
       1 = not a conversion

FLOOR A dummy variable for floor material.
       1 = hardwood floors

DRYWL A dummy variable for interior wall material.
       1 = dry wall

Equipment and Facilities

HEATA A dummy variable for heating (single family and duplex equations only).
       1 = area heat only

HEATB A dummy variable for heating.
       1 = central heat
       (Suppressed category: no owner-provided heat)

Table 2–3   continued

BTHRM A dummy variable for bathroom (single family and duplex equations only).
1 = contains full bathroom i.e., sink, tub, and commode in separate room

FREPL A dummy variable for the presence of a fireplace (single family and duplex equations only).
1 = contains a fireplace

Appraiser Judgment
IQUAL A continuous ranking of the quality of the original construction as assigned by the appraiser.

DEPTOT A continuous variable for the percentage decline in value due to physical and functional depreciation.

Neighborhood Factors
STREET A dummy variable for street paving (single family and duplex equations only).
1 = paved street

HIDEN A dummy variable for zoning class.
1 = high density

NONRES A dummy variable for zoning class.
1 = nonresidential
(Suppressed category: medium density residential)

RACE A dummy variable for race of occupant.
1 = nonwhite

Inflationary Factors
DATE1 1 = appraised during 1966–69

DATE2 1 = appraised during 1970–71
(Suppressed category: appraised during 1972–73.)

much of the worst quality stock consists of metal roofed, single family, or duplex units constructed on open foundations. These features represent generally cheap construction methods and are hypothesized to be strongly related to value. Another variable distinguishes brick from frame structures. It would, of course, be preferable to have measures for the condition of the roof, foundation, and exterior walls. Their unavailability is a weakness of the appraisal data, but presumably they are captured in the quality grade and depreciation variables.

Building age was hypothesized to be negatively related to value since it indicates the wear to which a building has been subjected and is a proxy for the building standards which were prevalent at the time of construction. A nonlinear effect was hypothesized since the absolute amount by which a structure depreciates would not be expected to be constant over time. Consideration of a number of functional forms between age and value indicated that a semilog relationship provided the best fit. This formulation implies more rapid depreciation in the early years, with the loss in value tapering off as the building ages.[6]

Three interior condition variables are included in the equation. Conversions are distinguished from structures originally built for multiple occupancy in an effort to capture a number of otherwise unrecorded factors. The process of conversion is often accomplished as cheaply as possible and may represent a last-ditch effort to milk whatever returns are possible from obsolete structures. Consequently, we expect the conversions variable to stand as a proxy for generally poor interior features such as bad wiring, old plumbing, and poorly constructed partitions. The floors variable indicates the presence of hardwood floors; dry wall construction, which may be a proxy for other modern features, is distinguished from other interior wall materials (primarily plaster). Both variables are expected to be positively related to value.

The ability of the dwelling to provide nonshelter services is measured by four dummy variables. The contributions to value of various types of heating systems are measured by variables which indicate the presence of an installed area heater or central system. Although all the dwellings are served by city utilities and all have interior plumbing facilities, a substantial portion do not contain a full bathroom. Finally, the presence of a fireplace is hypothesized to increase value, even though fireplaces are generally found in older dwellings for which they are often the sole heating source. To the extent that the fireplace variable captures unincluded negative features, its estimated contribution to value will be biased downward.[7]

The quality grade of the original construction, as judged by the appraiser, is a proxy for numerous construction characteristics which were not specifically recorded or had only partial coverage.[8] The other judgment measure is the total amount of depreciation assigned by the appraiser. Although depreciation is highly correlated with age, which is also included in the model, buildings of similar age may have been subjected to different intensities of use over their lives, and depreciation rates may have been diminished by increased levels of regular maintenance or by investments in capital improvements.[9]

To test whether neighborhood characteristics bias the tax evaluation of the structure, we include in the equation street paving, zoning classification, and race variables. The high density and nonresidential zoning variables are intended to capture adverse environmental factors and are postulated to be negatively related to building value. Race was entered to measure potential appraiser bias and neighborhood effects that may be correlated with nonwhite occupancy in these highly segregated cities. It is, of course, possible that race may be measuring the effect of omitted building features, but the likelihood is low, particularly since the quality grade and depreciation variables are expected to pick up residual dwelling attributes not captured by the objective features.

The final variables primarily measure inflationary trends over the seven-year period during which the appraisals were done, but there may be some confounding effects, since appraisals within a given city generally were performed at the same time. Thus the dummy variables for appraisal date tend to cluster dwellings which are located in one or two of the four cities. Although the correspondence between locations and date is not perfect, the date variable may be accounting for systematic differences in the evaluation procedures and tax equilization bases as well as for inflationary trends. Since dummy variables which distinguished the four cities did not prove as useful as the two date variables, however, city-specific differences probably do not influence value to a great extent.

Partitioning the Sample

The multiplicity of housing types across the market suggests that the dwelling unit is not a homogeneous commodity. The disaggregation of the dwelling into a number of presumably homogeneous attributes is designed to facilitate analyses which would otherwise be impossible given the severity and extent of housing differentiation. If dwellings are not characterized by the same set of attributes, or if these attributes are not combined and evaluated in the same way for all dwellings, then the housing stock must be segmented into homogeneous classes. At the extremes, for example, it is unlikely that modern garden apartments and shotgun shacks represent different quality levels of the same commodity, although both satisfy consumer needs for basic shelter.

In practical terms, the homogeneity issue can be examined by testing for differences across dwelling types in the quality-determination function. Thus we derived functionally similar estimating equations for the full sample, for the subsample of units in multifamily structures (3+ dwellings), and for the subsample of single family and duplex structures combined. A test of whether the value determination function differs for different structure types was performed by estimating the statistical significance of the reduction in the residual sums of squares resulting from the partition.[10] The test produced a highly significant F-ratio; the coefficients of determination were larger for each subsample than for the composite; and the coefficients of variation are each lower. The same test was applied to single family and duplex units, and, although the relationship is not as strong, the results suggest that they too have different value determination functions. Accordingly, the analyses that follow are disaggregated by structure type, allowing us to vary the specification for each subsample depending on the characteristics that are relevant to each group of dwellings. In the final section of the chapter we demonstrate that once the index is derived, it corresponds to similar quality levels for each structure type. No analytical power is lost, therefore, by recombining the subsample indexes into a single ranking of structural quality.

Adjustments for Multicollinearity

In order to provide an adequate test of the hypothesis that tax value is a useful indicator of the objective, quality-related characteristics of dwellings, it is important to eliminate any serious multicollinearity in the independent variable set. Particular problems were anticipated for variables which reflect summary appraiser judgments of the unit. The depreciation estimate, for example, should be based on the quality and condition of the structure, and its entry into the equation, therefore, may cause the estimated coefficients of variables related to construction features to become insignificant. In that case, it would be improper to deduce that the appraiser's estimate of depreciation is the strongest predictor of tax value when, in fact, that estimate is itself based on objective features. Conversely, if we have eliminated the multicollinearity problems and still find such summary judgments to be more important than the objective measures, our confidence in tax value as an indicator of dwelling quality would be diminished because of the subjectivity inherent in the appraisal process.

Potentially serious problems of multiple dependency were identified by regressing the independent variable set against those explanatory variables suspected of being highly collinear. Any variable whose multiple correlation with the remainder of the independent variables was excessively high was considered to be a serious problem [Farrar and Glauber, 1967], and four such cases were found. Three—building age, quality grade, and depreciation—are in a sense summary measures of dwelling characteristics. Regressing each against the remainder of the dependent set produced coefficients of determination ranging from .70 to .90. Similarly, multifamily units that are conversions tend to have very similar characteristics; the R^2 for the equation relating the independent set to the conversion dummy was .90. Each of these variables was adjusted by subtracting from it the variation attributable to the other independent variables.[11] This procedure, which Ridker and Henning [1967] refer to as "residualization," allows one "to retain all the explanatory power of [highly correlated variables] while assigning the joint variation to what is believed to be the true cause" [King, 1973:90]. Although the coefficients of the "residualized" variables are not meaningful, their standard errors indicate the strength of the relationship between them and the dependent variable, and their independent contribution to the explanatory power of the equation is unaffected.

The Determinants of Tax Value

The estimating equations for the three structure types (Table 2-4) indicate that the objective features of the dwelling unit are systematically related to tax value in the predicted manner. Single family units which have nonmetal roofs and are built on closed foundations are valued, on average, at $1.09 per square foot above the intercept value of $1.94.[12] Another $1.02 is added if the building is of brick construction. Drywall interiors and hardwood floors together add another $1.63 to value, which suggests that both variables are likely standing as proxies for other desirable interior dwelling features we could not measure.

The quality of the equipment and facilities also contributes heavily to value: over one dollar per square foot for built-in area heaters; more than two dollars for central heat; and $.57 for a complete bathroom. Among the single family dwelling characteristics, only the fireplace variable is statistically insignificant. The "residualized" age, depreciation and quality variables also have highly significant coefficients and indicate the importance of factors related to wear, aging and general condition that we were not able to measure more specifically. Finally, the scale economies effect, as measured by the size variable, indicates that the value per square foot of single family units is reduced by about $.10 for every one hundred square feet of living area. This suggests that for an average dwelling, the appraised value of $3.96 reflects a downward bias of $1.18, while a 500 square foot unit is undervalued by $.52. For the index to measure structural quality, this relative difference of $.66 must be taken into account in our adjustment of tax value.

The neighborhood variables do not behave entirely as expected in the single family equation. The lack of significance of the race variable suggests the absence of appraiser bias resulting from negative neighborhood features associated with black-occupied areas, and it implies that there are no important dwelling-specific characteristics that have been omitted from the model. Although we postulated that high density and nonresidential zoning would reflect inferior residential environments and might, therefore, bias building appraisals downward, both zoning variables have significant positive coefficients. Even if these variables were picking up some building characteristics, we would expect the quality of single family dwellings to be highest in low to medium density zones; thus, this influence would be expected to produce negative coefficients. It would appear, therefore, that the potential for a higher re-use of the land, which should be reflected in the land valuation only, is producing an upward bias in appraised building values.

The duplex and multifamily estimators have essentially the same characteristics as the single family equation. All the objective features of

Table 2–4. Estimating Equations for Dwelling Unit Value

Variable	Single Family	Duplex	Multifamily
FDN	.809[a]	1.226[a]	x
	(.126)	(.255)	
ROOF	1.157[a]	.699[a]	.771[b]
	(.123)	(.208)	(.332)
STRUC	1.024[a]	.904[a]	1.224[a]
	(.142)	(.208)	(.233)
AGELN*	−1.333[a]	−1.663[a]	−3.307[a]
	(.147)	(.178)	(.367)
DUSQFT	−.00104[a]	−.00089[a]	−.00255[a]
	(.0001)	(.0003)	(.0005)
CONV*	x	x	6.249[a]
			(.794)
FLOOR	.706[a]	.406[b]	.673[a]
	(.126)	(.222)	(.215)
DRYWL	.924[a]	1.079[a]	1.499[a]
	(.099)	(.168)	(.221)
HEATA	1.092[a]	1.615[a]	x
	(.144)	(.390)	
HEATB	2.190[a]	2.957[a]	2.002[a]
	(.160)	(.251)	(.270)
BTHRM	.568[a]	.515[b]	x
	(.142)	(.284)	
FREPL	−.087	.412[b]	x
	(.109)	(.207)	
IQUAL*	1.452[a]	1.460[a]	xx
	(.122)	(.196)	
DEPTOT*	−.095[a]	−.119[a]	−.203[a]
	(.005)	(.009)	(.017)
STREET	.402[b]	.218	x
	(.196)	(.268)	
HIDEN	.358[a]	.316	−.189
	(.145)	(.228)	(.282)
NONRES	.369[b]	−.111	−.147
	(.166)	(.280)	(.305)
RACE	−.102	.072	−.763[a]
	(.117)	(.261)	(.283)
DATE1	−.671[a]	−1.625[a]	−.185
	(.119)	(.209)	(.269)
DATE2	−.114	−.232	−.257
	(.128)	(.212)	(.246)
Constant	1.935	1.269	4.183
Corrected R^2	.910	.913	.900
SEE	.685	.747	.786
C_v	.173	.165	.147
F	138.38	60.67	62.12
N	270	110	87

Notes

Figures in parentheses are standard errors of coefficients.

x Variable not included in equation.

xx Variable not entered; $t < .1$.

* Indicates variable adjusted for multicollinearity.

Significance levels for coefficients:

[a].01 or higher

[b].05

[c].10

the dwelling are significantly related to value, but the neighborhood variables behave somewhat erratically. In neither case are the zoning variables significant, and race is significant only in the multifamily equation where the size of its coefficient suggests that it is either picking up strong negative environmental factors or acting as a proxy for omitted building characteristics. Inasmuch as we were better able to specify dwelling features, we are inclined to accept the former interpretation.

The variables that account for the time period over which the appraisals took place all carry the expected negative sign. The only statistically significant inflationary effects are associated with single family and duplex units appraised before 1970. In the multifamily equation, neither of the appraisal date variables has a significant coefficient.

Appraisal Consistency

The significance of the coefficients of the variables which measure the objective building characteristics is an indication that the tax appraisal process provides consistent estimates of value across the market. Further inferences about the objectivity of the appraisals can be drawn by examining each variable's contribution to the explanatory power of the equation. The adjusted R^2 values of .90 or higher for each equation indicate that we have accounted for the most important factors that enter the appraiser's calculus. Our interest in utilizing the tax records as a basis for measuring dwelling unit quality, however, makes the source of this explanatory power as important as its magnitude. The contribution made by each category of variables was monitored by specifying the order of variable entry in the stepwise regression to be: dwelling unit, appraiser judgment, neighborhood and price trend.[13]

Together, the measures of the dwellings' structural and interior features account for 73 to 80 percent of the ability of the equation to explain tax value. Once these factors have been controlled, the appraiser judgment variables increase the explanation to over 90 percent of its final value. While there is undoubtedly some subjectivity inherent in these variables, that they account for only 20 percent of the variation in value suggests that the appraisal process is reasonably objective and consistent. Moreover, we would expect the quality and depreciation estimates to capture structural characteristics that we were unable to specify explicitly. Finally, the additional contribution provided by the neighborhood variables indicates that the building appraisals are not strongly affected by environmental factors.[14]

STRUCTURAL QUALITY INDEX

In order to convert the appraised building value per square foot into an index of structural quality (QS), it is necessary to adjust tax value for the influences of the nonstructural factors which are identified in the above estimating equation. The computation derives directly from Equation (2–1):

$$QS = V - cS - \sum_j d_j P_j - \sum_k e_k N_k \qquad (2-2)$$

where the terms are as defined earlier, and the values of the coefficients are those estimated for each structure type (Table 2–4). The quality index computed in this manner is, for all intents and purposes, a continuous variable which ranges from about zero to fourteen. Multifamily units, which have a mean index score of 7.6, are apparently of much higher quality as a group than are single families and duplexes, whose respective scores are 4.7 and 5.5.

All that remains is to demonstrate that the index is both a valid and useful measure of housing quality, a task which is accomplished by reference to external criteria that were not used to derive the index. Specifically, three issues are addressed: (1) the collapsing of the index values into a single ranking which ignores structure type differences; (2) the inclusion of index values estimated from Equation (2-2) for observations that were omitted from the regression analyses becuase of missing data; and (3) the correspondence between the index and the external criteria.

These tests are based on the correlations between the index and a number of housing and neighborhood quality indicators. The external criteria that are used for the analysis include: rent; an independent quality ranking based on an inspection of photographs which were taken of each dwelling; and census measures of neighborhood quality. The overall pattern of correlations (Table 2–5) indicates a fairly strong relationship between the index and the external criteria; moreover, comparison of the correlations for the structure type classes and for the single ranking suggests that a recombination of the indexes is valid. For the entire sample, the index has a simple correlation of .66 with annual rent, a value which indicates the strong relationship between market value and physical quality. Another indication that the index provides an accurate measure of structural quality is its high correlation with the photo-based quality ranking.[15] This ordinal ranking is not "correct" in any sense, nor does it have the analytical flexibility and utility of the index. Nonetheless, the correlation between the index and the photographic ranking is over .70 for each structure type and .76 for the single ranking, which indicates both the consistency of the index and the utility of combining the structure types into a single ranking scheme. The latter point is important in that it provides evidence that units with the same score, regardless of structure type, are of similar quality. Finally, the mean value of the index for the omitted cases is not statistically different from that for the included

Table 2-5. Tests for Validity of Structural Quality Index

External Criterion	First Order Correlations with Index[a]					
	Structure Type Class			All Dwellings Used in Estimator	Omitted Dwellings	All Ranked Dwellings
	Single Family	*Duplex*	*Multifamily*			
Annual Rent	.686	.731	.484	.663	.816	.697
Photographic Rating	.732	.715	.765	.759	.800	.768
Neighborhood Factors:[b]						
Average Rent	.544	.479	.483	.525	.644	.549
Percent Black	−.469	−.416	−.340	−.443	−.511	−.460
Percent Plumbing Deficient	−.462	−.492	−.509	−.485	−.540	−.501
N	270	110	87	467	108	575
Mean Index Value	4.71	5.56	7.85	5.50	5.00	5.40
(Std. Dev.)	(2.32)	(2.59)	(2.40)	(2.67)	(3.14)	(2.77)

[a] All correlations significant at $p < .001$.
[b] Census Enumeration District.

observations, and in every instance these cases have at least as strong a relationship with the external criteria as do the included cases. Thus we can estimate quality scores for those cases which we could not use in the estimation of tax value without introducing any bias into our analyses which utilize the quality index.[16]

HOUSING QUALITY LEVELS

Substandard Housing

In the first section of this chapter, we derived a lower-bound estimate of substandard occupancy using APHA criteria related to the presence of certain dwelling facilities. Relying on the more subjective household evaluations of the units, we expanded the estimate to include a wider range of structural inadequacies. This analysis suggested that from 20–54 percent of the occupied rented stock is below code. Our objective in this section is to use the index to identify a minimum standard level of housing quality. Although the index provides a fairly fine-grained measure of housing quality, its values are not specifically associated with particular structural deficiencies, and thus we cannot, for example, automatically define dwellings as being dilapidated or deteriorated. Even if we utilized all the data available from the tax records, however, we would still not be able to define substandard units unambiguously since the records indicate the presence or absence of features and not their condition or functional utility.

The index-based definition of substandard, therefore, must rely on the concept of community standards, which is consistent with our earlier discussion of the relative nature of housing standards. Since the index enables us to rank all dwellings in the market, it is ideally suited to the task of establishing a relative minimum standard level. The combined quality ranking reveals, for example, easily identifiable upper and lower tails in the distribution. The lowest 10 percent is dominated by single family units, while multifamily units predominate the group of clearly superior dwellings in the upper 10 percent. Although the best and the worst housing can easily be identified, a more detailed consideration of the correspondence between the index and the incidence of housing problems is required to differentiate the remainder of the stock.

The relative concept of standard was operationalized by examining the distribution of housing deficiencies across six quality classes which were defined according to the percentile ranks of the index. Group 1 includes the lowest 10 percent of the units and group 6, the highest 10 percent; the remainder of the units were divided into four equal size classes. In general, the incidence of housing deficiencies is substantially higher than average in group 3, while for group 4 it is consistently below average (Table 2–6). In fact, the difference between groups 3 and 4 is considerable

Table 2-6. Correspondence Between Quality Classes and External Criteria

Percentile Ranking by Quality Index	Percent Rated Poor by Photographic Inspection	APHA Code Violations			Mean Annual Rent per Square Foot
		Percent Failing Plumbing and Kitchen	Percent Below Code	Percent with Three or More	
(1) 0–10%	78.5%	68.6%	86.3%	47.1%	.512
(2) 11–30	23.3	27.5	72.5	33.9	.614
(3) 31–50	19.3	25.3	74.7	22.5	.702
(4) 51–70	2.6	7.4	42.6	6.5	.863
(5) 71–90	0.0	3.7	35.2	5.6	1.098
(6) 91–100	0.0	0.0	9.8	2.0	1.592
Total	16.8	19.5	54.7	18.5	.859

in every case. While 19 percent of the units in the former group are rated poor based on their exterior condition, less than three percent in the latter group are so classified. The rate of APHA code violations, as they were defined in the first section of this chapter, also reveals sharp differences between these two groups. Over one-fourth of the units in group 3 lack complete plumbing or kitchen facilities, compared to only seven percent in group 4. Nearly 69 percent of the group 1 dwellings, compared to none of the group 6 units, suffer from this basic deficiency. Including the more subjective criteria related to structural condition, 86 percent of the group 1 dwellings fail the APHA code. The failure rate declines slightly to 75 percent in group 3, but ranges only from 43 percent in group 4 to 10 percent in group 6. Finally, the portion of dwellings with multiple code violations follows the same pattern; the incidence of three or more deficiencies (out of a possible seven) is more than three times as great in group 3 as in group 4.

Based on these patterns of physical deficiencies, all dwelling units which fall below the midpoint of group 3 (i.e., those which are below the 40th percentile) are defined as failing to meet the community norm of minimum housing quality; this definition corresponds to an index value of 4.13. About 48 percent of the single family, 39 percent of the duplex, and 9 percent of the multifamily units are thus classified as substandard. Conversely, the composition of the substandard stock is approximately 73 percent single family, 22 percent duplex, and 5 percent multifamily. Although it is very likely that on a dwelling by dwelling basis there will be some error in our quality designation, the dwellings we have identified as being inadequate are, as a class, clearly inferior to the remainder of the stock (Table 2–7). Almost all of the substandard units are wood frame buildings; nearly half have open foundations; and almost two-thirds have metal roofs. On average, substandard units are almost twice as old and command rents that are less than 60 percent of those charged for standard dwellings.

Although it appears that a large portion of the dwellings that are standard according to the distribution of the index scores fail the APHA code requirements, virtually all of the indicated violations are based on the subjective household evaluations of structural quality. Using the objective, facility-related criteria, only a very small portion of the standard units are APHA-deficient. Considering only the objective factors, the index values and the substandard definition derived from them correspond well to the incidence of code violations. Thus, nearly 40 percent of the substandard units lack complete plumbing or kitchen facilities, while 78 percent are below the APHA code if all the requirements are considered. The comparable figures for standard dwellings are 6 and 39 percent. Conversely, the substandard category includes about 80 percent of the units lacking at least one basic facility.

Table 2–7. Characteristics of Dwellings by Quality Standard

		Substandard			Standard
		Unrehabilitatable			
		Shotgun	Based on Rent Elasticity	Rehabili- tatable[a]	Total	
Structure and Facilities						
Wood Frame Exterior	(%)	100.0	90.5	95.8	93.9	59.0
Open Foundation	(%)	87.5	35.6	26.1	45.2	3.3
Metal Roof	(%)	89.6	49.6	68.8	62.7	10.4
Mean Age	(yrs)	45	43	47	45	23
Mean Size	(sq.ft)	870	895	1,347	994	1,043
Mean Rent	($)	33	51	42	45	81
APHA Code Violations						
Incomplete Plumbing	(%)	69.6	30.8	29.8	39.3	6.3
Below Code	(%)	87.0	74.2	78.7	78.0	39.2
Three or More	(%)	45.7	31.7	36.2	36.0	7.0
Neighborhood[b]						
Mean Rent	($)	44	51	49	49	68
Plumbing Deficient	(%)	30.2	17.0	18.2	20.0	7.5
Portion Black	(%)	65.6	37.9	34.9	42.9	17.9

[a]Assumes post-rehab rent of $.702 per square foot. See text.
[b]Census Enumeration District

Rehabilitation Potential

Beyond designating dwellings as being standard or substandard, it is relevant to classify units in the latter group according to their potential for being upgraded to standard quality. Unfortunately, our data do not permit us to provide a detailed, cost-based analysis of rehabilitation feasibility. Ideally, one would identify specific housing deficiencies, estimate the cost to remedy them and, finally, make a judgment about the economic feasibility of the necessary repairs. Since our dwelling condition information was not derived from independent inspections, we are able generally to measure only the presence or absence of various features and not their current condition or original quality. Using the quality index, however, we are able to provide at least a statistically-based approximation of the number of unrehabilitatable dwellings in the nonmetropolitan rental inventory.

A lower-bound estimate was obtained by defining as unsalvageable all units in the lowest nine percent of the quality distribution ($QS < 2.0$); over 80 percent of these are single family, and the remainder duplexes. Most of the dwellings are shotgun shacks which are inherently incapable of supporting rehabilitation capital by any reasonable standard (Table 2–7). On average, they rent for $33 a month and contain less than 900 square feet of living space. None has built-in heat, over two-thirds lack a complete bathroom and nearly 90 percent have an open foundation and/or metal roof. The extent of the basic structural deficiencies that characterize these units would necessitate substantial investment simply to render them safe and sanitary; they are, moreover, located in the least desirable neighborhoods in the city. The size of the required investment is thus not likely to be justified by the rent-generating potential of these houses.

Elasticity of Housing Quality: While it is a relatively simple matter to isolate the pool of unrehabilitatable shotgun houses, it is more difficult to estimate the upgrading potential of the higher quality substandard inventory. Our general approach to the problem is to estimate the elasticity of quality, as measured by the index, with respect to rent. Those dwellings for which a given exogenous rent increase would not produce a quality response sufficient to reach the minimum standard ($QS^* = 4.13$) can thus be classified as unrehabilitatable. The analysis assumes that the rental market is price competitive and that the quality of a dwelling is, therefore, a direct function of its rent.[17] Substandard housing will persist until some exogenous factor disturbs the present market equilibrium and permits landlords to increase rents in the lower-quality sectors of the market.

Although values of the index do not identify specific deficiencies, the values do, in general, account for the more important structural factors that are likely to impinge on rehabilitation feasibility. The substantial housing quality variations in the rental market, however, suggest that the response of quality to a change in rent is likely to vary across the market. In order to examine this possibility, we estimated the elasticity (b) from the simple relationship:

$$QS = aR^b. \qquad (2\text{-}3)$$

We then partitioned the sample and derived separate estimates for standard and substandard dwellings, as we defined them earlier. The partition resulted in a substantial and statistically significant reduction in the estimating residual; therefore, the analysis focuses only on substandard dwellings, which constitute a fairly homogeneous group (Table 2–7). Because there is relatively little variation in basic structural features, and because of sample size problems, no further partitions were made.

Irrespective of building quality, the presence of neighborhood externalities will also affect housing investment and, thereby, the potential for upgrading. Otherwise identical dwellings which are located in neighborhoods characterized by different amenity levels will differ with respect to the feasibility of supporting capital investments; specifically, we would expect the interaction between dwelling and neighborhood quality to cause the profitability of given investments to increase with the environ-

mental amenity level. Contrary to this expectation, however, the introduction of neighborhood factors has no material effect on the estimated
elasticity. The response of dwelling quality to changes in rent is, therefore, based on an estimate of Equation (2-3) for currently substandard
units only and thus assumes a constant elasticity in this sector of the
stock. The resultant estimator is:[18]

$$lnQS = -2.353 + .532 \, lnR \qquad (2\text{-}4)$$
$$(.066)$$
$$R^2 = .238$$
$$N = 210$$

The response of quality to a given rent change is thus:

$$\frac{\delta QS}{QS_0} = .532 \, \frac{\delta R}{R_0} \qquad (2\text{-}5)$$

or,

$$QS_1 = QS_0 \, [1 + .532 \, (R_1 - R_0)/R_0] \qquad (2\text{-}6)$$

Where QS_0 and R_0 are the current quality and rent and QS_1 is the
postrehabilitation quality level. Any dwelling for which

$$QS_1 \geqslant QS^* = 4.13 \qquad (2\text{-}7)$$

is assumed to be feasible to rehabilitate.

Postrehab Rent: Estimating the portion of the rental stock that cannot
feasibly be upgraded requires the specification of the postrehabilitation
rent, which was established by multiplying dwelling size times a base rent
per square foot (RSF) in order to control for size variations. At minimum,
a rehabilitated unit of a given size should be able to generate a rent
equivalent to that earned by similarly sized units which are currently
standard. In our earlier analysis we defined the minimum standard quality
level (QS^*) as the midpoint of the class containing dwellings in the
31–50th percentiles in the quality index ranking. Accordingly, the mean
annual square foot rent for that quality class, $RSF^* = \$.70$ (Table 2-6),
represents the minimum postrehabilitation rental rate we should expect
currently substandard housing to be able to generate; this figure is used to
generate our lower-bound estimate or upgrading potential. For each substandard dwelling, QS_1 is estimated from Equation (2-6), and those units
for which QS_1 does not satisfy the minimum standard requirement are
classified as unrehabilitatable.

Although this estimate is based on a crude procedure, the proportion
of the stock that is unrehabilitatable is relatively insensitive to changes in

either the postrehab rent or in the estimated elasticity of rent with respect to quality. Increasing *RSF* from the minimum standard rent of $.70 to the mean market rental rate reduces the unsalvageable portion of the stock from 31 to 26 percent, and an increase to a highly unlikely, but clearly upper-bound, $1.00 produces a further reduction to 23 percent (Figure 2–1). Similarly, if we increase the elasticity to 1.0—nearly double the value we estimated—the indicated extent of unsalvageable housing is not affected substantially. At *RSF**, the most likely postrehab rent level, virtually doubling the elasticity reduces the estimated unrehabilitatable portion of the stock from 31 to nearly 28 percent, a difference which is too

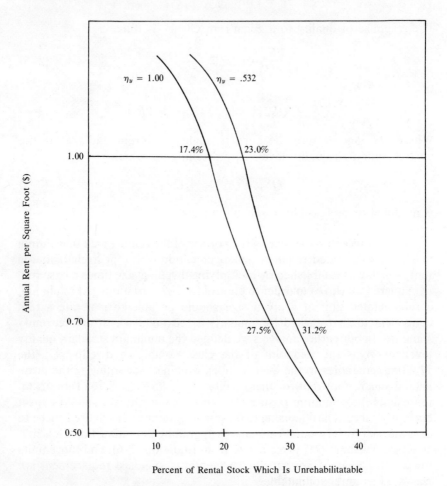

Percent of Rental Stock Which Is Unrehabilitatable

Figure 2–1. Estimated Unrehabilitatable Housing as a Function of Rent

small to have any policy or program significance. In sum, our best estimate is that 31 percent of the rental stock is unrehabilitatable; less than
nine percent is substandard and rehabilitatable.

The major distinction between dwellings which are potentially rehabilitatable and those which are not is that the former are larger units
which are currently renting at relatively low rates (Table 2–7). Units
which can be upgraded are half again as large and currently rent for nearly
20 percent less; the combined effect of these factors is to produce among
rehabilitatable dwellings a considerably larger increment in earnings potential after rehabilitation. On average, those units which are feasible to
upgrade currently command rents which are nearly $37 per month less
than they would be at the minimum standard rate. For more than one-
third, the gross earnings would be at least double at the standard rent level
compared to the current rent. Over half, however, are feasible to upgrade
given a rent increment of less than 75 percent.

Rehab Investments: The relationship between the investment required to bring a unit to standard and its current value can provide
additional insights into rehab feasibility. If we consider a simple model in
which capital investments are assumed to produce a perpetual income
stream, then the relationship between the rent change and the investment
(I) depends only on the capitalization rate (r_c):

$$I = \Delta R / r_c \qquad (2\text{-}8)$$

This model is conceptually identical to the gross rent multiplier analysis
which is presented in Chapter 7. There we demonstrate that, based on
owner estimates of total market value, the gross capitalization rate for low
quality units ranges from about 10 percent for single families to 15 percent
for multiunit buildings. When asked directly, landlords ·generally responded that they expect a gross return of 12 percent on their investments. As a first approximation of rehabilitation capital requirement,
therefore, we assumed a gross capitalization rate of 12 percent—a figure
which is consistent with the average market.

When capitalized at 12 percent, the mean annual rent increment of
$440 for rehabilitatable dwellings corresponds to an average investment of
about $3,700 (Table 2–8). Nearly one-third of these units could, according
to our estimates, be upgraded at a cost of $2,000 or less, while 23 percent
would require an investment of more than $5,000. For many of these
dwellings, these figures represent a substantial increment to current
value, which may or may not be justified for units which are located in
certain neighborhoods or which suffer from certain major deficiencies.
Ignoring these factors, a sense of the relative magnitudes of the rehab
investments can be gained from an examination of dwelling values as

Table 2-8.   Estimated Capital Investment to Upgrade Substandard Rehabilitatable Dwellings*

Investment Amount	Percent of Rehabilitatable Dwellings	Investment as a Percent of Value	Percent of Rehabilitatable Dwellings
≤$2,000	31.2%	≤25%	4.2%
2,001–3,000	14.6	26–50	20.8
3,001–4,000	14.6	51–75	29.2
4,001–5,000	16.7	76–100	20.8
5,001+	22.9	100+	25.0
Total	100.0	Total	100.0
Mean	$3,666		79.9%
N = 48			

* Postrehab RSF = $.702/sq.ft.
Capitalization Rate = .12

assessed for tax purposes.[19] The capital investments to which these rent increases correspond represent less than 50 percent of building tax value for one-fourth of the rehabilitatable dwellings (Table 2-8). At the other extreme, however, one-fourth of the dwellings would require investments in excess of their current tax value.

The magnitudes of rehab investments which can be justified depend on specific factors which we cannot readily take into account; it is true, however, that the larger the investment as a proportion of value, the less feasible will be rehabilitation. Keeping in mind that tax value tends to be less than actual market value, a plausible rule-of-thumb would define as unrehabilitatable those units for which the rehab investment is equal to or greater than the current tax value of the building. The application of this criterion would increase the unrehabilitatable stock from 31 percent of the total to almost 34 percent. Even if the criterion were 75 percent of value, the unsalvageable stock would be only 35 percent of the total. The overall crudeness of our rehab feasibility estimates does not justify this further refinement, but it is worth noting that a percent-of-value criterion would not substantially alter our estimates.

SUMMARY

The main purpose of this chapter has been to develop a quantitative measure of the physical quality of dwelling units. To this end, we presented a detailed statistical analysis of tax appraisal records, from which we concluded that the appraised building value per square foot, as adjusted for certain specified biases, is an accurate and consistent summary measure of the objective characteristics of the unit. Moreover, the relationships between the index and a number of external criteria indicated the utility of the derived index as a housing quality measure. Throughout our work, the index is employed in three ways to measure the housing consumption levels of renter households. For multivariate analyses, such as hedonic price estimations, the index is treated as a continuous variable. As we have demonstrated, the index values range from about one to fourteen, and their distribution, although skewed to the high values, is approximately normal. For essentially descriptive analyses, such as examining relative levels of housing quality and consumption across various population cohorts, we rely on the six-category ordinal classification. Finally, we have used the index to identify the quality level that corresponds to minimum adequacy as defined by community norms of standard housing. It is important to keep in mind that the designation of substandard units is, in many cases, less significant than is their distribution among renter households cohorts, a subject we consider in the next chapter, where we examine the consumption side of the rental market.

With respect to more substantive issues, the analysis in this chapter indicated a high rate of substandard occupancy in the rental market. Applying the most basic plumbing and kitchen criteria identifies a minimum of 20 percent of the stock as being below code. The addition of a heating facility requirement increases this baseline estimate to over 50 percent of the stock, although, as we have noted, this is an overly stringent requirement given the nature of the market. Finally, the application of a community norm concept of standard indicates that 40 percent of the stock is physically deficient.

From a policy standpoint, two significant facts emerge from this analysis. First, a large segment of the nonmetropolitan renters are underhoused in the sense that the dwellings they occupy are of poor structural quality. Second, these dwellings, by and large, are incapable of rehabilitation. Together, these observations suggest that any nonmetropolitan housing strategy would have to include new construction as a major element. Vigorous code enforcement is likely to accomplish little more than upgrading at the margin in conjunction with extensive withdrawals from the market. Subsidizing rehab efforts would probably be both inefficient and ineffective. We return to these policy matters in later chapters.

NOTES TO CHAPTER 2

1. Conceptually and methodologically, this method is analogous to the hedonic price analysis presented in Chapter 5. Here, however, only the attributes of the dwelling unit per se are considered, and the summary measure of worth is not derived from actual market transactions.

2. Eisenlauer [1968] argues that mass appraising can be as accurate in the aggregate as fee appraising, particularly since the former can make use of large quantities of data not available for individual appraisals.

3. C_v is the standard error of the estimate divided by the mean value of the dependent variable. In this case is indicates that the predicted values will be within 25 percent of the actual figure about 68 percent of the time. This relative measure of prediction accuracy is useful for comparing different regression equations.

4. For the 360 units for which we obtained estimated market value, tax value explains only 52 percent of the variation in the owner estimates, and the coefficient of variation (C_v) of .58 indicates a very low level of prediction accuracy. These results suggest that owner estimates are more reliable the more recent the last transaction.

5. The explanatory power of variables added in stepwise fashion depends on the order of inclusion; Berry and Bednarz [1975] do not present an estimate of land assessment in which the environmental factors were entered first.

6. Similarly, Lapham [1971] found a semilog relationship between age and house value to give the best fit. Emerson [1972], however, used an exponential form which contained explicit estimates of the depreciation rate (1% per year) and the economic life of the building (200 years).

7. Although a number of additional items are contained on the tax appraisal records, variations in the record formats limit the usable set of variables to only those items that were common to all the cities. Other items were eliminated from consideration after preliminary analyses revealed either that there was virtually no variation in them or that they had no systematic relationship with value. Rather than estimate values for important items that were missing on haphazard basis from individual records, we included in the analysis only those cases (467) with complete information. Evidence supporting the absence of systematic biases resulting from missing data is presented in our discussion of the validity of the derived index. It is likely that the effects of the omitted items are measured by the age, grade, and depreciation variables.

8. The letter scores ($A–E$) were converted to a numerical ranking ranging from 1 to 5 with increments of 0.25 for plus or minus grades (e.g., $A- = 4.75, B+ = 4.25$, etc.). This conversion is consistent with the appraisal procedure in which the difference between two letter grades represents approximately a 20 percent difference in the quality of the materials and workmanship used in construction. This rating is used to estimate the basic square foot replacement cost, which is then adjusted according to the presence and quality of various facilities and features. Current market value is computed by estimating the depreciation of the structure and multiplying that factor times replacement value [Cole, Layer, Trumble Co., 1972].

9. Although the depreciation variable may include economic obsolescence due to neighborhood factors that reduce the desirability of the property for residential use, the error this might introduce is small. In three of the cities, depreciation was separated into physical and functional components, where the latter should capture whatever neighborhood factors detract from value. In all cases functional depreciation is only a small fraction of the total; moreover, the

adjustments for multicollinearity, which we discuss below, remove the variation in depreciation attributable to the neighborhood variables included in the model.

10. If there are n observations, which can be disaggregated into two sets of i and j observations, respectively, then an F statistic is computed from:

$$F_{k,n-2k} = \frac{[RSS_n - (RSS_i + RSS_j)]/k}{(RSS_i + RSS_j)/(n - 2k)}$$

where k is the number of independent variables plus one, and the RSS terms are the residual sums of squares for each equation [Johnston, 1963:136].

11. For example if X_1 is found to be collinear with X_2 and X_3, we estimate

$$X_1 = a + bX_2 + cX_3 + u,$$

and then compute

$$X^*_1 = X_1 - (a + bX_2 + cX_3) = u.$$

Since X^*_1 is the residual of the regression of X_2 and X_3 on X_1, X^*_1 is orthogonal to X_2 and X_3 and will not bias their estimated standard errors [Ridker and Henning, 1967:251]. The regression equation thus becomes:

$$Y = a + bX^*_1 + cX_2 + dX_3.$$

12. The intercept value may be interpreted as that for a newly constructed ($AGELN=0$; $DEPTOT=0$), low quality unit ($IQUAL=0$) for which all dummy variables are zero. The dwelling size variable, however, complicates the meaning since it is difficult to conceive of a unit with zero square feet. For single family dwellings which contain 1,000 square feet, the base value is $.90 [$1.94-(1000) (.00104)]; at 500 square feet, it is $1.42.

13. Since our primary interest lies in the building features, it is unimportant that altering the order of entry would change the amount of explanation provided by the other categories of variables.

14. The precision of the estimating equations is indicated by the coefficients of variation which range from 15 to 17 percent. A plot of the residuals against square foot tax value displayed no evidence of heteroscedasticity, nor were there any signs of either linear or nonlinear trends that would suggest specification errors, [Hu, 1973:65]. Both the mean error and the error slope are close to the theoretically expected value of zero.

15. Using the pictures, each dwelling was assigned to one of five quality classes based on the condition of its exterior. As a rule, newer brick units were classified as being of high or medium quality, while buildings with exterior walls out of plumb, broken windows, sagging front porches and/or open foundations were ranked as poor or very poor. A marginal category captured those units falling between medium and poor.

16. The first set of tests was performed using only the 467 observations for which complete data were available and which could be used in the tax value

estimation. Because the actual derivation of the index using Equation (2–2) required considerably less information, it was possible to rank virtually the entire sample (575 dwellings).

17. We demonstrate in Chapters 5 and 6 that, while competitive pricing apparently prevails across the market, various independent submarkets can be identified, as can certain market imperfections that lead to price differentials. These influences, however, are not likely to affect our approximations of rehabilitation potential.

18. Although the explanatory power is low, this is a result of the small variation in both rent and quality among substandard units. For the full sample, an R^2 of .54 was obtained. If neighborhood factors are included, the estimated elasticity is .548, which is not statistically different from that for the two variable model. Dwelling unit size effects were also tested but found to be insignificant.

19. Tax values were adjusted for the nonstructural factors we identified in the index derivation in order to standardize the basis for these analyses. Since the index represents adjusted tax value per square foot of the dwelling unit, we computed:

$$\hat{V}' = QS * \text{Dwelling Size},$$

an estimate of building tax value which is more comparable across dwellings and cities than is the actual tax value.

※ *Chapter 3*

The Demand for Rental Housing Services

INTRODUCTION

The theory of the consumption function holds that if housing is
a necessity of life, then the elasticity of housing expenditures
with respect to income should be less than unity. Morton, for
example, has argued that "housing stands with food very high on the
order for urgency" and that "housing expenditures, accordingly, do not
bear a constant but a decreasing ratio to income" [cited in Muth,
1960:146]. When housing is viewed within a broader social context, however, an alternative understanding of housing expenditure patterns over
the income cycle becomes relevant. Marshall suggested some years ago
that "where the condition of society is healthy . . . there seems always to
be an elastic demand for house room, on account of the real conveniences
and the social distinction which it affords" [cited in Muth, 1960:146–147].
In essence, the theoretical link between these two apparently contradic-
tory understandings of housing consumption is a recognition that the
demand for housing space is relatively income inelastic, while the demand
for nonessential housing services is relatively income elastic. As Reid has
determined, "With housing as with food, increase in quality rather than
sheer quantity accounts for most of the rise in consumption with normal
income" [Reid, 1962:378].

Despite the fact that today's housing consumer might choose to
purchase, in addition to more and better housing space, higher quality
municipal services, swimming pools, saunas, tennis courts, private open
space and 24-hour security services, few empirical studies have estimated
rental housing expenditures to increase more than proportionately with

income. This is particularly striking inasmuch as today's rental contracts can be negotiated to include the costs of a vast array of housing-related amenities that, if available at all 20 years ago, were not directly chargeable to monthly rental costs. As a matter of fact, de Leeuw's systematic review of the existing major empirical studies on the subject, which tend to be metropolitan or nationally based, concludes that, when differences in research designs are taken into consideration, "overall, the elasticity of rental housing in the United States is probably in the range of 0.8 to 1.0" [de Leeuw, 1971:1].

Because our traditional assortment of housing assistance programs are primarily supply oriented and specify the cost and quality of the housing that will be consumed by participating families, the changes in housing expenditure patterns that might accompany the receipt of housing subsidies have received relatively little attention by housing policymakers. Despite the fact that the receipt of direct or indirect housing subsidies has the effect of lowering relative housing prices and of increasing real incomes, the supply emphasis of our program approach has given rise to production-oriented measures of program performance rather than to measures of the changes in housing consumption brought about by the respective programs. Inquiries into the nature of housing demand which have been undertaken by academic economists interested in consumption theory have remained far removed from the federal housing establishment.

Recent changes in the housing policy environment, however, have not only rekindled an official interest in the structure of housing demand but have also renewed the relevance of the few existing empirical studies of consumer housing expenditure patterns. On the evaluation front, Smolensky was one of the first economists to estimate the real resource cost to the government of building low-rent public housing, and to ask "if a larger number of low-income families could be induced to occupy standard housing . . . if the funds currently devoted to public housing construction were spent in some other way" [Smolensky, 1968:253]. His analysis suggested that a system of unrestricted cash grants in an amount less than the cost to the government of financing the public housing program would likely lead to greater improvements in the housing circumstances of poor families. More recently, program evaluation efforts within HUD are based increasingly upon the relationship between the welfare increase an unrestricted cash grant would provide households, and the extra housing consumed by virtue of a household's participation in any one of the existing supply programs. The justification for this approach is based on the suggestion that "the tenant may not value his extra housing as highly as its market price because the in-kind nature of the transfer restricts his flexibility in choosing between various housing options and other goods" [U.S. Department of Housing and Urban Development, 1974a:IV–13]. The value of the in-kind subsidy to the tenant "can be measured by the size of the unrestricted cash grant which he would accept in lieu of the subsidy" [U.S. Department of Housing and Urban Development, 1974a:IV–12].

Not only do the above evaluation efforts place a premium on empirically derived estimates of income and price elasticities of housing demand, but an a priori understanding of elasticities lies at the heart of the large-scale, federally supported experimental housing allowance program now under way in several metropolitan areas. Under this demonstration, thousands of consumers are receiving income transfers to increase their housing consumption. Changes in family expenditure patterns under various earmarking requirements are being monitored and analyzed in an effort to field test the proposition that a restricted income transfer program is a more cost-effective means of increasing the quality of housing consumed by low-income families than are programs which subsidize the costs of new construction.

Our systematic examination of rental housing expenditure patterns in nonmetropolitan communities will determine the extent to which household groups differ with respect to their levels of housing consumption and incidence of housing deprivations. Particular emphasis is placed on the influences of life cycle, household composition, race, and income. The analysis of the previous chapter demonstrated that the rental stock in these cities is both very shelter-oriented and characterized by extensive basic deficiencies, and we shall further demonstrate here that the renter population is dominated by low and moderate income families. Inasmuch as household demand for basic shelter services should be relatively income inelastic and lower-income families are likely to seek to satisfy these needs before they elect to consume higher quality service flows, we would presume that Morton's concept of income elasticities is more appropriate to the smaller city than is Marshall's. In short, not only is a systematic analysis of income elasticities an efficient way of summarizing the relative importance of housing to a given population but, since most empirical studies are metropolitan-based, the comparative element of our demand analysis may have important national policy implications, particularly with respect to the potential impact of demand-oriented housing programs in the nonmetropolitan housing market.

HOUSING EXPENDITURE PATTERNS IN THE RENTAL MARKET

Household Composition and Housing Consumption

The 45-year mean age of all nonmetropolitan renter household heads suggests either that there is a relatively large concentration of elderly tenants who rely upon the rental stock to meet their housing needs, or that relatively more households in the so-called home-ownership age categories are heavily represented in the rental market (Table 3–1). Although there is some truth to both of these propositions, the renter population is in fact relatively evenly dispersed over the age groups.

Table 3–1.   Composition and Socioeconomic Characteristics of Renter Households by Race

	White	*Black*	*Total*
Age of Head:			
<25	22.5%	9.9%	18.3%
25–34	21.9	15.5	19.8
35–54	24.4	38.1	28.9
55–64	12.6	16.0	13.7
65+	18.4	20.4	19.0
Mean Age (yrs)	43	48	45
Household Type:			
Male Head			
Single Person	4.7%	11.0%	6.8%
2–4 Persons	44.7	28.2	39.2
5+ Persons	9.0	11.6	9.9
Total Male Head	58.4	50.8	55.9
Female Head			
Single Person	26.6%	16.0%	23.1%
2–4 Persons	13.7	16.6	14.7
5+ Persons	1.3	16.6	6.3
Total Female Head	41.6	49.2	44.1
Mean Household Size	2.4	3.1	2.6
Education of Head:			
No High School	28.8%	54.1%	32.8%
Some High School	20.8	26.2	22.5
High School Graduate	18.8	16.3	18.0
Post-High School	37.6	3.4	26.7
Employment of Head:			
White Collar	34.1%	3.3%	23.8%
Skilled Labor	31.0	33.2	31.7
Unskilled Labor	8.5	22.6	13.3
Total Employed	73.6	59.1	68.8
Unemployed	1.1	7.2	3.1
Not in Labor Force	25.3	33.7	28.1
Mean Household Income	$6,756	$4,726	$6,073
Mean Wage of Full-Time Employed Heads	$5,739	$4,030	$5,273
Mean Household Nonwage Income	$1,989	$1,415	$1,760
N	365	181	546

Nearly one in five household heads is age 65 or more, but the dependence of this older group upon the rental market is balanced by an almost equal portion of household heads less than 25 years of age.

Further disaggregating renter household heads by race and sex, however, reveals variations in the age structure which contribute greatly to differences in housing circumstances. One-third of nonmetropolitan renters are black, and black household heads tend, overall, to be somewhat older than whites, the higher average being accounted for by the presence of more black households in the intermediate age group of 35 to 54 years (Table 3–1). Generally high levels of female headship prevail among nonmetropolitan renters. Approximately 40 percent of the white and about half the black households are headed by women, who are substantially older than their male counterparts. Almost 40 percent of white and over a quarter of black female heads are elderly, compared with only four and thirteen percent respectively for white and black men.

Generally, nonmetropolitan renter households tend to be quite small (Table 3–1). Mean household size is 2.6, and 80 percent of all households have three or fewer members. Although the average size is virtually the same both for black and white male-headed households, this disguises the fact that black males are about two and one-half times as likely as white males either to live alone or to head households with six or more members. Nearly two-thirds of the white female heads live alone, which was suggested by the earlier discussion of their higher ages. Although one-third of black, female-headed households contain five or more members, it is the frequent presence of nonspouse adults, relatives, and nonrelatives that swells their average size. Although larger numbers of children do influence the size of these households more than households headed by males or by white females, it is nevertheless the case that the large, black, female-headed households which figure prominently in the metropolitan, inner-city housing market play a much smaller role in the nonmetropolitan market where they account for only three percent of the renters.

For the entire nonmetropolitan renter population, the mean annual contract rent is $798, or $67 a month (Table 3–2). With a standard deviation approaching one-half the mean, the rent distribution is reasonably dispersed. Although this suggests widely varying expenditures across the market, the rent distribution is far more clustered than is the distribution of rent-income ratios. While the average renter devotes 19 percent of gross current income to contract rent, the relative housing expense distribution is characterized by a coefficient of variability of .89. No matter how the renter population is disaggregated, household cohorts are far less homogeneous with respect to the proportion of current income devoted to housing than with respect to absolute housing expenses.

According to Maisel and Winnick [1960:149], "housing expenditures, like total consumption, follow the cross-section life cycle of rising and declining income.'' Though the expected amplitude would be lower than in the income cycle, we would expect mean housing expenses to be low for very young household heads, to peak in middle age, where income earning capacity is at a maximum, and to decline among the elderly. From the perspective of the permanent income hypothesis, however, we would expect less sharp distinctions in housing expenditures among the different age groups. If present levels of housing consumption are related to household expectations of long term income possibilities, then younger households will be likely to overspend relative to their current incomes. Similarly, because of the lag in the downward adjustment of the housing circumstances of older households to declines in their current incomes, their mean expenditures are also likely to be relatively high.

As a matter of fact, the nonmetropolitan rental market is characterized by small differences in mean expenditures across most of the age cohorts. Overall, mean annual rents are highest by far for the youngest households, and are relatively constant across all remaining age groups (Table 3–2). Indeed, mean monthly rents vary by only $6 between households headed by individuals in the 45–54 year age group and those aged at least 65. Within each age group, however, widely differing expenditure patterns are reflected in high coefficients of variability.

Despite the relative constancy of rents across the majority of age cohorts, the pattern of relative housing expenditures follows a priori expectations. Rent-income ratios are a relatively high .18 for the youngest

Table 3–2. Housing Consumption by Household Composition

	Mean Annual Rent	Mean Rent-Income Ratio
Age of Head		
16–24	$957	.183
25–34	904	.152
35–44	731	.123
45–54	755	.156
55–64	702	.245
65+	679	.266
Race		
White	$920	.191
Black	557	.177
Household Size		
1	$761	.247
2	845	.185
3–4	848	.156
5+	712	.134
Total	$798	.186
N	535	496

families, decrease to a mean of .12 for families in the 35–44 year age group and increase thereafter with age to .27 for elderly households. Although great variability exists within each cohort, this pattern does support the contention that "housing expenditures over the family life cycle tend to be much 'stickier' and affected by more discontinuous changes than is the case for many other forms of consumption" [Maisel and Winnick, 1960:149]. The failure of households to reduce housing expenditures with advances in age and with declines in income is reflected in the high relative housing expense burden of older renters.

Differences in mean housing expenditures among household sizes are very small. Average rents are virtually identical for households with between two and four members, and are only $4 a month higher for single individuals than they are for large families (Table 3–2). Relative housing expenses, on the other hand, decrease from a high of 25 percent for single person households to a low of 13 percent for families of five or more. Within income groups, however, patterns of expenditure vary, as we will discuss in detail later.

Socioeconomic Characteristics and Housing Consumption

Overall, the heads of nonmetropolitan renter households do not have high levels of formal education. One-third never attended high school, and fewer than half are high school graduates (Table 3–1). Levels of education are substantially lower for black heads, over half of whom have received no high school training. In contrast, over half of all white heads have at least graduated from high school; nearly 40 percent have some education beyond high school, and 18 percent are college graduates.

Slightly more than seven out of every ten heads of renter households are members of the labor force, and the unemployment rate is only 4.3 percent. Labor force participation varies considerably with sex and race, however, as does the incidence of unemployment and underemployment. Almost nine out of 10 white male household heads are in the labor force, compared with only three-quarters of black males. In every age category below age 54, white males are more likely to be in the labor force and to be employed, while at age 55 or over black males are considerably more likely still to be in the labor force and employed. Unemployment rates are substantially higher for blacks than for whites and for female than for male household heads. While only one-half of one percent of all white male heads in the labor force were unemployed at the time of our survey, the corresponding rate for black males was closer to six percent. Among black female heads, 18 percent were unemployed and an additional 14 percent were working part-time despite their expressed desire to hold a full time job.

The majority of all employed renter household heads are manual workers: nearly 50 percent are employed as skilled laborers, and nearly a fifth are unskilled laborers. Whites are nine times as likely to be employed in white collar jobs; conversely, blacks are four times as likely as whites to be employed in unskilled blue collar jobs. Although black male heads are seriously underrepresented in white collar occupations, it is the concentration of black female heads in private household or domestic employment that exerts the single strongest influence on the differences between the black and white occupation distributions.

Among nonmetropolitan renters, total household income from all sources averages about $6,100, with the mean for blacks being only about 70 percent of that for whites (Table 3–1). Similarly, the mean wage income of employed black household heads is 71 percent that of whites. Although blacks are more likely to be receiving nonwage income, there is no difference in the number of wage earners per household for each racial group. Overall, 40 percent of all households have two or more working adults. Within occupation classes, mean wages for whites are generally higher than those for blacks, although in fact the occupational structures for whites and blacks are so different that these comparisons are in many cases not meaningful. It is significant, however, that the class of low-paid workers making less than $4,000 accounts for one-quarter of white compared with over half of black household heads. Conversely, 70 percent of white household heads earn annual wages of $4,000 to $10,000, while fewer than half of black household heads do. In general, however, there does not exist among white nonmetropolitan renters any substantial group with both high income and job status. Indeed, although no employed black heads of households earn more than $10,000 a year, only six percent of whites make that much. While about a quarter of white household heads are employed in professional or managerial occupations, fewer than one-fifth of them, representing about four percent of all household heads, earn over $10,000.

Despite the fact that nearly 40 percent of all renter households have total annual incomes of $4,000 or less, fewer than one-third of these low-income families had received any kind of public assistance payments over the year prior to our survey. Nearly 40 percent of black and almost a quarter of white households in this income class received such transfer payments. Of those who had received payments, one-third were elderly, one-third were households with dependent children, and one-third were disabled or receiving payments for which no program source could be identified.

In their analysis of national housing consumption patterns, Maisel and Winnick [1960] found that more education and higher job status lead to higher levels of housing consumption, but when either of these two variables is controlled, variation in the other is associated with little additional variation in mean housing expenditures. They thus concluded that "higher status can be reached either through higher education or occupation" [Maisel and Winnick, 1960:152], and that one route is as good as the other. In the nonmetropolitan rental market, mean housing expenditures are a monotonically increasing function of education (Table 3–3) as we would expect, but the relationship between rent and occupa-

Table 3–3. Mean Annual Rent by Occupation and Education of Household Head[a]

Education	White Collar	Skilled Labor	Unskilled Labor	Not in Labor Force	Total
<8th Grade	$ 601	$ 643	$ 549	$ 541	$ 576
Some High School	912	732	614	663	714
High School Grad.	909	734	794	960	812
Some College	1,082	1,069	b	1,312	1,102
College, Tech. Grad.	1,235	864	b	1,230	1,214
Total	$1,045	$ 732	$ 691	$ 738	$ 804

$N = 521$

[a] Excludes full-time students.

[b] Fewer than five observations.

tion is somewhat less consistent. Within each occupation group, however, housing expenditures vary significantly by education. Among white collar workers, for example, mean rents are lowest for those with less than eight years of schooling, increase for those with some high school, are still higher for workers with some college, and are highest for college graduates. A similar pattern holds for skilled laborers, with the exception that those with some college outspend graduates of college and technical schools.

A further examination of the interaction effects of education and occupation on mean housing expenditures reveals that higher status on one dimension compensates for lower status on the other dimension. Thus, for example, while the mean expenditures of unskilled laborers are generally lower than those of white collar workers, laborers who have graduated from high school spend more for housing than do white collar workers who have less than eight years of schooling. Similarly, skilled laborers with some college outspend white collar workers who have had no post-high school education.

We would expect mean rent to increase monotonically with income and mean rent-income ratios to be inversely related to income, with the relative rate of decline moderating beyond the middle income cohort. In fact, none of these a priori expectations holds entirely. Although mean rents virtually double from a low of $540 a year for families with incomes below $2,000 to a high of $1,018 for those with incomes above $10,000, households with incomes between $4,000 and $10,000 average approximately similar rents (Table 3–4). Thus, ignoring the two extremes, mean rents do not vary significantly across income groups. Strikingly, too, the within-group variations in housing expenses are generally as large as those for the entire population.

Table 3–4. Mean Annual Rent by Household Size and Income

Household Income	Household Size				
	1	*2*	*3–4*	*5+*	*Total*
⩽$2,000	$ 513	$ 638	$505	$521	$ 540
2,001–4,000	691	682	573	526	644
4,001–6,000	886	880	811	880	872
6,001–8,000	880	856	909	740	854
8,001–10,000	1,230	1,020	826	639	860
10,001+	1,284	1,095	998	895	1,018

N = 494

In contrast, the mean relative housing expenditure is a monotonically decreasing function of income (Table 3–5). The lowest income renters devote 41 percent of current income to housing, and each successively higher income group allocates a lesser percentage of total resources to rent. Nevertheless, there is great variation in relative housing expenditures at each income level, suggesting that current income is but one of many factors influencing the relative share of resources that is allocated to the housing component of the family budget.

Table 3–5. Mean Rent-Income Ratio by Household Size and Income

Household Income	Household Size				
	1	*2*	*3–4*	*5+*	*Total*
⩽$2,000	.370	.457	.529	.391	.412
2,001–4,000	.223	.221	.196	.203	.215
4,001–6,000	.180	.178	.179	.182	.179
6,001–8,000	.132	.121	.129	.106	.122
8,001–10,000	.146	.115	.095	.072	.098
10,000+	.115	.084	.079	.067	.080

N = 494

Earlier we noted that mean housing expenditures vary little by household size. An analysis of the joint effects of income and household size, however, does produce some interesting distinctions in expenditure patterns. Holding income constant, the pressure to expand both housing and nonhousing consumption increases with household size. In actuality, among lower-income nonmetropolitan renters, mean housing expenditures tend to be stable or to decline slightly with increasing household size (Table 3–5). Within household size cohorts, mean rent tends to increase with income. In most cases the variability of behavior within the respective household size and income cohorts is significantly less than in any previous tabulation thus far examined.

In the lowest income group, relative housing expenses increase with size up to 3–4 person households and then decrease sharply for larger families. In the middle of the income spectrum, rent-income ratios are remarkably stable across household size classes. In the $4,000–$6,000 range, ratios are a constant .18, while they only range from .13 for single person households in the $6,000–$8,000 group to .11 for families of five or more persons. In the two highest income groups, however, small households allocate almost twice the proportion of their incomes to rent as do their larger counterparts. And, as was the case with absolute expenditures, rent-income ratios are tightly clustered around their respective group means. Overall, then, the analysis indicates that large households satisfy, to the extent possible, their nonhousing needs before increasing their housing consumption.

Confounding the effects of the socioeconomic variables on housing expenditure patterns in the above analyses is the influence of race, the importance of which can be isolated by simultaneously controlling for income, household size, and race (Table 3–6). The most interesting aspect

Table 3–6. Mean Annual Rent by Income, Race and Household Size

Household Size	< *Median Income*		≥ *Median Income*		
	White	*Black*	*White*	*Black*	*N*
1	$ 736	$ 518	$1,071	$ 680	140
2	862	480	1,056	617	147
3–4	834	499	948	678	125
5+	1,092	558	808	668	82
					494

of the resulting rent distribution is the relative stability across household size cohorts among blacks and the directly opposite patterns exhibited by lower-income as opposed to higher-income whites. Less than two dollars a month separates the mean rents of small and large black households within each of the two income groups. On the other hand, among lower-income whites, average rents tend to increase with household size, while among higher-income whites, the reverse is true. In the latter case, single-person white households pay slightly less than $1,000 a year for rent, while households with five of more persons pay an average rent of only $808.

Housing Deprivation

Although the nonmetropolitan rental market may in fact be characterized by a number of serious imperfections, for which we test in subsequent chapters, relatively high rates of substandard occupany may be fully consistent with a smoothly functioning competitive market. As Rothenberg [1967:36] notes, "If there is poverty, this means that some people are living a 'substandard' way of life [and] such a way of life must necessarily contain some 'substandard' elements—perhaps inadequate food, or clothing, or recreation, or shelter, or various combinations of these." Ignoring for the moment any serious market immobilities which may affect the housing allocation process in nonmetropolitan cities, we would expect the incidence of substandard occupancy to vary inversely with income. Essentially, this is the case. Almost 60 percent of all renters with incomes of less than $4,000 occupy substandard housing (Table 3–7).

Table 3–7. Housing Deprivation by Household Cohort

	Housing Deprived as a Percent of All Renters	Percent of Deprived Households:		
		In Substandard Dwellings	In Standard Dwellings at Excessive Costs	In Overcrowded Standard Dwellings
Age of Head				
16–24	39.8%	75.7%	24.3%	-0-%
25–34	44.0	61.4	29.6	9.0
35–44	53.2	78.8	3.0	18.2
45–54	67.5	82.1	8.9	8.9
55–64	76.5	71.2	28.8	-0-
65+	72.2	63.2	35.1	1.7
Total Household Income				
≤$2,000	98.6	59.4	40.6	-0-
$2,001–4,000	80.1	73.9	25.0	1.1
$4,001–6,000	51.1	69.6	23.9	6.5
$6,001–10,000	38.0	83.3	3.7	13.0
$10,000+	29.7	77.3	-0-	22.7
Race				
White	43.7	60.3	34.7	5.0
Black	84.7	83.3	10.2	6.5
Total	57.5	71.7	22.6	5.7

$N = 485$

These lower income renters are almost twice as likely to be poorly housed as are households with moderate incomes, and two and one-half times as likely to occupy substandard dwellings as are the highest income renters. Despite a general confirmation of the income-quality hypothesis, however, it should be noted that the rate of housing inadequacies among more affluent households is relatively high, reflecting either low housing preferences or substantial stock constraints.

Because of the relationship between income and life cycle we would also expect to find the incidence of substandard housing to be higher among young and old consumers and somewhat lower among the middle age cohorts, but this is not the case. Overall, the two youngest cohorts are less likely than any others to occupy substandard housing while the incidence of substandard occupancy among elderly renters is less than that among household heads between the ages of 45–64. While we are not able to explain this pattern without controlling for additional socioeconomic variables, it is the case that larger proportions of elderly and young renters are consuming standard housing at the cost of allocating substantially larger shares of their incomes to rent than are middle-aged consumers. Essentially, then, the distribution of housing quality is affected by the degree to which different types of households are willing or able to sacrifice their consumption of nonhousing goods in order to consume standard housing.

Within the context of a microeconomic equilibrium model of the urban housing market, Rothenberg [1967] argues persuasively that the poverty-inadequate housing nexus calls for an income rather than housing attack. More recently, a macroeconomic analysis of our national housing condition also takes note, though somewhat differently, of the interface between housing deprivation and income. Frieden and Atkinson [1975:5] argue that the limited definition of substandard, "based on structural deficiencies and the presence or absence of plumbing facilities, is no longer a meaningful discriminator of conditions in the urban housing stock." They argue that "increasingly, the [urban housing] problem is one of excessive cost rather than of poor physical condition" [Frieden and Atkinson, 1975:6].

In support of this proposition, national statistics indicate that "the number and proportion of households living in physically inadequate units have declined sharply since 1960 but the number paying more than a reasonable portion of income for housing has risen sharply" [Frieden and Atkinson, 1975:6]. Indeed, in 1970, one out of every five American households suffered from at least one of three kinds of housing deprivation. Of these, 53 percent occupied physically inadequate housing, 42 percent consumed standard housing at excessive costs relative to their incomes, and five percent were overcrowded though living in standard housing and not spending excessively. A decade earlier, 71 percent of all the housing deprived suffered solely from physically inadequate shelter, while only 24 percent consumed adequate housing at excessive costs [Frieden and Atkinson, 1975:7]. Obviously, any estimate of the size of the housing-deprived population across the nonmetropolitan rental market will be sensitive to the housing quality measure that is used to establish minimum standards of adequacy. Nevertheless, it is worth noting that, on the basis of physical housing inadequacies alone, a nonmetropolitan renter is four times as likely to be inadequately housed as the average American.

By defining the housing-deprived nonmetropolitan population to include not only households who occupy physically inadequate shelter, but also those who consume standard housing at the cost of being overcrowded or spending more than one-quarter of their incomes, the marketwide incidence of housing problems rises to 58 percent, compared to the national average of 20 percent. In short, the magnitude of small city housing problems increases some 25 percent when overcrowded and overconsuming households are added to the substandard universe, while in the nation as a whole, the addition of these same two cohorts swells the deprived population by some 90 percent. Overall, about 72 percent of all housing-deprived renter households in the nonmetropolitan city occupy physically inadequate housing, 22 percent have standard housing at excessive costs, and six percent are overcrowded (Table 3–7). Whether coincidental or not, the composition of the housing-deprived pool of renters in the smaller city in 1972 is almost identical to that which characterized the nation as a whole almost a decade earlier. At this point in time, contrary to the national experience, physical stock inadequacies still dominate the housing problems of nonmetropolitan renters.

In general, stock deficiencies dominate the deprivation pool among all cohorts, although, expectedly, the incidence of excessive housing costs is very high among isolated population groups. As we indicated above, high rent burdens are a more important cause of housing deprivation among younger and older households than among middle-aged renters. In many ways, however, the split between substandard occupancy and excessive housing costs is most pronounced between black and white nonmetropolitan renters. First, blacks are twice as likely as whites to suffer housing deficiencies. Second, upwards of 80 percent of all deprived blacks consume substandard housing, while the corresponding rate among whites is 60 percent. Third, around 35 percent of all deprived white renters consume standard housing at high costs, while among blacks, excessive expenditures for standard housing account for just 10 percent of the deprivation pool. Whites are nearly twice as likely as blacks to occupy standard housing at the cost of high rent-income ratios. Essentially, then, stock inadequacies characterize the problems of black renters more than white, and excessive housing costs are more characteristically a problem for whites. These summary statistics reflect significant problems relating to market discrimination, which are discussed more fully in our demand analysis, and extensively in Chapter 6. Problems of stock deficiencies, access restrictions, and income limitations are also considered in our later analyses of policy and program possibilities.

INCOME ELASTICITY OF DEMAND

A number of insights into housing demand were developed in the previous sections where consumption patterns were examined across household types. With respect to current income, for example, rent-income ratios monotonically decrease as income rises, while mean rents vary by less than $2 per month for households with incomes between $4,000–$10,000. Without simultaneous multiple controls, these relationships are somewhat ambiguous; they do, however, indicate that certain expected housing consumption patterns either are not observed in the smaller city, or are not as strong as one might hypothesize. In particular, they suggest that the income elasticity of housing demand in the nonmetropolitan rental market is considerably less than one. In the remainder of this chapter, we examine in a more systematic fashion the relationship between income and housing consumption. The analysis is based on estimated permanent household income so that the elasticities do not reflect the downward bias that would be caused by transitory components of income. We first estimate income elasticity using a two variable rent-income model; stratified estimates are made for white and black consumers and for cohorts differentiated by household size. We then expand our simple elasticity model into a more generalized model in order to assess the impacts on housing expenditures of nonincome characteristics of renters. The results of our analysis suggest that general levels of housing consumption and expenditure responses to changes in income horizons are substantially lower in nonmetropolitan rental markets than in the nation as a whole or in large metropolitan areas.

Model Specification

As is most often the case in studies of this kind, our income and housing consumption data are derived from a cross-sectional survey. For all intents and purposes, therefore, the price per unit of housing can be assumed to be constant across the market, and we cannot estimate a demand curve relating housing price to the amount of housing consumed. Our focus is on estimating the effect of income on housing demand and, therefore, on shifts of, rather than movement along, the demand curve. If we assume that the consumption of housing is a monotonically increasing function of income (i.e., that housing is a normal good), and that the income elasticity (β) is constant over the relevant income range, then:

$$H = \alpha Y^{\beta} \tag{3-1}$$

where: H is the amount of housing consumed, and
            Y is household income.
A logarithmic transformation of Equation (3–1) produces:

$$lnH = \alpha + \beta ln Y. \tag{3-2}$$

The parameters of Equation (3–2) can be estimated in the usual manner through multiple regression techniques. A unitary elasticity ($\beta = 1$) would indicate that rent-income ratios are constant across all incomes. An elasticity of less than one would suggest that housing consumption increases at a slower rate than income, which corresponds to Morton's conception of housing as a basic necessity. An elasticity exceeding one would suggest that once a household has purchased a basic minimum amount of housing, further expenditures, which increase at a more rapid rate than income, are related to increased consumption of nonessential housing services.

   Rent: Both the varied nature of the housing commodity and the multidimensional services it provides make it difficult to measure unambiguously the quantity of housing consumed. The market price of housing is a function of numerous characteristics, including the size and physical quality of the dwelling and the features of the neighborhood in which it is located. In the next chapter, we estimate a hedonic price model and demonstrate that rent can be accurately predicted from empirical knowledge of these characteristics of the dwelling. This suggests that the prices of various dimensions of the housing services flow are relatively constant across the market and, therefore, that market rent can be employed as a reasonable measure of total housing consumption. Nevertheless, the relationship between total expenditures and the amount of the commodity consumed is probably less perfect for housing than for most other consumer goods. For example, we demonstrate in Chapter 6 that certain market immobilities and imperfections result in variations in the price of housing services across the market. Despite these problems, we follow the common practice of using rent as the measure of housing consumption.
   A further complication in the definition of the dependent variable is the fact that in some cases contract rent includes payment for services unrelated to the building structure or to the neighborhood. For households

who live in unfurnished dwellings and who are responsible for paying for their own utility service, contract rent represents basic shelter costs. For the relatively small proportion of the renter population that occupy furnished dwellings (10%), or for whom part or all of their utility services are included in their rent (6%), contract rent represents more than just shelter costs. Reid [1962:45–47] suggests that, since the income elasticity of utility services is considerably lower than that for housing consumption, the use of gross rent data will create a downward bias on the elasticity estimate. Lee [1968:485], however, found no evidence of a systematic bias as a result of using contract rent, which in some cases included the provision of nonshelter services. In the nonmetropolitan cities, utilities or furnishings are more likely to be provided in the higher rent units, which would result in a slight upward bias in our estimate of income elasticity. Since there are relatively few instances in which these services are provided, however, the error should not be large.

Income: According to de Leeuw [1971:1], there is now "widespread acceptance of the proposition that the elasticity of housing with respect to normal income is higher than the elasticity of housing with respect to measured income of a single year." This is because "housing demand reacts less to a change in current income precisely because a consumer's expectations of his normal income level change less rapidly than his current income" [Muth, 1960:163]. In accordance with the theory and empirical evidence relating to housing consumption patterns, we have estimated permanent or normal household income using a technique developed by Ramanathan [1971] which is fully explained in Appendix B.

Briefly, the methodology is based on the assumption that within well-defined household types, the expected value of the transitory components of household income is zero. Households were disaggregated according to the age and education of the head, and for each cohort the average earnings of the head were determined. Using secondary data sources, we then estimated the annual rate of change in mean wages between age groups and the annual rate of growth of earnings for persons in each education group. Given these estimated income changes, normal income was computed by discounting anticipated future earnings back to the present and taking a weighted average of the current and expected annual income of household heads. Following Ramanathan [1971], we assumed a 10-year horizon for the 55–64 year age cohort, 0-year horizon for the 65 and over group (i.e., average current income equals permanent income), and a 20-year horizon for all other age groups. In short, the head of every nonmetropolitan renter household was assigned a normal earnings figure that is pegged to one of 24 age-education cohorts.

To this amount, we added all nonwage income received by the house-

...der the assumption that it is stable over time and represents a component of income. In the large majority of cases in which ...ge income is a substantial portion of the total, the head is over age ..., ...d the income is a form of retirement or disability payment; the assumption of stability is, therefore, reasonable. The wage incomes of other adults in the household were not included in permanent income because such earnings are likely to vary substantially from year to year among lower-income consumers and reflect transitory components of total income. The independent variable is thus the sum of nonwage income and the estimated permanent income of the head. The effect of the income of secondary wage earners on housing consumption is considered independently in the more fully specified model which we discuss later.

Estimated Elasticity

The estimated permanent income elasticity of demand for rental housing in nonmetropolitan markets is about .37 (Table 3–8). Instead of the housing expenditure responses of nonmetropolitan renters being close to proportionate to long-term income changes, on average their housing expenditures increase by only around four percent for every 10 percent change in permanent income. This figure is considerably below de Leeuw's estimate that the income elasticity for renters across the nation is in the range of 0.8–1.0 [de Leeuw, 1971]. Recent evidence presented by Carliner [1973], however, indicates that the elasticity for renters is about 0.5. While one could argue that our low elasticity estimate is a function of the way in which we defined normal income, it is the case that when

Table 3–8. Estimated Income Elasticity of Demand for Rental Housing Based on Permanent Income Two-Variable Model[a]

| | | Elasticity[b] | | | |
	Constant	Value	Std. Error	R^2	N
All Renters	3.393	.374	.035	.190	491
Race[d]					
White	3.127	.418	.045	.212	329
Black	5.000	.155[a]	.044	.072	162
Household Size[e]					
1–2 Persons	3.087	.413	.043	.247	281
3–4 Persons	3.558	.357	.083	.132	124
5+ Persons	4.637	.218[c]	.089	.067	86

[a] Estimated from: $R = \alpha Y^\beta$
where Y is defined as permanent earnings of head plus nonwage income.
[b] All elasticities significant at $p < .001$.
[c] Elasticity significantly different from that for full sample at $p < .05$ or better.
[d] Elasticities between groups different at $p < .001$.
[e] $b_{1-2} > b_{5+}, p < .05$.

measured income is used, the average income elasticity is lowered by some 70 percent to .11. Moreover, the elasticity estimates are fairly stable with respect to the definition of permanent income. The use of discount rates ranging from 0 to 8 percent produced elasticities ranging only from .34–37. This is consistent with de Leeuw's [1971:1] conclusions that differences in the definition of income used in cross-sectional demand studies do not account for much of the variation in estimated elasticities. Carliner [1973] experimented with two weighting schemes to estimate permanent income from a four-year panel study, and he also concluded that the exact definition of permanent income had very little effect on the derived elasticity.

The significance of the extremely low average elasticity across the entire rental population cannot be overstated. It is likely that stock constraints are primarily responsible for the very weak housing expenditure responses to income changes in smaller cities. Not only are broad segments of the smaller city rental market relatively undifferentiated with respect to cost and structural quality, but relatively low levels of housing-related services are included in contract rent. To the extent that contract rent reflects shelter cost in the narrowest sense, our finding that the demand for shelter is relatively income inelastic is fully consistent with the precepts of general consumption theory. One might plausibly argue that such a low elasticity indicates that housing is rather low on the priority lists of nonmetropolitan renters. Recently developed, convenience-laden apartment complexes, however, seem to attract proportionately greater shares of household incomes than do the older, more spartan segments of the rental stock, suggesting that such an argument may be only partially true.

A likely possibility, given the relatively narrow range of options available in the rental stock, may be that any substantial interest in expanding housing consumpton in response to increases in income is ultimately felt in the fee simple market as renters become homeowners. This may be particularly true for families requiring more space than is available in higher quality apartments. Nearly 60 percent of the housing stock in these cities is owner-occupied, which indicates a relatively strong preference for ownership. Moreover, ownership opportunities outside the city, where land is relatively inexpensive and where mobile homes provide a low-cost housing option, are likely to provide close substitutes for renting in the city. Because of the compact size of the city, families locating in these areas do not make a significant tradeoff between accessibility and housing consumption. In sum, we can infer that an important role of the rental sector in these cities is to provide housing for households who have low preferences for housing or who are economically constrained to consume low levels of housing.

city Variations

cit in the above analysis is the assumption that rent responses to
changes are invariant for all households; essentially this implies
r all consumers there is a single family of preference functions. This
assumption can be relaxed by disaggregating the renter population into
more or less homogeneous cohorts and examining variations in the elasticities across the groups.[1] While this approach can provide some insights
into the differences in household preference patterns, the results are
somewhat ambiguous. If, for example, the rental market is segmented
into relatively independent submarkets, observed differences in income
elasticities may reflect supply-side factors as well as demand influences.
In Chapter 5 we will consider the submarket segmentation problem more
explicitly in the context of hedonic price estimation; because of the
complexities inherent in the analysis of housing consumption, we do not
attempt to estimate market parameters from a simultaneous equation structural model.

Race: We noted earlier that race is an important factor in the small
city rental market. Here we consider whether the differences in housing
consumption between black and white households are in part the result of
differences in the relationship between rent and income changes. In his
study of housing demand for metropolitan areas across the nation, de
Leeuw [1971:8] observed that while nonwhites devote a larger proportion
of their incomes to housing, the relative amount they spend declines more
rapidly than average as their incomes rise. Among nonmetropolitan renters the same relationships are found (Table 3–8), but the differences are
considerably greater than those found by de Leeuw for all U.S. renters.
While a 10 percent income increase would induce a four percent increase
in housing expenditures among white households, the response among
blacks would be less than half that amount. Although the rent response to
income changes is much weaker among blacks, the intercept term is
considerably larger, which suggests that a higher average expenditure is
required for blacks to purchase basic shelter services. Employing the
estimating equations to compute total rent expenditures at the respective
mean permanent incomes for blacks and whites reveals that the former
pay lower rents in both absolute and relative terms. While the computed
$552 annual rent for blacks represents 11.6 percent of permanent income,
the comparable figure for whites is $885, which yields a rent-permanent
income ratio of 14.7 percent.

These results suggest that blacks have lower housing preferences or
that their lower incomes leave little for housing after other basic household needs are met. It is equally likely, however, that racial segregation,
restricted access to the housing market at large, and price discrimination

are contributing to the differences in the observed expenditure patterns. If the segregation patterns of these cities are the result of either formal or informal pressures to restrict black households to well-defined neighborhoods where low quality housing predominates, then blacks will have limited opportunities to expand their housing consumption as their incomes increase. In effect, the operative factor would not be low preferences but an inelastic housing supply for the black-occupied submarket.

A likely result of artificial supply restrictions is that blacks pay higher prices for housing than do whites, *cet. par.* While this issue is pursued more fully in Chapter 6, we can draw some important inferences from the demand equations. Blacks may pay higher prices because of explicit discriminatory behavior or as a result of excess demand pressures in submarkets in which expansion of the stock does not keep pace with household growth or increases in income. In either case the net result will be the same. If the demand for housing is price elastic, as is commonly believed, then blacks confronted by higher housing prices than whites will consume less housing at all levels of permanent income. In short, the higher intercept value, lower elasticity, and lower mean expenditure derived for black households are all fully consistent with the existence of racial discrimination in the housing market.

Household Size: It is reasonable to expect elasticities to differ by household size since it is this factor that determines the household's requirement for space—the most basic dimension of shelter service. If, for example, large households must make a larger "base payment" for housing than do smaller households, the regression intercept will increase with household size. The expected rent responses to income changes across household size cohorts are somewhat less clear. If we assume that all households are satisfying minimum space requirements, then additional rent expenditures will be related to increases in the quality of housing consumed. Since large households are likely to be underconsuming nonhousing goods, their income elasticity of demand for housing should be lower than that for small households. That is, a greater proportion of any marginal increase in income is likely to be spent on nonhousing consumption than on nonessential housing services. The same conclusion can be reached if we consider the situation of two households of different size but with the same incomes. If the larger household, because of its greater space requirements, were spending more for housing, then it would have to devote a larger proportion of any given marginal increase in income to rent than would the smaller household in order for the respective elasticities to be equal.[2]

If the assumption that all households are consuming at least a minimally sufficient amount of space is relaxed, however, the conclusion is not as clear. If lower-income, larger households cannot satisfy their basic space requirements, they should be willing to devote relatively larger portions of their marginal income increases to rent. Were this the case, we would expect to observe a higher elasticity among large households. Overall, however, the incidence of overcrowding is relatively low, indicating that pressures that would contribute to higher elasticities among larger households should be minimal.

The results of separate regressions for three household size groups tend to confirm the hypothesis that large households spend more than average portions of their incomes for rent, but that they increase their expenditures more slowly with income increases. The intercept value increases monotonically with household size, while the elasticity declines as the number of persons increases. For the largest households as compared to the smallest, the elasticities differ by a factor of two, and there is a 50 percent difference in the intercepts. We can conclude, therefore, that, at least at the extremes, income increases will result in small households increasing their consumption of housing services at a much faster rate than large households. Computing the marginal propensity to consume housing at the mean for each size cohort indicates that the smallest households devote about 6.3 percent of their marginal income to housing; the corresponding figure for the largest households is only 2.8 percent. It is possible, however, that the overrepresentation of blacks in the larger household cohort contributes to these results. Overall, blacks represent about one-third of the renters, but they comprise 58 percent of the five-or-more person households. The low expenditures among blacks thus appear to be the result of price discrimination and restricted access on the one hand, and low income and large family size on the other.

A SOCIODEMOGRAPHIC MODEL OF HOUSING DEMAND

Model Specification

The coefficient of determination in the two-variable rent-income model for the full sample equation indicated that income alone explains less than 20 percent of the variation in rent. This suggests that other household-specific factors in addition to income may have an important influence on housing demand. Therefore, a number of sociodemographic characteristics were incorporated into the estimating equation in order to investigate further those characteristics of housing consumers that produce shifts in the demand curve.

In general, the sociodemographic variables included in the expanded model (Table 3–9) are intended to explain taste-related variations in housing consumption, controlling for income. With the exception of

Table 3-9. Definition of Variables Included in Generalized Demand Equation

YPERM*	Estimated permanent income of household
SUPEARN*	Income of secondary wage earners
HHSIZE*	Number of persons in household
SEX	1 = Female head of household
YRSCTY	1 = Household in city one year or less
EDUC1	1 = Household head has 9–11 years of school
EDUC2	1 = Household head is high school graduate
EDUC3	1 = Household head has at least some post-high school education
WHITCOL	1 = Head is white collar worker
GASELEC	1 = Gas and/or electricity included in rent
FURN	1 = Furnished apartment

Dependent variable: Natural logarithm of annual rent (ANRENT)
* Variable entered in natural log form

household size, they are entered as dummy variables which indicate the presence or absence of relevant household characteristics. The income of secondary wage earners, which was not considered to be a component of permanent income, is included in the expanded model to provide an estimate of the elasticity associated with this presumed transitory component of household income. In addition, we have introduced dummy variables to control for the inclusion of utilities in contract rent. The expanded model of housing demand is thus:

$$R = \alpha Y^\beta Y_s^\gamma S^\eta \left[\prod_i \pi e^{\delta_i D_i} \right] \qquad (3-4)$$

where: Y = estimated permanent income;
Y_s = supplementary wage income;
S = household size;
D_i = socioeconomic characteristics and utility services measured as dummy variables.

The model is intrinsically linear in logarithmic form:

$$lnR = a + blnY + clnY_s + hlnS + \sum_i d_i D_i \qquad (3-5)$$

The coefficients of the continuous variables represent the elasticities of rent with respect to the corresponding variable. The percentage increase in rent attributable to the presence of a characteristic D_i can be computed from the antilog of its coefficient, d_i.[3]

Nonincome Determinants of Demand

The fully specified demand model (Table 3–10) explains twice the variation in rent as does the permanent income of the household head

Table 3-10.   Estimated Socio-Demographic Demand Equation

	All Renters	White	Black
YPERM*	.119[a]	.132[a]	.142[a]
	(.041)	(.053)	(.058)
SUPEARN*	.017[a]	.017[a]	.013[b]
	(.005)	(.006)	(.008)
HHSIZE*	.017	.055	.038
	(.032)	(.047)	(.043)
SEX	−.023	.040	−.084[b]
	(.035)	(.049)	(.051)
YRSCTY	.143[a]	.195[a]	−.163
	(.059)	(.062)	(.143)
EDUC1	.099[b]	.213[a]	−.115[b]
	(.046)	(.059)	(.066)
EDUC2	.141[a]	.168[a]	.040
	(.057)	(.071)	(.085)
EDUC3	.444[a]	.459[a]	.168
	(.061)	(.071)	(.152)
WHITCOL	.130[a]	.082[b]	.098
	(.042)	(.045)	(.136)
GASELEC	.240[a]	.187[a]	x
	(.069)	(.069)	
FURN	.082[c]	.022	x
	(.056)	(.057)	
Constant	5.271	5.147	5.093
$\bar{R}^2$	.421	.409	.140
SEE	.341	.333	.307
C_v	.052	.050	.049
F	33.40	21.65	3.91
N	491	329	162

* Variable entered as natural logarithm.
x Too few observations.
Standard errors shown in parentheses.
Significance levels, one-tailed test:
[a] $p < .01$
[b] $p < .05$
[c] $p < .10$

alone, thus confirming the hypothesis that housing demand is a function of a variety of household characteristics other than income. Although our interest lies primarily in the sociodemographic demand factors, we should note that the permanent income elasticity estimated by the model is only about one-third of the value derived from the two variable model. Lee's [1968:485] analysis of housing demand indicated that the permanent income elasticity for renters fell from about .61 to .46 when sociodemographic factors were incorporated into his model. He suggests that excluding these variables, which are related to permanent housing consumption, will create an upward bias on the estimated elasticity [Lee, 1968:488].

Viewing the problem somewhat differently, de Leeuw [1971:5], argues that since the sociodemographic variables "tend to be closely related to normal income, . . . the estimated elasticities omit that part of the income response reflected in [these] variables." The dramatic reduction in the values of our estimates seems to confirm de Leeuw's view. One could argue, however, that the results suggest that housing consumption responds much less to income changes than it does to changes in the social status of the household as reflected in educational attainment and employment. The relationships among the status and income variables make it very difficult to establish which factors are more important.[4]

As we would expect, the impact of secondary wage income on housing is small. The secondary-income elasticity of demand for housing of about .02 indicates that, at the mean, less than one percent of this income is spent on housing consumption.[5] This supports the hypothesis that such earnings represent a transitory component of household income. The positive coefficient associated with the household size variable confirms the expected relationship between expenditures and family size, but its lack of statistical significance precludes the drawing of any firm conclusions about the relationship. The age of the head showed no consistent relationship to housing consumption and was subsequently deleted from the analysis. The model also indicates that female-headed households exhibit no statistically significant differences in their willingness to spend their incomes on housing from otherwise similarly situated renters. The lack of significance of these variables is clearly the result of collinearity among household size, age, sex, and income. A substantial portion of the female-headed household cohort consists of elderly women living alone; it is, therefore, difficult to determine the independent effects of each factor.

The variables which measure the occupational and educational status of the household head all have statistically significant relationships to housing consumption, and they are in the predicted direction. Their performance in the model reveals the importance of social status to housing consumption; if income is held constant, higher levels of educational and occupational attainment are associated with higher rents. Although no difference was found between the rents paid by households headed by blue collar workers and those in which the head is not currently employed,[6] households headed by white collar workers spend 13 percent more than others. Education is treated as an ordinal varible on the theory that there are qualitative status differences associated with specific levels of educational attainment. Dummy variables are included, therefore, to indicate households whose heads have completed 9–11 years of school, are high school graduates, or have at least some post-high school education. The last category includes graduates of college, business or technical school, as well as those who did not complete or have not yet completed their post-high school education; sample size restrictions precluded a finer categorization of this group. Compared with household heads who have completed eight or fewer years of school, those with at least some high school spend about 10 percent more for rent, and high school graduates spend over 14 percent more. The two coefficients are not statistically different from each other, implying that the importance of high school graduation may be less than we hypothesized.

According to these estimates, household heads with at least some post-high school education spend 55 percent more for housing than otherwise similarly situated households. While one would expect relatively high housing preferences among these households, a consumption difference of this magnitude may be the result of other factors as well. In cases where household heads are currently college or technical school students, there may be some error in the income data. Although we attempted to document all sources and forms of income over the year, student households may have neglected to include income from their parents. Students may also draw heavily on accumulated wealth for current consumption during the relatively brief period in which they are not working. Although we omitted a few cases in which it appeared impossible for a household to exist on its reported income, less obvious errors may remain. Even in the absence of measurement error, however, the procedure for estimating permanent income may not fully reflect the expectations of young college-educated families.

Particularly for renters, moving is the most important way that housing consumption can be altered as income changes. Thus, de Leeuw [1971:5–6] argues that renters who have a high income elasticity may be the most likely to move. Carliner [1973:530] estimated separate regressions for mover and nonmover households, but a test of the equality of the regression equations failed to confirm that the income elasticities were statistically different for the two groups. In the nonmetropolitan market, where the rental stock offers only a limited range of housing opportunities, we would expect increases in housing consumption to be realized, in large part, by households moving from the rental to the owner sector. Nevertheless, it is of interest to examine the relationship between housing consumption and mobility.

The measurement of the elasticity difference between movers and nonmovers is complicated by two problems. As we demonstrate in the next chapter, landlords are apparently willing to forgo rent increases in order to avoid losing a good tenant. That long-term residents of a dwelling tend to pay lower rents may, therefore, indicate less about household preferences than it does about the market pricing mechanism. Second, King and Mieszcowski [1973] suggest that recent immigrants to a city, *cet. par.*, will pay more for housing because of their lack of information about the market and because they have not established themselves as reliable tenants. Their paying of higher rents, therefore, would not be an unambiguous indication that housing is a relatively high priority for them.

In preliminary analyses using the two variable rent-income model, we divided the sample according to moving status and estimated individual regressions for each group. Although the income elasticity of recent arrivals to the city appears to be very high, we could not attach statistical significance to the differences between the various estimates. When the sample is divided according to the length of time the household has been in the dwelling, the estimated elasticities are in fact lower than those for the entire sample. In part the differences between immigrants to the city and those who have recently moved into the dwelling unit reflect demographic characteristics which are correlated with the respective mobility measures. Recent movers to the city tend to be white and to have higher than average incomes and levels of educational attainment; a very small portion of the black population are short term residents.

In order to isolate the effects of status and mobility on housing consumption, a dummy variable to indicate recent arrivals to the city was included in the sociodemographic model. Length of residence in the dwelling itself was not included because of the strong supply effect related to it and because it had no discernible effect as a partition variable in the rent-income equation. According to the results, households who have come to the city within the last year consume about 14 percent more housing than do longer term residents. Whether the difference reflects the extent to which mobility is the primary method whereby renters can increase their housing consumption or the competitive disadvantage of immigrants to the city is difficult to assess. Since we have controlled for socioeconomic status, however, we can be sure that the mobility is not simply reflecting these factors.

Racial Variations

Since the income elasticities of blacks and whites differ substantially, we estimated separate demand functions for each group. Although an analysis of variance test [Johnston, 1963:136] confirmed that the overall demand relationships are statistically different, the income elasticities in the expanded model do not differ significantly by race. This virtual equality in the two elasticity estimates is attributable to the substantial differences in the socioeconomic characteristics of the two racial groups. While only four percent of the black household heads are white collar workers, the corresponding figure for whites is 34 percent. Similarly, 55 percent of the whites have at least graduated from high school, but only 22 percent of the blacks have completed 12 or more years of school. We have already noted that the effect of introducing these variables into the model is to drain a substantial portion of the income-related rent response. By segmenting the population into two disparate groups, the domination of the socioeconomic characteristics in the demand relationships causes the differences in the income responses to disappear.

The importance of education and occupation in housing consumption is highlighted even further in the separate equations. White households whose heads are employed in white collar occupations are willing to spend eight percent more for housing than otherwise identical renters. As was the case in the equation for the full sample, white household heads with at least some post-high school education spend more than half again as much for housing. Finally, white households who have recently arrived in the city spend about 20 percent more than do established residents.

Among black households, none of the status variables is related to rent in a systematic or predictable fashion. Since the black renter population is considerably more homogeneous than the white, the absence of any occupation or education effects must be interpreted cautiously. Because of the lack of a sufficient number of higher status black households, it may be that we are unable to detect housing consumption responses to status differences that do, in fact, exist. These considerations notwithstanding, the explanation of these phenomena must lie in part in the structure of the rental market itself. We have already suggested that the relatively undifferentiated nature of the rental stock and an inelastic supply function may cause the income elasticity to appear unusually low. The same effects occur with respect to status-related consumption patterns among blacks. There apparently is no outlet available to black households for improving their housing conditions within the rental market.

Another perspective on the racial dichotomization of the market can be gained by introducing race as a dummy variable in the expanded model. The highly significant coefficient suggests that, *cet. par.*, blacks will pay 22 percent less than whites for housing, which tends to support the accessibility restriction argument. If, in fact, the rental market is artificially dichotomized into racial submarkets, then the supply responses in the two sectors are likely to differ and the simultaneous interaction of supply and demand factors will result in different price equilibria. In short, it is highly likely that race is more important as a supply characteristic than it is as a factor of housing demand in the nonmetropolitan rental market.[7]

NOTES TO CHAPTER 3

1. An assumption that cannot be relaxed is that within each cohort households that have an income of Y_0 and consume an amount of housing, H_0, would consume H_1 units of housing if their income increased to Y_1, where H_1 is the amount

consumed by those households in the market that currently have incomes of Y_1. That is, to each household we attribute a response pattern which is determined by the marketwide, cross-sectional relationship between housing consumption and income.

2. For small and large households, denoted by subscripts s and l, respectively, we have:

$$b_s = (\delta R_s/\delta Y_s)(Y_s/R_s) \quad \text{and} \quad b_l = (\delta R_l/\delta Y_l)(Y_l/R_l).$$

If: $Y_l = Y_s$ and $\delta Y_l = \delta Y_s$, then $b_s = b_l$ implies:

$$\delta R_l/R_l = \delta R_s/R_s.$$

If we assume that $R_l > R_s$, this requires that: $\delta R_l > \delta R_s$. Equal elasticities between two size groups imply, therefore, that the larger households devote larger portions of their income increases to increased housing consumption, or that their marginal propensity to consume housing ($M = \delta R/\delta Y$) is greater.

While de Leeuw [1971] found the income elasticity to increase with household size for all groups except those with six or more persons, he presents these results without attempting to provide a theoretical reason for them.

3. In a two variable case,

$$R = ae^{dD}$$

and the difference in rent attributable to the presence of the characteristic is:

$$R_1 - R_0 = ae^d - a.$$

Therefore:

$$(R_1 - R_0)/R_0 = e^d - 1,$$

and, for small values of d,

$$d \simeq e^d - 1.$$

4. The sociodemographic factors explain over 55 percent of the variation in income, which substantially exceeds our ability to explain rent. This would suggest a serious collinearity problem [Farrar and Glauber, 1967]. To some extent, we have built in this multicollinearity by defining permanent income in terms of age and educational cohort averages. It would be possible to "re-sidualize" the socioeconomic variables with respect to income in order to retain the full explanatory power of the model without diluting the income elasticity [Ridker and Henning, 1967]. Were we to do that, the elasticity would be the same as that derived in the two variable model, but the meaning of the socioeconomic variables would not be clear.

5. Unlike the elasticity of permanent income, this elasticity is not appreciably affected by the sociodemographic variables. Including just the income variables yields:

$$lnR = 3.518 + .352 \, lnY + .020 \, lnY_s$$
$$ (.036) (.005)$$

$$\bar{R}^2 = .208$$
$$SEE = .399$$
$$C_v = .061$$

6. A dummy variable for the blue collar workers had a t-value considerably below 1.0 and was omitted from the model.

7. The problem of restricted access as a result of discrimination against blacks is explored more completely in Sumka [1976]. The analyses presented there confirm the existence of market separation and indicate that blacks, relative to socioeconomically similar whites, consume less space and less quality as well as less total housing services.

Chapter 4

Rental Housing Suppliers

INTRODUCTION

To suggest that nonmetropolitan rental housing market dynamics can be best interpreted through an understanding of who owns and operates the inventory would be a gross oversimplification of the issue. Nevertheless, in order to be implemented successfully, many proposed housing programs require the active participation of key market participants. Especially since national housing policy has begun to focus more closely on ensuring a better utilization of the standing stock and reducing the loss rate of existing dwellings which can still provide reasonable shelter, more systematic information about the suppliers of rental housing can provide important insights into the workings of the nonmetropolitan market. While it may be possible, for example, to predict certain important market outcomes under a direct cash assistance program, assuming renters and owners behave as if they are utility and profit maximizers, a more thorough and realistic evaluation of such a program's potential would require insights into consumer housing search processes, mobility patterns, and supplier behavior patterns.

Although a static equilibrium analysis of the market can provide estimates of price and quality levels in the postintervention equilibrium, it cannot address important issues related to the market adjustment process. Severe immobilities of capital, land, and other factors, as well as restrictions on the housing choices of certain household groups, can cause long delays in the achievement of the new equilibrium, if not undermine the policy objectives entirely. Moreover, while a cross-sectional analysis may produce price-quantity relationships that conform to the neoclassical model, certain segments of the market may be characterized by quite different behavioral patterns that are lost or averaged out in the statistics. Well-intended public policies may, therefore, do nothing more than create bottlenecks and distortions in localized segments of the market. In short, while hard estimates of income, price, and supply elasticities may lie at the heart of housing policy evaluations, such parameters, were they to be generally available across markets, would still provide a less than fully satisfactory basis for building a thorough understanding of the potential impact of various housing programs.

The major distinction between strict economic theories and those which relax the narrow assumptions embedded in the competitive model is that the former are outcome-oriented, whereas the latter would be more behavior and process-oriented. Specifically, a model of the latter type would posit the existence of nonprice directed behavior on the part of both suppliers and consumers, although the importance of traditional economic variables in the market equation would still be maintained. Kornai [1971:226-8], for example, defines the market as a system of information processing and decision preparation that operates over time. The assemblage of overlapping events that collectively constitute market operations involves the appraisal of both price and nonprice information by buyer and seller alike. Contrary to the assumption of the competitive model, Kornai argues that market decisions are based as much on nonprice as on price information, and that neither buyers nor sellers are truly indifferent to the organizations with which they do business. With respect to the market for housing, tenants and landlords would, for example, vary in their previous market experiences, their levels of sophistication and the quantities of information they possess, their market expectations, and, consequently, in their overall housing search and marketing processes. These and related differences among market actors, it may be argued, affect important outcomes. Resulting price-quantity relationships would be far different from those that would obtain in a competitive market under equilibrium conditions.

The obvious limitation of behaviorist models is the difficulty of developing a rigorous specification which is subject to empirical testing and verification. One interesting and at least partially testable theory views small-scale, resident landlords as "peasant producers" who are not motivated by profit maximizing objectives [Krohn and Tiller, 1969; Krohn and Fleming, 1972]. This theory evolved out of an empirical study of local market organization in older Montreal neighborhoods that had undergone substantial ethnic changes since the mid 1950s. During this period the predominantly native born, middle-class residents were replaced by an immigrant, working and lower class population. Characteristic of these older neighborhoods was a landlord-tenant selection process that operated to maximize compatibility between owners and renters. Long-term, native born, resident landlords showed great personal attachments to their rental units and tended to overmaintain their dwellings beyond what the market could reasonably justify. They knew little of the economics of rental housing, rarely advertised their vacancies, carefully screened tenant applicants, frequently held their units vacant for long periods of time until good tenants were found, and rarely raised rents once their units were occupied. Established immigrant owners who, like their native counterparts, were reasonably long-term resident landlords also placed a high personal value on their rental units. Although of more limited means than native landlords, and more heavily mortgaged, they too purchased their houses for the long term, did not view their investments in strictly economic terms, and put as much as they could possibly afford into maintenance. They tended to be less selective than long term residents in maximizing ethnic compatibility, but they typically enjoyed low turnover rates and had few tenant problems because of their good maintenance practices.

Absentee owners, on the other hand, were the least homogeneous group of landlords in the older neighborhoods; they held professional or managerial occupations and tended to view their rental housing investments in strictly economic terms. While native-born absentees generally owned relatively few rental units, had long-term investment horizons and exercised reasonable care in tenant selection, immigrant absentees had shorter investment horizons and less commitment to their more extensive holdings. They exercised less care in selecting tenants and tended not to make any repairs unless literally forced to do so under the terms of their rental agreements. Overall, the exterior maintenance of their units was poor, and the inflationary spiral of rising taxes, wages, and high costs of skilled labor made good maintenance increasingly uneconomical.

Struck by the inverse relation between the quality of rental housing and the investment sophistication of landlords, these studies concluded that such older areas would suffer substantial deterioration were the incidence of absentee ownership to increase substantially over the years. Indeed, it was felt that the strength and vitality of these neighborhoods lay in the fact that much of the rental housing was in the hands of "economic amateurs, people who are only part-time or incidental owners of property, who do not invest in and manage property toward maximum gain, and who are not sophisticated in economic concepts or techniques" [Krohn and Fleming, 1972:1]. These older neighborhoods apparently had managed to withstand the traumas of social change and the limited invasion of lower income groups because the local housing market was not yet controlled by professional real estate operators and because there had yet to emerge, on the demand side, any permanently exploitable tenantry.

Krohn and Fleming [1972:3] suggest that market operations in these areas
parallel the workings of peasant markets, in which suppliers are also
small-scale, often part-time operators who do not consciously attempt to
"expand or rationalize for efficiency."

Essentially, the peasant model holds that there is an inverse relationship between housing quality and the extent to which older, local markets
meet the conditions necessary for the existence of a perfectly competitive
market. Given the aging physical stock in changing neighborhoods and
the low incomes of current and potential demanders for this housing, the
pursuit of profit maximization policies on the part of owners would likely
lead to higher rates of housing deterioration. As long as substantial
segments of the landlord population remain uninvolved with the larger
market economy and continue their pursuit of nonmonetary, nonprofit-
related objectives, rental housing quality can be maintained in older
areas. Thus, according to Krohn and Fleming [1972:2], the "amateur-
rental housing economy is troubled not when it fails to participate in the
progressive national economy, but when it does."

While it may be stretching the analogy somewhat to classify nonmetropolitan landlords as "peasant producers," it is the case that a substantial portion of the owners are not professional real estate investors. If
these nonprofessionals are, in fact, motivated by nonprice objectives, the
impact of price-oriented public policies would be diluted in those sectors
of the market where nonprofessionals predominate. Moreover, their behavioral patterns could hold prices below the level one would expect in a
competitive market, thus depressing new construction and maintenance
by profit-motivated investors.

In this chapter we present a profile of nonmetropolitan landlords,
exploring their market motivations and investment experiences. Particular efforts are made to compare this profile with available data from
metropolitan-based, inner-city market studies. The question of whether
significant differences exist between the suppliers of rental housing in
small and large cities is part of the larger policy question of whether
remedial programs aimed at correcting market disabilities and improving
housing conditions and opportunities should be tailored more specifically
to local conditions. In the following section, we test for the existence of
particular kinds of nonprice-directed behavior among nonmetropolitan
suppliers. The chapter concludes with a brief discussion of the relationship between nonrational investor behavior and housing policy.

THE NONMETROPOLITAN LANDLORD

General Owner Characteristics
Perhaps the most important reason why scale of ownership is relevant
to housing problems in small and large cities alike is that, because of its

effect on such matters as a landlord's permanency of operations, capitalization, market sophistication, visibility, and commitment to the stock, it has important implications for determining the most efficient means of reaching suppliers with any kind of public sector program. All other things equal, as Sternlieb [1966:128] has noted, "programs may be more easily explained and more easily sold to the professional than to the amateur." In Baltimore, Stegman [1972:27] estimated that "over one-fourth of the private, inner-city, rental inventory is owned or controlled by about 50 professionals, with the largest having in excess of 1,500 units and the smallest, about 100." Sixty percent of the Baltimore stock is owned by nonprofessional operators, each of whom owns no more than 24 units. Consistent with Sternlieb's view, Stegman [1972:28] concluded that "small and casual owners are, almost without exception, amateurs who are difficult to reach through any potential upgrading program." Accepting this premise, the even more fractionated ownership pattern in the nonmetropolitan market suggests a potentially more troublesome problem of gaining significant leverage through a public program aimed at existing operators. Ninety-two percent of small city landlords own five or fewer units; the average number of units owned is 2.4 (Table 4–1).[1] At the other end of the scale, only three percent own more than 10 units, compared with Sternlieb's [1966:132] finding that 16 percent of Newark's owners have holdings of more than 12 units.[2]

As we would also anticipate in a rental housing market dominated by small-scale owners, individual title is held by more than nine out of ten nonmetropolitan landlords, who own over 84 percent of the rental stock. Only two percent of the landlords use a corporate form of ownership,

Table 4–1. General Owner Characteristics

Scale of Ownership:	
Average Number	2.4 dwellings
Fewer than 6 Dwellings	92.1%
Individual Ownership Form	92.6%
Born in City or County	59.5%
Reside in City or County	82.8%
Demographic Characteristics	
Average Age	58 yrs.
Aged 65+	33.2%
Female	38.3%
Black	19.5%
Years Owned Rental Housing:	
0–5	18.2%
6–10	17.2%
11+	64.6%

Base for percentages is all landlords.

while about four percent own in other forms: trusts, estates, or nonprofit corporations. In the inner cities, corporate and institutional ownership forms are far more prevalent: they accounted for the ownership of 37 percent and 20 percent, respectively, of the parcels in New York's West side renewal area and in Newark in 1971 [Rapkin, 1959:14; Sternlieb and Burchell, 1973:56].

Consistent with their small-scale operations and individual form of ownership, small city landlords are predominantly local people. Sixty percent were born in the same county in which they eventually acquired their rental units. More importantly, seven out of ten currently reside in the same city as their rental properties, and more than eight out of ten live within the same city or county as their properties. This represents substantially higher local residency than that which Sternlieb and Burchell [1973:61] found in Newark, where only about 57 percent of the landlords live in the city.

The mean landlord age is 58, with one-third of all owners being 65 or older and an additional one-quarter being between the ages of 55 and 64. Female owners, who comprise more than one-third of the landlord population, are significantly older than males, with over half of the former and only 21 percent of the latter having reached their sixty-fifth year.[3] The larger proportion of elderly female owners, together with the finding that over twice the percentage of male as female owners are under age 55, reflects the fact that many women have survived their husbands and are owners through inheritance and not design.

Comparable data on the age distribution of core city rental operators indicate that higher percentages of landlords are beyond age 60 in the nonmetropolitan market than in either New York or Newark. In the core cities it has been reported that many large operators are not able to keep on top of their inventories because of problems of age or health; in Baltimore, for example, it has been suggested that one cause of the deterioration of the rental stock is the inability of older landlords to cope with today's burgeoning management problems [Stegman, 1972:114]. It may be, however, that despite their greater age, the nonmetropolitan landlords will be better able to handle the maintenance of their considerably smaller inventories. More importantly, because the holdings of these small scale-owners are more scattered than those of larger-scale metropolitan owners, a rapid deterioration of a block or neighborhood could not be triggered as easily by individual landlord neglect as in the unstable market environments of Newark and New York.

Nearly a fifth of all nonmetropolitan landlords are black. Although this represents a lower proportion of black ownership than exists in the decaying cores of New York and Newark, and although the scale of ownership is even smaller for black than white nonmetropolitan owners, it is significant that the number of years of experience in rental housing is greater among black owners in the nonmetropolitan city. Only 11 percent of the black owners entered the rental business within the last five years, compared with 20 percent of the whites.

Although similar proportions (about 65 percent) of nonmetropolitan and metropolitan owners have owned rental housing for more than ten years [Sternlieb and Burchell, 1973:58], the nonmetropolitan tradition of long-term black ownership stands in sharp contrast to the recent trends in metropolitan core cities. In the latter, the advanced age of white landlords and the growth of black investors are related through a succession-type hypothesis. In New York, black investors are buying into a heavily welfare-dependent, deteriorating sector of the multifamily stock in predominantly nonwhite areas [Sternlieb and Indik, 1973:184]. In Newark, younger, black households with modest capital, seeking investment and home-ownership opportunities, are taking up the void left by white landlords who are either dying out or fleeing the inner-city; even here, however, new black buyers are avoiding the old hard core areas, leaving them to the big-time professionals. In the more desirable, outer areas of Newark's inner-city, "as white resident owners die out, they will in all probability be replaced, not by equivalent white single parcel resident owners, but either by Negro residents or by white major real estate holders. . . ." [Sternlieb, 1966:143]; the latter would move in only if there should be no demand for these tenements among black would-be resident owners.

In addition to being relatively long-term owners, black investors in the small city are over twice as likely as whites (38 versus 17 percent) to have entered the market through inheritance rather than acquiring properties for income-related purposes. In view of these facts and the added information that little trading occurs in the smaller market, which will be discussed below, it is reasonable to conclude that black owners are not succeeding whites in any significant numbers in the nonmetropolitan market.

The Landlord as Investor

Only three percent of all small-city owners are professional real estate brokers, managers or investors; about a fifth of the small number of corporate and other ownership entities are also real estate businesses. In Newark and New York, on the other hand, 20 and 30 percent, respectively, of the owners considered real estate as their primary occupation [Sternlieb, 1966:130; Sternlieb, 1970:722]. Furthermore, some 37 percent of the landlords in Newark's inner-city and 43 percent of the owners of welfare housing in New York receive at least one-third of their annual incomes from their rental holdings [Sternlieb, 1966:129; Sternlieb and

Indik, 1973:183]. In the nonmetropolitan market, only 16 percent of all landlords count very heavily upon their rental income, and over 60 percent said it was inconsequential to them.

To a great extent, the fairly low importance of rental income in the smaller city appears to be consistent with the relatively small percentage of owners who first acquired rental properties for the purpose of supplementing their current incomes. Only 14 percent entered the rental market for current income purposes, compared with eight percent who were motivated by capital gains concerns. Overwhelming all investment-related motivations, however, is the fact that 34 percent of the landlords entered the market through a decision to rent out a dwelling originally built or purchased as their primary residence. Furthermore, a fifth of nonmetropolitan landlords came into the market as a result of inheriting a dwelling. This group is particularly insensitive to potential policy manipulation since, all other things equal, "the owner by inheritance has little information and less interest in his parcel than the owner by deliberate purchase" [Sternlieb, 1966:152].

Market Activity: An interesting dimension of the supply side of the nonmetropolitan market is the fact that many landlords have built, as well as purchased, rental housing. As a matter of fact, almost a quarter of the owners built their first rental unit, while another 50 percent acquired their first property through purchase. More than twice the percentage of whites as blacks entered the landlord business via construction. Collectively, almost 30 percent of the landlord population has built rental units and, of those, 12 percent constructed units within the past five years, while 57 percent last built more than 21 years ago. Overall, blacks are far less likely to have been active in the construction phase of the rental market than whites. Nine out of ten black owners have never constructed a unit; in fact, no construction by black owners has taken place within the last 10 years.

Although 42 percent of the landlords have never purchased any rental units, of those who have, 21 percent have bought at least one unit within the past five years. An additional 20 percent last acquired a rental unit between six and ten years ago. Black owners are as likely to have purchased units as whites; as was the case with construction, whites are significantly more likely to have been active recently in the market, although the differences are not as great.

Regardless of whether landlords have acquired properties through inheritance, purchase or new construction, very few have ever sold a rental property. Fully 89 percent of owners report never to have sold a rental unit; only five percent have sold a unit within the last five years. Unlike metropolitan owners, small city investors appear to be nontraders by choice and not by market circumstance. That such a high proportion have never sold a rental property does not seem to be a function of a lack of purchasers or a consequence of present owners' being locked into their holdings because of current high earnings and low capital values, as is the case in Baltimore [Stegman, 1972:96-97]. This aspect of the investment side of the nonmetropolitan rental market is explored more fully in Chapter 7.

Investment Perspectives: As implied earlier, the nonmetropolitan landlord is neither highly sophisticated nor well capitalized, although there are several significant exceptions to this proposition. When asked what minimum profit requirements or returns would be required to make a rental housing investment competitive, approximately one-half of the landlords were unable to answer the question. Of those who could respond, only 42 percent indicated that they were currently earning at least the minimum return that they felt they ought to be receiving from their properties.

In an effort to organize our own thinking, interviewers assigned each owner to one of six classes based upon a subjective evaluation of the landlord as an investor. We first classified the respondents according to their profit orientation. Profit-maximizers were defined as landlords who frequently responded to questions in terms of dollars and cents, and who were aware both of local market conditions and of such concepts as rates of return, alternative investment opportunities and the like. We defined semimarket operators as those landlords who, while aware of profit implications of various policies and practices, explicitly placed nonprofit objectives on a par with profit motivations in the course of their rental housing business. Nonmarket landlords were those who seemed to pay little attention to the financial aspects of rental housing investments and who took pains to maximize some nonmonetary objectives, such as tenant compatibility. A second dimension was added to indicate the interviewer's estimate of the respondents' sophistication or lack thereof. The further refinement was necessary to reflect, for example, the fact that some profit-maximizers were more knowledgeable than others; some claimed to be pursuing profit maximization objectives, but clearly were not. According to this typology, 23 percent of the owners are profit-maximizers, 45 percent are semimarket oriented, and 32 percent pursue nonmarket objectives. Two-thirds of the owners were classified as unsophisticated. While this distribution is purely subjective, it still gives some sense of the perceptions and thinking processes of nonmetropolitan rental housing suppliers. It is also consistent with the body of evidence we have presented relating to the characteristics of the owners and to their attitudes toward their rental housing investments.

Management Policies

Considering the predominance of very small scale owners in the non-metropolitan market, a surprisingly high proportion (28 percent) contract the management of their units to professional firms. Controlling for residency, three-quarters of all nonlocal operators use managers, compared with 19 percent of all resident landlords. On the other hand, scale of ownership is not an important determinant of whether a landlord uses a manager: owners of five or fewer units are only slightly less likely to use a firm than are large owners. Though hard data regarding managers is not available for Baltimore, managers did not appear to play a major role in the inner-city market there [Stegman, 1972:46]. In Newark, where the percentage of owners using managers is around 25 percent, slightly lower than the nonmetropolitan figure, the incidence of professional management has increased dramatically from around 11 percent in the middle sixties [Sternlieb and Burchell, 1973:109]. Although we cannot say whether the use of managers is a growing phenomenon in the nonmetropolitan market, the current extent of professional management appears significant and will be examined later with regard to differences between this segment of the stock and investor-managed portions of the inventory.

Additional distinctions between metropolitan and nonmetropolitan landlords relate to their attitudes in the important matters of tenant selection and screening, particularly with regard to discrimination toward minority households. In addition to those small city landlords who rely upon their managers to deal with tenant matters, 50 percent use their own homes as the base for tenant contact, while another 11 percent request their tenants to call them at their places of business when the need arises. Consistent with their small scale and the personalized way of doing business in the smaller city, half of all owners rely upon word of mouth and other informal means of locating renters, preferring not to advertise vacancies or post "for rent" signs. For screening potential tenants, personal interviews are relied upon most heavily, with eight percent of the landlords requiring personal references and fewer owners requiring credit checks, references from previous landlords or the like.

Where dwelling unit quality allows, the personalized procedure used for filling vacancies permits tenant-screening processes to be rather discriminating (Table 4–2). Nearly 60 percent of all the landlords either would rather not or would definitely not rent their units to female-headed families receiving public assistance. Although to some landlords, welfare families and black households may be viewed synonymously, 57 percent said that they would not rent to blacks if they could help it, and an additional 13 percent said they would only rent to blacks in already black-occupied areas. Nor, for that matter, was there any strong desire to rent to young, unattached males or females. As expected, elderly tenants

Table 4–2. Landlord Preferences for Household Types

	Elderly	Welfare	Young Males	Young Females	Black
Prefer	43.7%	1.6%	6.4%	4.0%	1.7%
OK	41.5	25.6	23.2	30.1	19.7
Rather Not Rent to Them	7.8	27.6	22.7	31.3	22.1
Definitely Would Not Rent to Them*	2.2	31.4	38.6	26.6	47.3
No Opinion	4.8	13.8	9.1	8.0	9.2
Total	100.0	100.0	100.0	100.0	100.0
$N =$	2614	2603	2590	2600	2246

* Includes response: "only in black neighborhoods" for race.

were preferred. Although equally large numbers of landlords indicated a distaste for renting to young, unattached men or women as did for blacks, the fact is that far less than 10 percent of all nonmetropolitan rental households fall into the former category, while 34 percent of the tenant population is black. In Newark, as in Baltimore, larger scale operators were less likely than smaller owners to discriminate against blacks, the larger forces of neighborhood change likely having overpowered any personal prejudices [Stegman, 1972:48-49]. In the small urban community, in which the black population is not growing rapidly, processes of racial transition or expansion can be deterred or directed significantly by suppliers, if not halted entirely.

Attitudes Toward Government Involvement in Rental Housing

Though the majority of the landlords are unsophisticated in the ways of real estate investment, they generally agreed with the proposition that the government ought to have the right to tell owners that their properties must either be improved or taken off the market (Table 4–3). More than seven out of every ten owners supported this notion, while even higher proportions were in favor of requiring all rental housing to have hot running water, complete kitchen and bathroom facilities. Only 50 percent, however, would be in favor of requiring all rental housing to have built-in heating facilities. Inasmuch as most of the poorer quality housing in the nonmetropolitan market does not contain central heating facilities or space heaters provided by the landlords, but does contain hot running water, and kitchen and toilet facilities, many landlords seemed to be reflecting the actual state of the housing stock in their responses to this question.

It is interesting to note that while there is overwhelming support

Table 4-3. Landlord Attitudes Toward Government Involvement in Housing

	Approve	Disapprove	No Opinion	Total Percent	Total N
Code Enforcement in Principle	76.5%	17.5%	6.0%	100.0%	2,888
Code Requirements for:					
Hot Water	78.1	16.8	5.1	100.0	2,842
Complete Kitchen	85.2	8.9	5.9	100.0	2,842
Complete Bathroom	92.4	4.2	3.4	100.0	2,838
Built-in Heat	49.9	45.1	5.0	100.0	2,813
Housing Allowance	28.5	46.8	24.7	100.0	2,725
Revenue Sharing for Housing	50.4	30.7	18.9	100.0	2,550

among landlords for some form of code enforcement activity in the nonmetropolitan market, fewer than one-third are in favor of any government effort that would give to low-income families income supplements for housing or other life necessities (Table 4–3). Since many landlords would be indirect beneficiaries of any so-called housing allowance program, the fact that 47 percent are opposed to such an effort may seem shortsighted, to say the least. The majority of those opposed to such a program indicated that they are against any form of public assistance, or that they did not think that participating families would choose to spend their allowances on housing unless the grants were earmarked solely for that purpose.

Consistent with the above conviction, only one-half of the landlords believed that the city should spend any of its General Revenue Sharing monies to improve housing conditions. The opposition to any housing-directed effort is based on the belief that housing is basically a private responsibility and that maintenance of housing quality is a personal matter between landlord and tenant. That this sentiment seems to contradict their general attitudes toward code enforcement evidently posed few dilemmas to the majority of the respondents.

NONPRICE DIRECTED BEHAVIOR

The preceding profile suggests that small-city landlords are primarily nonprofessional investors who, more often than not, became owners of rental housing either by chance or through a passive rather than an active decision. Sixty percent entered the business through inheritance or by deciding to rent a house first acquired as a primary residence. In view of this, and consistent with our subjective determination that 77 percent of the owners do not seem to place the highest priority on profit maximization, it may well be that nonmetropolitan operators are motivated quite differently than is a substantial segment of metropolitan landlords.

The introductory discussion of the peasant model implied that small-scale and resident owners would be insulated from the economy at large and would be as concerned about nonprice related objectives as with maximizing profit. A number of specific, testable hypotheses are suggested by this model. First, resident and small-scale landlords would be less likely to have nonrental housing investments. Next, ignoring the thin new construction sector, the average quality of holdings should be highest for resident owners and lowest for absentees. If quality and living space are held constant, rents should be highest for dwellings owned by large-scale and absentee owners, who are hypothesized to be pure profit-maximizers, and lowest for small-scale and resident owners. Similarly, one would expect a larger proportion of the latter to be guided by nonmarket objectives and thus to invest more heavily in maintenance and routine upkeep. If resident and other small-scale owners are more likely to seek tenants compatible with themselves, we would also expect them to be more selective in their tenant screening processes; in this regard, we would expect significantly higher proportions of resident owners to evidence strong racial biases than absentees. On the other hand, large-scale landlords and absentees would be more likely to employ the services of professional management firms to screen and select their tenants and otherwise operate their inventories.

In the remainder of this chapter, the above and related hypotheses are examined, with the analysis focusing on two general themes. First, we consider the market significance of variations in the objectives of different landlord types. If the peasant model framework were relevant in this regard, one would expect to observe systematically lower prices and higher quality among the dwellings owned by small-scale, resident landlords. From a policy standpoint, the confirmation of these hypotheses would suggest that public intervention programs should actively encourage the continuation of nonprofessional ownership.

The second, and essentially independent, theme relates directly to the operating procedures of the different owner types. Even in the absence of systematic, landlord-based differences in price and quality, housing policies may have to be designed specifically to account for nonprofessional ownership, at least to the extent that these owners control large portions of the low-quality rental stock. Upgrading programs that require the active participation of landlords may be ineffective unless special efforts are made to stimulate the interest of nonprofessional investors. Regardless of price and quality effects, policies to encourage nonprofessional ownership of the stock may be important if the relationships between these owners and their tenants are more congenial and less strife-ridden than those between more impersonal large-scale investors and their tenants. In essence, amateur ownership may be an important stabilizing influence on the market, the effects of which may contribute to a generally more desirable social environment.

Landlord Typology

The operating characteristics of landlords reported in this section are related to the quantities of stock they control and not to all landlords, as was the case in the profile. The shift in base is required because our primary interest is now in identifying the impacts of different operating policies on the housing circumstances of nonmetropolitan households. Each owner's response is effectively weighted by the number of dwellings sampled from his portfolio to provide an accurate representation of his influence on the rental market as a whole.

Both the proximity of owners to their rental housing and the size of their portfolios are likely to be related to key landlord behavioral characteristics, such as profit orientation, pricing patterns, and tenant selection processes. While scale and residency may act independently of each other as far as some aspects of owner behavior are concerned, one would expect that, in general, they would have an interactive effect. Accordingly, the hypothesis testing is based on a unidimensional landlord typology containing three cells. Resident owners are those who live in the same neighborhood in which their rental unit is located, including owners resident in the structure. These owners are not further classified by scale since most of the analysis concerns the sampled dwelling, and a resident owner's behavior with respect to a unit in his neighborhood is not likely to be strongly related to the number of other dwellings he owns. In total, resident owners control about one-fifth of the rental stock. Local nonresidents, who live in the city or county, are further classified by scale. Nonresidents are hypothesized to be more profit-motivated than residents, and large-scale (6 or more dwellings) nonresidents are expected to display more market sophistication than their small-scale counterparts. Small-scale nonresidents own about one-fourth of the rental stock, and large-scale, slightly over one-half. Owners living outside the city or county are excluded from these analyses because of their unusual characteristics and their small market influence.[4]

Housing Quality and Price

Although our primary interest is to examine market processes and modes of owner behavior, it is useful to begin by examining market outcomes as a function of landlord type. If the model of owner behavior has important marketwide significance, one would expect the housing units of owners with less personal attachment to their rental investments to be, on the average, of relatively low quality. Owners proximate to their rental housing, on the other hand, should be relatively insulated from the market forces that determine price-quality relationships; regardless of the prevailing price, they would be expected to make an effort to maintain their housing in above-average condition.

The relationship between housing quality and owner type is not, however, consistent with this hypothesis (Table 4–4). While large-scale non-residents control a disproportionate amount of the worst quality stock, they also own a relatively large proportion of the highest quality housing. The latter point is no doubt a function of our definition of large-scale, since the best quality stock is dominated by newly constructed multifamily complexes, all of which contain more than six dwellings. When the highest quality class is ignored, the distribution of high quality housing across owner types is essentially random; that is, it is close to what one would anticipate given the overall distribution of owner types. The lack of association between quality and owner type is indicated by the small values of both gamma and tau, the statistics employed here as measures of association.[5]

Although it does not appear that resident ownership is tantamount to good housing quality in nonmetropolitan rental markets, it would seem probable that rent levels are lower in the housing owned by resident and small-scale landlords, whose efforts are directed toward tenant compatibility, neighborhood homogeneity, and other objectives not related to profit. Again, however, the relationship does not hold true. Owner type and rent per square foot, which controls for dwelling unit size variations, are not consistently related (Table 4–5). In four of the six quality classes, large-scale nonresidents charge more than residents; in the other two, the

Table 4–4. Housing Quality by Landlord Type

Landlord Type			*Quality Level*				
	1	*2*	*3*	*4*	*5*	*6*	*Total*
	(Low)					*(High)*	
Resident	17.4%	17.1%	24.5%	21.4%	17.6	23.2%	20.2%
Small-Scale Nonresident	15.2	25.8	26.6	31.0	26.5	7.2	24.1
Large-Scale Nonresident	67.4	57.1	48.9	47.6	55.9	69.6	55.7
Total	100.0	100.0	100.0	100.0	100.0	100.0	100.0
N =	46	105	94	103	102	56	506
Gamma	.001						
Tau	.001, Not sig.						

Table 4–5. Annual Rent per Square Foot by Quality and Landlord Type

Landlord Type	Quality Level							
	1	*2*	*3*	*4*	*5*	*6*	*Total*	*N*
	(Low)					*(High)*		
Resident Small-Scale	$.546	.572	.739	.934	.994	1.525	.877	95
Nonresident Large-Scale	$.632	.650	.599	.901	.952	1.229	.791	121
Nonresident	$.520	.626	.751	.816	1.156	1.580	.904	278
Total	$.542	.634	.707	.866	1.074	1.540	.871	494

Analysis of Variance by Landlord Type: $F = 2.32$, NS

reverse is true. Ignoring quality, resident-owned units are on average less expensive than those owned by large-scale nonresidents, but housing owned by small-scale nonresidents has the lowest average price. Since no statistical significance can be attached to this pattern of price variation, we reject the hypothesis that owner-type strongly influences rental housing prices.

Consistent with the lack of any systematic variation in rent or quality is the absence of a significant relationship between owner types and maintenance and repair expenditures (Table 4–6). While residents spend an average of $40 per year more than large-scale nonresidents and $73 more than the small-scale nonresidents, these differences are significant in neither a statistical nor a market sense. It is doubtful that these differences are sufficient to retard the further deterioration of the lower quality

Table 4–6. Income and Expenditure Characteristics by Landlord Type

Landlord Type	Variable Expense per Unit	Net Cash Before Debt Service per Unit
Resident	$202.24	$370.30
Small-Scale Nonresident	129.37	442.06
Large-Scale Nonresident	162.45	430.31
Total	$158.40	$424.96
N	200	180
Analysis of Variance: $F =$	1.57	.45
	NS	NS

stock or to preserve the higher quality stock held by smaller operators relative to the large-scale owned inventory. That there is no significant difference in the average condition of the stock held by the various owner groups, despite the fact that residents spend more on maintenance, may imply that residents are less efficient operators rather than more committed landlords. On average, nonresidents, regardless of scale, realize a net cash flow of about $35 per month per unit before debt service. Residents earn a lower $31, but again the differences are not statistically significant. Thus while the observations that resident owners invest more in repair and maintenance costs and realize a lower net income are consistent with the peasant model, we can draw no inferences from these relationships.

In general, we can conclude that the important market outcomes of price and quality are essentially unrelated to the characteristics of the housing suppliers. This does not, however, imply that a behavioral analysis of owners can provide no insights into the nature of the rental market. While it does suggest that market forces are sufficiently strong to produce relatively consistent pricing patterns across owner types, from a public intervention standpoint it is still relevant to know whether different landlord types respond to different market cues.

Investment Orientations

While landlord involvement in the larger community and national economy cannot be simply measured, indications of the investment and market orientation of nonmetropolitan suppliers can be gauged by reference to supplier experiences with nonhousing investments, their lack of trading in the resale market, their reliance upon mortgage capital, and by related measures. Of the six indicators of investment orientation which were tested, for four the association with landlord type is statistically significant and supportive of our hypotheses. Resident and small-scale owners are much less likely than large-scale nonresidents to participate in the larger economy. Over 84 percent of the last group acknowledged having nonhousing capital investments, compared with only half of the small-scale nonresidents and less than 60 percent of the resident owners (Table 4–7). In general, one would expect landlords who have built or purchased their units to be more market-oriented than those who entered the rental business through passive or unintentional means, such as inheritance or assuming ownership upon the death of their spouse. Similarly, one might anticipate that the greater an owner's market orientation, the greater the likelihood of his ever having sold any rental housing.

In fact, the pattern of property acquisition methods, although statistically significant, is in the opposite direction from that hypothesized. Rather than indicating a stronger market orientation among residents, however, this is partially a result of the greater tendency of residents to

Table 4–7.　Investment Orientations by Landlord Type

Landlord Type	Percent of Units for Which Owner:				
	Has Nonhousing Investments	Built or Purchased Unit	Ever Sold a Unit	Has a Mortgage	Ever Lived in Units
Resident	59.0%	83.3%	12.1%	31.6%	18.1%
Small-Scale Nonresident	50.0	75.0	13.9	28.6	25.6
Large-Scale Nonresident	84.4	70.5	34.5	32.7	2.8
Total	71.9	74.3	24.8	31.4	11.1
N	448	513	504	458	487
Gamma[a]	.515	−.225	.504	.046	.612
Tau[b]	.291***	−.105***	.229***	.023	.267***

[a]Significance level not tested

[b]Significance level for tau:　*** .001
　　　　　　　　　　　　　　　　　 ** .01
　　　　　　　　　　　　　　　　　　* .05

All tests constructed so that positive values of gamma and tau support hypotheses.

have acquired their units for their own residences rather than as rental properties. Whereas fewer than three percent of large-scale nonresidents once lived in their rental units, more than 18 percent of the residents and over a quarter of the small-scale nonresidents were previous occupants of their units. In many cases, therefore, the decision to purchase or construct these units was not investment-related.

Although the nonmetropolitan market is not characterized by frequent trading of rental housing, there is a strong relationship between owner-type and the frequency of the owner's having sold a rental unit. Overall, the owners of fewer than 25 percent of the rental stock have ever sold a unit. For resident-owned units, the figure is only 12 percent, but nearly 35 percent of the large-scale nonresidents have engaged in some rental unit sales. The selling of a rental unit represents a conscious effort to increase the efficiency of an operation either by changing the relative composition of a portfolio, converting unrealized equity and capital gains into cash, or by cutting losses by unloading a problem property. Whatever the reason, short of forced sale or liquidation, the act of selling a rental property is an indication of higher rather than lower market awareness and profit motivation. Thus, the above data on sales supports the hypothesis that large-scale landlords are more market-oriented than other suppliers.

Finally, large-scale nonresidents are three times as likely as their small-scale counterparts to rely heavily on their rental income for their livelihood. More than half of the residents, compared with slightly more than one-third of the large-scale nonresidents, considered their rental income to be inconsequential to them. This does not suggest that landlords are indifferent about whether or not their housing investments return a profit, but it does indicate the priority which they attach to it. That 44 percent of the rental stock is controlled by owners for whom the generated income is inconsequential is an indication of the substantial influence of amateur and part-time investors on the market. The policy implications of this level of amateurism could be considerable. Programs which depend for their success on active landlord participation and cooperation could face serious obstacles if these nonprofessionals are simply not interested in investing the requisite time and energy needed to produce the desired results.

Operating Characteristics

An important dimension of the housing market which pure economic analysis does not address is the relationship between the owner and the tenant. No matter how well market outcomes conform to a competitive model, rental housing transactions are characterized by continuous interactions between landlords and tenants. Contracting for a rental unit establishes an ongoing relationship that is reinforced with every rent payment and every tenant complaint about the dwelling. We hypothesize, therefore, that resident owners exercise the greatest care in tenant selection and attempt to maintain a relatively close relationship with their tenants. At the other extreme, large-scale nonresidents are likely to operate in a much more detached and impersonal manner.

A second factor which will affect operating policies is the greater economic dependency of small-scale owners on their tenants. Vaughn [1972:83] suggests that, depending on their relative market strength, investors in the low-income market adopt particular operating patterns that are designed to minimize overt tenant hostility and collective action against landlords. Large-scale landlords generally operate from a position of strength, since they are economically independent of any individual or small group of tenants. Their tendency is to be more formal and businesslike in their operations, to surround themselves with a support staff that insulates them from individual tenant contact and protects them from strong tenant identification of the rental housing with its owners. Tenants may not like their housing, but they tend not to relate that unhappiness to the landlord as an individual. Many small landlords, however, are not significantly better off than their tenants. To maintain their relative superiority in the rental relationship requires a more personal and informal mode of operation. By assisting tenants in meeting nonhousing needs—such as lending them money or, on occasion, providing transportation in cases of emergencies—landlords personalize the relationship and bind their tenants to them, thus increasing the psychological dependence of these families on their providers of shelter. Through this means, open tenant hostility against the smaller, less secure owners is minimized. Dissatisfaction with housing conditions generally is not translated into disaffection with the landlord.

In nonmetropolitan cities, large-scale landlords do not generally own rental units in sufficient number to produce enough net cash flow to support themselves financially. To that extent, at least, the distinction between large and small-scale modes of operation is blurred. Even though rental income is important to more large than small-scale owners, it is, nevertheless, considered unimportant by 35 percent of large-scale owners who are likely involved in other occupational endeavors and can maintain an independence from their tenants because of their nonrental housing sources of income.

Management Policies: One set of hypotheses suggested by the above discussion relates to the manner in which investors handle their rental properties and the degree of personal attachment which they display toward the units and tenants. Overall, about 26 percent of the rental stock is professionally managed, compared with only eight percent of the resident-owned stock (Table 4–8). The propensity to contract with a

Table 4–8. Operating Characteristics by Landlord Type

Percent of Units for Which Owner:

Landlord Type	Uses Management Firm	Knew Tenant Before Renting	Would Not Rent to Blacks	Has Been Inside Unit in Last Year	Has Had Personal Contact with Tenant in Last Year
Resident	8.3%	47.1%	54.2%	73.4%	76.2%
Small-Scale Nonresident	29.0	30.1	65.6	65.7	36.0
Large-Scale Nonresident	30.9	24.5	33.6	54.5	30.0
Total	25.8	30.1	44.3	61.0	29.1
N	520	389	409	418	384
Gamma	.349	.298	.408	.281	.507
Tau	.162***	.156***	.229***	.149***	.315***

See notes to Table 4–7.

management firm is more a function of residency than scale; nonresidents, regardless of the size of their holdings are three and a half times more likely to use professional managers than are residents. This relationship reveals a large degree of detachment among nonresidents and is consistent with our expectations.

If renting their dwellings to family members or to tenants with whom they have had some prior contact and experience is indicative of nonmarket behavior, then resident landlord experiences conform to the peasant model. Resident owners are far more likely to rent through nonmarket channels than are nonresidents. Over 47 percent of the former, compared with fewer than one-third of the latter, rent to a family member or an acquaintance. Indeed, the fact that almost 30 percent of all owners knew their tenants before renting to them may be a distinguishing feature of the small city market generally.

We have argued that resident owners, seeking compatibility between themselves and the households to whom they rent their units, will be more discriminating in tenant selection. Among the renter household types discussed earlier, landlord preferences vary systematically only with respect to race. Here, scale rather than residency appears to be the operative factor, with 54 and 66 percent of the resident and small-scale nonresidents, respectively, expressing an unwillingness to rent to blacks. About one-third of the large-scale nonresidents admitted to this prejudice; overall 44 percent of the rental stock is unavailable to black consumers solely on the basis of their race. These prejudicial supplier attitudes are in part the source of access restrictions imposed upon black housing consumers and are reflected in substantial price premiums, as is demonstrated in Chapter 6.

Resident owners are considerably more likely than nonresidents to keep close tabs on their rental housing through personal visits. Nearly three-fourths have been inside the unit one or more times during the year. The same is true of about two-thirds of the small-scale and 55 percent of the large-scale nonresidents. A more striking indication of the lack of landlord-tenant anonymity in the small city is that 76 percent of all resident owners have had some personal contact with their tenants in matters unrelated to their respective roles as landlords and tenants.

Each of the operating characteristics examined here has a statistically significant and moderate-to-strong association with owner type. As scale increases and residency becomes more remote, so too does the landlord's personal association with the property. Since neither rent nor housing quality differs across landlord types, it is reasonable to assume that resident owners, who sense their vulnerability and their financial dependence on one or perhaps a few tenants, are attempting to soften any natural antagonism resulting from their role and status differentials with families who rent their housing.

Tenant Satisfactions: The extent to which such landlord efforts are successful is difficult to assess. One objective measure is the length of time tenants have been in the unit. A third of the rental stock has been occupied by the same tenant for five or more years, but this is true of only 27 percent of the resident-owned units (Table 4–9). It would thus appear that efforts to establish good relationships with their tenants do not result in the resident owners' experiencing longer term tenancies in their units.

On a more subjective level, however, they do seem to succeed in establishing good rapport with their tenants. Despite the fact that neither rent nor quality varies systematically by owner type, nearly 92 percent of the tenants of resident owners think their rent is fair, compared with 78 percent of large-scale nonresidents. Similar differences were revealed when tenants were asked if their landlord does a good job and if they are satisfied with the condition of the dwelling unit. As expected, the proportion of dissatisfied tenants decreases with increases in housing quality regardless of ownership type, but the differences in satisfaction levels among owner classes at the top and bottom of the market are particularly large. More than two-thirds of all tenants living in the worst quality housing owned by small-scale operators think their landlords are doing a reasonable job of keeping up their dwellings, compared with just 32 percent of those who occupy similar quality stock that is owned by larger investors. In the highest quality stock, 100 percent of the former are satisfied compared with just 85 percent of the latter.

CONCLUSIONS

Although housing suppliers in the nonmetropolitan rental market are not rigidly segmented along the lines hypothesized by the peasant theory, the

Table 4–9. Tenant Satisfaction by Landlord Type

	Percent of Tenants Who:			
Landlord Type	*Think Rent Is Fair*	*Think Landlord Does a Good Job*	*Have Lived in Unit 5 or More Years*	*Think Dwelling Condition Is Not a Problem*
Resident	91.7%	83.7%	27.1%	82.3%
Small-Scale Nonresident	83.5	69.8	35.9	72.6
Large-Scale Nonresident	77.9	64.3	34.8	67.8
Total	82.0	69.5	33.5	71.8
N	478	463	486	486
Gamma	.325	.289	−.086	.220
Tau	.129***	.142***	−.044	.108***

See notes to Table 4–7.

landlord profile reflects a substantial incidence of nonmarket motivation which, in our subsequent analysis, was attributed primarily to resident owners. That almost one-third of all small city rental dwellings are let to family members or acquaintances of the landlord, a proportion which reaches nearly one-half of all resident owner-held dwellings, suggests that supplier responses to changes in market conditions may not be in accord with those that would be anticipated in a competitive market. Nevertheless, it still may be the case that the domination of the stock by local, nonresident investors, a majority of whom are large scale and who seem to fit more comfortably within a market-orientation mold, may be sufficiently great to lend to the nonmetropolitan market an aura of competitiveness that can be understood within the context of conventional price theory. This argument is supported by our inability to detect any variation in price-quality relationships by owner-type.

To the extent that we have demonstrated a relationship among particular supplier characteristics and behavioral patterns which is antithetical to perfect market competition, it is necessary to explore the more salient policy implications of a peasant-type analog of market organization. Although owner residency is not clearly related either to better maintenance or to higher levels of housing quality, because of their strong personal ties to their limited holdings, the reasonably strict enforcement of occupancy standards could possibly encourage resident owners to improve their dwellings. At the same time, the further expansion of marginal housing inventories held by market-oriented investors could be discouraged. The ultimate test of this proposition, however, lies in a fuller understanding of the complex relationships among a landlord's income and capitalization, the nature of his relationship with his tenants, and price adjustment possibilities that may exist within the semi or nonmarket context in which he operates.

Beyond public attempts to keep the older stock in the hands of resident owners, Krohn and Fleming [1972] suggest that local programs must be developed specifically to appeal to the so-called peasant landlords. They argue that because of their small-scale and their lack of political visibility, the level of government awareness of their existence and problems is nowhere commensurate with the proportion of the older rental stock they collectively control. They also believe that assistance efforts cannot be highly leveraged and may entail relatively high unit administrative costs because of the small-scale and lack of sophistication of most peasant operators. Contributing to high overhead costs would be the substantial efforts needed to sell any programs that may be devised, including the "door-to-door" delivery of the assistance being provided. A not unfamiliar model which may bear some relation to the "need to sell" concept is the low interest rehabilitation loan and grant programs which provide financial assistance to eligible homeowners in certain urban renewal areas. Before these programs can be institutionalized, homeowners must be contacted, informed, educated, and involved in the neighborhood development process. As is well known, the renewal process is long, complicated and costly. Yet it may well be that amateur, part-time operators must be approached in a manner not dissimilar to that which has been developed under traditional renewal programs.

Although we have previously deemphasized the potential role of rehabilitation in the nonmetropolitan city because of the small portion of the stock that can support rehab capital, the analysis in this chapter suggests that whatever rehab is encouraged would involve high overhead costs. This is true because of the lack of a nucleus of large-scale investors who control a substantial portion of the rehabilitatable stock. The holdings of the large-scale and well-capitalized investors are concentrated in the new supply sector. With respect to possible efforts to stimulate new supply, it is important to note a significant indirect association between potential suppliers of new housing and nonmarket oriented, small-scale landlords. To some limited extent, the marketing potential of new, multifamily housing is dependent upon the price structure established across the market by an aggregation of independent transactions that are heavily influenced by policies of nonmarket-oriented landlords. The greater the gap between prices in the existing stock and minimum supply prices for new construction, the less likely the stock will be expanded at any appreciable rate. Short of high levels of government subsidies, significant additions to the supply may not occur without generating upward price pressures throughout the existing stock by means of a systematic code enforcement effort.

In short, a market in which nonprofessional investors play such an important role may either support or impede systematic public efforts to improve community housing standards. How the investor mix in the smaller city will ultimately affect local developments is as much a function of program mix between new construction and rehabilitation of the marginal stock as it is of anything else. Although the demand versus supply emphasis of housing assistance programs will also have different market impacts for reasons to be discussed in later chapters, the analysis of supplier characteristics suggests that a supply strategy focusing on subsidized new construction would be relatively unhampered by the high incidence of nonprofessional owners in the nonmetropolitan market. On the other hand, a rehabilitation program, supported through supply or demand assistance, would have to overcome the amateur owners' natural aversion to public involvement in what heretofore has been viewed as a private responsibility.

NOTES TO CHAPTER 4

1. Distributions for the landlord population were estimated by weighting each observation by the probability of selecting a landlord given that the total number of units owned was known and that rental housing units, and not landlords, were selected at random (See Appendix A). The weighting procedure produces an effective sample size of 3,814 landlords, the estimated total for the four study cities. The number of cases reported for particular questions depends on the actual response rate for it.

2. Because of differences in the sampling and analysis plans employed by others who have studied the owners of urban rental housing, direct comparisons with our results are often difficult to make. The metropolitan data does, however, provide a useful reference point for developing a perspective on nonmetropolitan owners.

3. Sex, race, and residency status were assigned to nonindividual owners based on the characteristics of the principal(s) of the association or corporation. Husband-wife joint ownership is classified as "male."

4. Preliminary analyses revealed that the investment behavior of owners living outside the county is atypical of what one would expect. Rather than being an anonymous class of well-capitalized, large-scale investors, these absentees are more often unsophisticated, amateur investors, many of whom acquired their units by inheritance or other nonmarket means and once lived in their units. Because of their geographic separation from their investments, the vast majority of absentees employ local, professional management firms. Moreover, absentees have a limited influence on the market; in total they control less than nine percent of the rental stock. Thus, while absentees as a class may find it difficult to manage their holdings adequately, their heavy reliance on local, professional managers and their relatively small numbers make them less of a policy concern than otherwise might be the case. For these reasons, we have excluded from our subsequent analysis in this chapter absentee landlords and the housing they own.

5. Gamma is a symmetrical measure of association which is derived from the number of concordant and discordant pairs in the matrix. Its interpretation is analogous to that of the Pearson correlation coefficient for continuous data. Kendall's tau is a similar measure, but it is derived from a different computational form that yields lower values. It is reported since significance levels could be computed for tau, but the statistical significance of gamma could not be obtained from our computational package.

✳ *Chapter 5*

The Price of Rental Housing Services

INTRODUCTION

Market price is the summary measure which describes the ultimate outcome of supply and demand interactions in the housing market. Whether or not the market conforms well to the hypothetical assumptions of perfect competition, it is through the price mechanism that housing units are allocated to housing consumers, and it is from the prevailing price structure that housing producers determine their optimal output. In earlier chapters we examined independently the factors which determine the housing demand of households and the characteristics of housing suppliers which affect the ways in which they operate. The extreme heterogeneity of dwelling units, the importance of both consumption and production externalities, and the likelihood of market segmentation all contribute to the complexity of specifying a simultaneous structural model of housing supply and demand.

Nonetheless, it is possible to analyze the pricing process in the market by recognizing these problems and by imposing on the analysis simplifying structural assumptions which can later be relaxed. The purpose of this chapter is to present a positive theory of the market and to examine the pricing of housing within that framework. A theoretical understanding of market structure is necessary for the collection and measurement of data, the formulation of functional relationships that describe market phenomena, and the interpretation of empirical analyses, but the a priori specification of and strict adherence to any single positive market theory carry two significant costs. First, the parameters of the chosen theory set the bounds within which we can interpret the empirical data; only those forms of behavior that can be logically understood within the context of the theory are considered relevant. Second, while a positive theory may prove useful in evaluating the potential market impacts of certain programs and policies, it may be of little use in assessing the implications of normative proposals which are designed to change the basic framework of the system the theory describes.

The strength and utility of a positive theory lie in its ability to predict market outcomes given certain specified changes in important market variables. In an effort to achieve both simplicity and strong predictive power, however, positive theories generally make no attempt to explain fully the market processes that translate a given change in a market variable into a predicted outcome; in a sense, the market is treated as a "black box" within which certain combinations of inputs are combined to produce given quantities of outputs through market processes which are not necessarily explicit or descriptive of actual behavior. If one's purpose is to assess the potential for achieving a new market organization in which actors respond to a different set of cues, a positive theory would be of limited utility. While recognizing the shortcomings of a positive theory, however, we will rely heavily on the assumption that nonmetropolitan urban, rental housing market operations are consistent with those of competitive markets. Despite the limitations of a microeconomic theoretic approach to the analyses of market structure and prevailing price-quality relationships, few alternative market theories are equally plausible, comprehensive and empirically testable.

We first outline the parameters of a competitive market theory and summarize basic market operations and stock adjustment processes. In the second section, we analyze how the nonmetropolitan price mechanism functions in the consumption market by treating housing as a complex good which provides varying levels of services along several independent dimensions. The hedonic price equation we derive enables us to estimate price elasticities for each component of the housing service flow, assuming that the market is subject to a single equilibrium adjustment process. We then relax this assumption and test for evidence of submarket homogeneity based on a number of housing attributes. In the next chapter we develop and test a series of hypotheses related to price variations and market imperfections. The price model which is developed here provides the basis for these later analyses.

THE PERFECTLY COMPETITIVE HOUSING MARKET

The assumption that the housing market is perfectly competitive implies that four conditions are satisfied.[1] The first, that all market transactions are anonymous, includes the assumption of a homogeneous commodity, from which it follows that consumers have no preference for purchasing the product of one firm over that of another. Though necessary to force-fit a myriad of housing market transactions of a differentiated physical stock into a price-quality context that is amenable to traditional forms of microeconomic analyses, the assumption that housing is a homogeneous good is one which "most scholars would probably find . . . to be the least plausible . . ." [Olsen, 1969:613]. We will return to this point later and discuss in detail the problem of product heterogeneity and its implication for our analysis. Anonymity similarly implies that producers will sell to the highest bidder without preference or prejudice. The weight of evidence on housing market discrimination and spatial segregation makes this an equally implausible assumption which is also subjected to empirical examination in the next chapter.

The "many buyer, many seller" condition ensures that no single person can noticeably affect the market price through his transactions, and it precludes collusion. Each person behaves "as if he has no influence on price and merely adjusts to what he considers a given market situation" [Henderson and Quandt, 1958:86]. Third, we assume that all buyers and sellers have perfect information about prices and commodities and that this information is used by each in an economically rational way. Thus, all sellers act to maximize profits, and all buyers are utility maximizers. Finally, entry into and exit from the market are free, thus ensuring that resources are employed in the most productive manner. This condition implies that inefficient producers are eliminated by more efficient ones.

Beyond having to satisfy the above set of conditions, the assumption of a perfectly competitive market suggests that while the market may not be in long-term equilibrium, its natural tendency is to drift toward a steady state. Associated with long-run equilibrium conditions is a net rate of return on housing investments, with short-run deviations from this rate leading to changes in the aggregate supply of housing. By assuming that dwelling units differ ultimately only with respect to the quantity of housing service units they produce, we can describe long-run, demand-induced stock adjustments in terms of investor-initiated changes in the quantity of housing service units produced by their dwelling units. By altering the flow of housing service units produced by a given dwelling or cluster of dwellings, investors can, within specified technological limitations, cause the upward or downward filtering of their housing through the stock to take advantge of the higher than normal profits being earned in those submarkets in which demand exceeds supply [Muth, 1960; Olsen, 1969].

As a positive theory of market organization and behavior, the competitive model focuses on the price mechanism as the allocator of housing services, and not upon distributional implications of the resulting allocation. The concept of a perfectly competitive market under disequilibrium conditions, for example, is consistent with the existence of homeless families or high rates of doubling up. Short-run shortages exist when the quantity of housing services demanded at the existing market price is greater than the quantity of housing services supplied; these "shortages will be eliminated by a rise in the price of housing services . . ." [Olsen, 1969:614–15]. Similarly, since market-efficient operations are defined within the context of the existing income distribution that characterizes a community, equilibrium market conditions may be consistent with high rates of substandard occupancy and a large proportion of families whose shelter costs consume excessive portions of their incomes. Generally, it is only when serious market imperfections cause inefficient operations, or when necessary stock adjustments substantially lag behind changes in demand conditions, that positive economic theorists call for public intervention in the pricing and allocation process.

THE DETERMINATION OF HOUSING PRICES

Theory

The heterogeneity of the housing good is a major obstacle to the analysis of housing within the confines of traditional economic theory. A dwelling unit is a composite package of attributes that satisfies independent dimensions of household demand. Olsen [1969:613], however, argues that the concepts of neoclassical economic theory can be applied to the study of housing markets by defining a unit of "housing service" as a homogeneous commodity. In an equilibrium market, the price per unit of housing service is constant across the market for all dwellings and for all consumers. Since dwellings will contain varying amounts of housing service units, the market price or rent per period of time will be the product of the service units consumed and the price per unit. While this appears to be a useful and simplifying approach to the analysis of a commodity that provides multidimensional services, it does not provide one with the analytic capability of examining market pricing systematically. The reduction of a single measure of all the services provided by a dwelling unit suggests that in an equilibrium market all houses renting for the same price produce equal service flows and are, by implication, perfect substitutes among which consumers are indifferent. Logically this statement must hold, regardless of differences in dwelling size, physical quality, or neighborhood or locational characteristics.

Theoretically, however, one would expect the demand for various housing services to be somewhat independent, thus making it impossible to collapse all housing characteristics into a single index. For example, the demand for space is likely to be less elastic than that for quality. Put another way, households will first attempt to satisfy their minimum space needs and, given their budget constraints and preferences, will then purchase as much quality as they can. An index that combines size and quality into a single measure is thus based on a very weak theoretical foundation. A household is not likely to be indifferent to the difference between a high-quality, two-room dwelling and a low-quality, five-room dwelling, even if both contain an equal number of conceptually pure, but arbitrarily defined, units of housing service.

Lancaster [1966] has formalized a theory of consumer behavior that accounts for the complex nature of commodities like housing. His approach to demand analysis is based on the assumption that the consumer derives utility not from the good per se, but from the characteristics which the good contains. The explicit acknowledgment that commodities contain a number of characteristics and are, therefore, capable of satisfying various consumption needs renders market analysis more complex than it is in a world of unidimensional, homogeneous commodities. The relaxing of the rigid assumption of homogeneity does, however, allow one to construct empirical models of commodity markets that more closely approximate reality and that provide insights into market dynamics that would not otherwise be obtainable.

The realization that commodities satisfy multiple consumer needs and wants has given rise to so-called "hedonic" price measurement techniques [Triplett, 1971; Rosen, 1974]. The purpose of hedonic analysis is to disaggregate a composite good, such as a housing unit, into its component parts and to estimate the contribution each makes to the total worth of the good, where worth is generally measured by the market-determined price. The operational basis of analysis thus becomes the physical characteristics of the product, which serve as empirical referents for the derived service flow [Triplett, 1971:9–10]. If one can identify a group of commodities that contain a vector of attributes, X_i, then the general hedonic price function can be written as:

$$P = f(X_i). \tag{5–1}$$

In a simple linear specification:

$$P = \alpha + \sum_i \beta_i X_i. \tag{5–2}$$

A regression of market price onto the vector of characteristics yields a set of implicit prices associated with each attribute "as if each . . . can be purchased separately" [Triplett, 1971:11]. The major distinction from

Olsen's theory is that here we explicitly acknowledge that the market enables the consumer to select from a wide range of attribute combinations at each price level.

Lancaster [1966:144] suggests that this approach to consumer demand allows one to "discuss relationships between goods, as revealed in the structure of technology." The traditional concept of homogeneity is replaced by defining an intrinsic commodity group to include all goods among which "efficiency substitution effects will occur only for relative price changes within the group and will be unaffected by changes in the price of other goods." Working in a different analytical context, Blank and Winnick [1953:183–4] defined a similar concept for the housing market. In their view, all dwellings within a geographically defined market area comprised a "commodity" group of "very close substitutes" all of which "may be considered as being linked to each other." Whereas Lancaster [1966:144] defines "intrinsic perfect substitutes" to include all goods within the group which contain identical proportions of the same attributes, Blank and Winnick [1953:184], employing more traditional stock terms, noted the tendency of dwellings "to arrange themselves in clusters or submarkets by virtue of having some important characteristics in common." The parallelism of the two approaches, one based on a service and the other on a stock view of the market, is striking. For both, all housing units would be defined as more or less close substitutes as a result of their technological similarity and their ability to satisfy, to greater or lesser degrees, the same basic consumer needs.

Triplett [1971:40–41] views product heterogeneity in the context of hedonic measurement as a problem that is resolvable only through empirical study. He argues that quality variation is not synonymous with product differentiation or heterogeneity. The decision as to whether the members of a set of observations all belong to a homogeneous product group or are in fact different products can be made by examining the basic assumption that all varieties of the good, regardless of the combination of attributes they contain, conform to the same price structure. Analytically, two sets of observations constitute a single commodity if the set of quality characteristics is the same for both and if the estimated coefficients are the same in each estimating equation.

Although this procedure is useful for identifying housing submarkets, the interpretation of the results of this test do not rest solely on technological factors. As Rosen [1974:44] has demonstrated, a hedonic price function "represents a joint envelope of a family of value functions and another family of offer functions." The observed prices are the equilibrium levels resulting from the interaction of supply and demand in the market; one cannot, therefore, derive from the hedonic equation an understanding of the underlying structure of the supply and demand factors from which the prices result. While the application of the test suggested by Triplett [1971] will identify housing submarkets, the source of the submarket differentiation is not clear. Technological differences in the nature of housing units will account for some of the observed differences in the price functions, but market immobilities are likely to be equally important [de Leeuw, 1970a].

In the housing market, where consumption and production activities are spatially fixed, the tendency toward segmentation is particularly strong. Market externalities and consumer preferences for socioeconomic segregation could result in a submarket pattern which may be unrelated to characteristic differences among the housing units themselves. Straszheim [1974:404] contends that in metropolitan areas wide variations exist in both the kinds of housing available and in the demand for various housing types among geographically-defined submarkets. Household preferences, socioeconomic differences, and intertemporal variations in factor prices will produce widely different supply and demand functions in the various submarkets. In the small cities which are the subject of this study, location, as such, is probably less important than it is in metropolitan areas. Structure- and population-specific factors may, however, lead to segmentation of the market.

Within the limits of our data set we will test for the presence of distinct submarkets to determine the extent to which the housing market is actually comprised of a number of submarkets which are linked together in a "chain of substitution" [Grigsby, 1963:36]. Whether this differentiation is the result of supply or demand influences or of mobility restrictions, the analysis rests on the assumption that within each submarket, a homogeneous housing good is sold under competitive conditions. The individual price equilibria are, however, independently determined by the supply and demand interactions that pertain to each submarket. In reality, of course, these equilibria can never be completely independent. All housing units satisfy at least basic shelter needs, and all submarkets are governed by similar market forces. Nevertheless, it is reasonable to assume, for example, that the price of the poorest quality stock is relatively unaffected by new construction levels and that the demand for efficiency apartments will not decrease as the supply of six-room homes increases.

Model Specification

Even though dwelling attributes cannot be purchased independently, if the market provides a reasonable variation in the combinations and relative amounts of each feature available in housing bundles, we can derive the implicit price of each attribute using multiple regression analysis to relate the various housing characteristics to market rent. Specifically, we hypothesize that rent is a function of the structural quality of the dwelling, its size, the size of the lot, neighborhood and locational amenities, nonstructural services included in the rent, and certain market factors related to transactions between landlords and tenants.

We employ a multiplicative model since the assumptions and mathematical relationships it embodies conform, in most respects, to the way in which we would expect the housing market to operate. Although it requires constant elasticities, the formulation allows for negative second derivatives, which is consistent with the diminishing returns effects one would hypothesize. Thus, for example, the higher the quality level, the lower would be the increase in rent derived from a given marginal increase in quality. It also produces nonzero and normally positive cross partials, thus implying, for example, that the larger a dwelling unit, the greater will be the rent increase realized from a given marginal change in quality.[2]

Mathematically, the model is of the form:

$$R = \alpha \, \pi_i \, X_i^{\beta i} \, [\pi_j \, e^{\delta_j D_j}] \qquad (5\text{--}3)$$

where: R is the market rent;
   the X_i are housing characteristics measured as continuous variables;
   the D_j are variables which measure the presence or absence of characteristics not amenable to continuous measurement; and
   the β_i and δ_j are the equation parameters to be estimated.

The model is intrinsically linear in logarithmic form:

$$lnR = a + \sum_i b_i \, lnX_i + \sum_j d_j D_j \qquad (5\text{--}4)$$

The interpretation of the results is straightforward. The estimated coefficients b_i are the elasticities of R with respect to the corresponding variable, X_i. The percentage increase in rent attributable to the presence of a characteristic, D_j, can be computed from the antilog of its coefficient, d_j; for small values, d_j is approximately equal to the percentage increase in rent.

Independent Variables

The basic shelter services provided by the housing bundle are measured by three continuous variables: structural quality, dwelling unit size, and the exterior space associated with the unit (Table 5–1). Structural quality is measured using the index derived earlier by adjusting the

Table 5–1.   Independent Variables

Basic Dwelling Features

QIND*	Continuous measure of the structural quality of the dwelling unit
SIZE*	Dwelling unit square feet
LTSIZ*	Lot size in square feet

Utilities and Services

FURN	1 = furnishings included in rent
HEAT	1 = heat included in rent

Neighborhood

LTVAL*	Square foot value of the lot
POPDEN	1 = population density of ED greater than 8,000 persons per gross square mile
PLUM1	1 = ED with 5–9% of dwellings lacking one or more plumbing facilities
PLUM2	1 = ED with 10% or more units lacking one or more plumbing facilities
REN1	1 = ED average rent between $50–90
REN2	1 = ED average rent above $90
DSTCBD*	Standardized distance (0–100) from center of ED to center of downtown area

Market Factors

TENURE	1 = tenant in unit 5 or more years
LEASE	1 = presence of lease
RESLL	1 = owner resident in property or on adjacent lot

Dependent Variable: Natural Logarithm of annual rent (*ANRENT*)
* Indicates variable entered as natural logarithm.

appraised tax value of the unit for neighborhood bias and for variations in the appraisal dates. As we have demonstrated, the index provides a summary measure which reflects the basic structural characteristics of the unit, its interior features, equipment, and facilities. The ability of the index to summarize a large number of dwelling unit characteristics into a single measure enhances the ease and efficiency of obtaining our parameter estimates.[3]

Dwelling unit size is measured by the gross square footage as recorded on the tax appraisal record. Although this measure includes nonuseable space and, in some cases, small exterior areas, the error that might result from using gross area as opposed to net useable space is very slight. Moreover, square footage provides a far more homogeneous measure of size than does the number of rooms, a more commonly used size parameter. Lot size is also measured in square feet and is taken directly from the appraisal records. For multiple-unit structures, lot area is allocated proportionately to each dwelling in the structure.

In addition to these basic size and quality attributes, the rent for a dwelling unit will be affected by whatever nonstructural services are provided by the owner. Partially because of the high proportion of single family rental units in the nonmetropolitan inventory, relatively few units include utilities and other such services in the rent. Two variables indicating the inclusion of furnishings or heat in the rent are included in the model.[4]

The quality of the surrounding environment and the locational accessibility of the dwelling are important elements in the determination of market rent. Dummy variables to indicate high density and nonresidential zoning were examined but were not found to be useful. This is not surprising, since in many areas of the cities actual land uses predate the zoning ordinances. Moreover, the proximity of nonresidential uses may not be reflected by the zone classification for a particular parcel if an area is characterized by spot zoning. The square foot value of the lot, also taken from appraisal records, was employed as a measure of neighborhood quality on the theory that environmental and locational amenities are reflected in lot appraisals. No direction was predicted for lot value, however, since high values may reflect either a high residential amenity level or a potentially high nonresidential land value in neighborhoods of low residential amenity.

Other aspects of neighborhood quality were measured using 1970 Census data for Enumeration Districts (ED's) [U.S. Bureau of the Census, 1970f]. Although the ED may in some cases be too large to reflect accurately the environmental factors relevant to individual dwellings, it is the smallest geographical area for which the census routinely disaggregates data for cities of this size. Often an ED can be divided unambiguously into two or three neighborhoods, each having clearly distinct characteristics; the masking of true neighborhood attributes is, however, somewhat mitigated by the spatial segregation of rental housing within the ED. Because the sample was clustered in 21 ED's and due to the tendency of the census data to fall into discrete ranges, dummy variables were used to designate value ranges for particular characteristics. Two census variables were found to be useful in explaining rent: the mean rent for the ED; and the percent of units lacking one or more plumbing facilities. In addition, population densities were computed by measuring the area of the ED's and computing persons per gross square mile. The categorical groupings for these variables are shown in Table 5–1.

Intuitively, accessibility appears to be a less important factor in nonmetropolitan than in metropolitan cities; distances are not large enough to make travel time and cost major factors in a household's locational decision. To test the impact of accessibility on rent, we employ a single-center model in which access is measured by the distance from the geometric center of each ED to the main intersection of the downtown area. To account for the fact that the sample was taken from four cities having different geographic areas, the proximity of each ED to the center was entered as a percentage of the maximum distance between the center and the boundary of each city.

Finally, a set of dummy variables measures market factors that affect the nature of housing transactions and thereby impinge on rent, although they do not necessarily reflect services obtained by the household. Depending on one's viewpoint, these variables may be interpreted as lags in the adjustment of rent to changes in demand and supply parameters, imperfections in the flow of information, services provided to the tenant, or means by which owners attempt to reduce costs or minimize risk.

A lease prevents the owner from raising rents over a specified period of time; on the other hand, it also reduces turnover, thus helping to lower supply costs. In addition, a lease may contribute to the tenant's security, in which case it may be considered a service for which a premium is paid. The length of tenure of the tenant is somewhat less ambiguous in that we can hypothesize a negative effect on rent. The exact interpretation is, however, not clear cut. Long-term residence in a dwelling may be associated with lower rent simply because owners only raise rent on turnover—a policy many owners indicated that they followed. One can view this as a market lag or as an indication of nonrational (i.e., not profit-maximizing) behavior. Alternatively, the fact that many owners felt that it is self-defeating to raise the rent and risk losing a good tenant suggests a strategy of cost reduction and risk minimization. Finally, we postulated that rents would be lower in resident-owner structures (including single family homes when the owner's home is on the same or adjacent parcels). Kain and Quigley [1970] suggest that owners may lower rents to assure a compatible tenant, or that tenants subject to the constant scrutiny of the owner are not willing to pay a higher rent. Our interviews with landlords indicated that the former is more likely to be the operative factor in the nonmetropolitan market.

Empirical Results

The housing, neighborhood, and market factors included in the rent model account for 71 percent of the variation in the logarithm of annual rent (Table 5–2). Of the 15 variables in the equation, 13 have coefficients which are statistically significant, and all the variables for which direction was postulated have the correct sign. The standard error of the estimate and the coefficient of variation indicate that the estimator predicts rent with acceptable accuracy, and the residual pattern displays no signs of heteroscedasticity.[5]

Dwelling Unit Characteristics: The characteristics of the dwelling unit, including nonstructural services, account for 62 percent of the variation in rent.[6] As we would expect, given the theoretical arguments and the

Table 5–2. Estimating Equation for Annual Rent

Variable	Estimated Coefficient	Std. Error
QIND*	.439[a]	.025
SIZE*	.275[a]	.039
LTSIZ*	.048[a]	.020
FURN	.168[a]	.037
HEAT	.046[c]	.033
LTVAL*	.104[a']	.026
POPDEN	.115[a']	.039
PLUM1	−.088[a]	.035
PLUM2	−.093[c]	.059
REN1	.126[a]	.047
REN2	.291[a]	.068
DSTCBD*	−.027	.038
TENURE	−.087[a]	.025
LEASE	−.016	.047
RESLL	−.106[b]	.053
Constant	3.819	

Corrected R^2	.706	
SEE	.256	
C_v	.039	
F	85.04	
N	525	

Notes:
* Indicates variable entered as natural logarithm.
[a] Significant at .01 level or higher
[b] Significant at .05 level
[c] Significant at .10 level
(Except for significance levels marked with prime, all t-tests are one-tailed.)

empirical results cited earlier, the elasticity of rent with respect to quality is substantially larger than that with respect to size. While a 10 percent increase in quality, as measured by the index, will result in a rent increase of about 4.4 percent, a similar increase in dwelling unit size will increase rent by only 2.8 percent. Lot size has a substantially lower elasticity of only .05. The inclusion of furnishings adds about 17 percent to rent; at the mean this amounts to about $11 per month. Landlord-provided heat carries a 4.6 percent premium and adds about $3 per month at the mean. Even acknowledging that the climate in North Carolina is relatively moderate, this figure seems low, and we can only attach 90 percent confidence to it.

Neighborhood and Location Factors: Neighborhood variables contribute an additional eight percent of explanatory power after we have controlled for the characteristics of the unit itself. Each of the variables is significant, and there is no evidence of serious multicollinearity among them. The coefficients are interpreted as the premium that is paid for a dwelling unit located in a neighborhood characterized by particular amenities, but the magnitudes of some of the coefficients imply that they may be reflecting the influence of other, unmeasured, factors. For example, for the 11 percent of the sample located in areas with mean rents of $90 per month or more, the coefficient suggests that the amenities of the neighborhood increase rent by 34 percent over what the same unit would command in areas where the average rent is less than $50. These high rent districts primarily contain relatively new duplex and garden apartment units. To the extent that they are very homogeneous areas, the high rent dummy may be capturing some dwelling-specific characteristics.

In neighborhoods where the average rent falls into the $50–90 range, there is a rent premium of 13 percent. These results suggest that, at the mean, moving a unit into a moderate rent neighborhood from a low rent area would add $9 a month to rent; moving it into a high rent district would add about $23 a month. Similarly, the plumbing variables indicate a rent reduction of about nine percent in neighborhoods containing a high proportion of units which lack one or more plumbing facilities. Although both plumbing coefficients are significant, they are not statistically different from each other. A five percent level of plumbing deficient units appears to be a threshold in terms of rent; higher levels have no greater impact on prices. The square foot value of the lot apparently measures residential amenity; controlling for all other factors it has a positive, and highly significant, elasticity of .10. Thus, were a unit to be located in an area where lot values were, on average, 10 percent higher, we would expect a 1.0 percent increase in the average rent.

The population density variable suggests that a rent premium of 11 percent is paid in high density areas. One would normally expect rent to decrease with density; in large cities, neighborhoods of intense development lack public open spaces, play areas for children, and generally provide a less desirable residential environment. Although one of the key distinctions between metropolitan and nonmetropolitan cities is that in the latter the worst neighborhoods tend to be areas of low quality single family homes, this does not explain the density effect since we have already controlled for lot size per dwelling. Since density was computed on the basis of gross land area, the variation it explains after controlling for lot size must be related to the presence of nonresidential uses in the neighborhood. The density variable is thus measuring the absence of negative environmental factors as well as the general attractiveness of newer areas which tend to be developed more intensively.

As we have noted, we would not expect accessibility to be an important factor in the housing choice process in small cities. Distance from the center is, however, related in predictable ways to a number of other factors. Neighborhoods near the city center tend to have, for example, lower average rents, a larger incidence of plumbing-deficient units and higher population densities. The simple correlation of distance with density is only $-.13$, and with lot size, it is $.19$. Thus, while the commonly observed metropolitan pattern of lower densities in outer areas where unit land costs are cheaper [Muth, 1961] is also found in the small city, density is equally strongly related to neighborhood amenity factors. Even though rent and distance are positively correlated, controlling for housing and neighborhood factors reveals that a small premium is paid for locations closer to the city center. The lack of significance of the variable is apparently a result of its multicollinearity with the neighborhood amenity variables.

Market Factors:　As was hypothesized, the longer a tenant has been living in the dwelling unit, the lower the rent. Compared to dwellings which are currently vacant or in which the current tenant has lived less than five years, units occupied by the same tenant for five years or more carry a nine percent discount in rent. Assuming an owner incurs no major redecorating costs during a tenant's continued occupancy, over a five-year period he has given up, in the form of reduced rent, an amount ($360) which is less than the normal cost of preparing a unit for a new tenant every two years or so. Moreover, he has reduced his risk by encouraging a presumably good tenant to continue his occupancy, and he has avoided losing rent during the period it takes to prepare the unit for marketing and to find a new tenant. Kain and Quigley [1970] obtained a similar result, but their estimate of the rent reduction per year of occupancy was only $3.24, or about $16 a year for a tenant who had lived in the unit for five years.

For the seven percent of the tenants who have signed leases, our results indicate a slight rent reduction. The coefficient is, however, not significant, and we cannot assert with any confidence that owners are willing to discount rents if they are assured of a minimum occupancy period. Compared to the length of tenure variable, this is a reasonable result. First, many owners expressed the sentiment that a lease protects a tenant more than it does the owner. Second, new tenants are unknown; the fact that they sign a lease is no guarantee that they will prove to be desirable from the owner's perspective. Once owners get to know their tenants, however, they are more willing to provide a reduction in return for prompt rent payments and careful use of their property.

The presence of an owner-occupant in or near the building reduces rent by about 11 percent, or $88 a year at the mean. This is most likely the result of landlord efforts to maintain compatible tenants. Kain and Quigley [1970] estimated an annual reduction of $52 per year in owner-occupied structures, while King and Mieszcowski [1973] estimated a $10 annual reduction if the owner lived in or near the property.

SUBMARKET STRUCTURE

The preceding analysis was based on the assumption that the nonmetropolitan city contains a single, aggregate rental housing market. The observed price equilibrium should, therefore, reflect the interaction of the expressed demand of all renter households competing for housing units across the market. As we noted earlier in our discussion of hedonic price estimation, however, a number of factors may create an underlying structure of more or less independent submarkets. These include: the extreme heterogeneity of the housing good; indivisibilities and market immobilities; and market externalities resulting from the spatial aspects of housing consumption and production. Factor immobilities, for example, may retard adjustments in the supply of different types of housing as demand changes over time. The physical quality of a given dwelling is determined to a large degree by the basic characteristics of the original structure, and it may not be amenable to major alteration as the demand for housing quality changes. Dwelling size is even less susceptible to alteration. On the demand side, immobilities may be the result of artificial market restrictions or characteristics that confine certain households to particular dwelling types.

Blank and Winnick [1953] proposed that submarkets within the rental housing market be defined on the basis of the number of units in the structure.[7] In their model, structure size acted as a proxy for scale of ownership, for variations in operating costs and pricing behavior and, to some extent, for nonrational behavior by small owners. They provided a partial confirmation of their theory using data relating the response of rent levels to vacancy rate changes for 28 cities during 1938–41. In the majority of cities, single family rents increased more rapidly than those in large apartment units during this period of rising demand. In the development of the Detroit prototype of the NBER Urban Simulation Model, Ingram et al. [1972:135–8] defined 26 housing submarkets based on structure type, lot size, unit size, unit quality and neighborhood quality, although they provided no statistical validation of their submarket grouping procedure. Straszheim [1974:406] argues that the primary focus of hedonic analysis should be directed toward the identification of factors which "define homogeneous submarkets." In his work in the San Francisco SMSA, he relied on geographic clustering to identify housing submarkets.

Within the methodological frame of hedonic analysis, an explicit test can be made for the existence of submarkets using the same techniques employed in our earlier analysis of dwelling quality (Chapter 2) [Johnston, 1963:136; Straszheim, 1974; Gillingham and Lund, 1970]. A number of market characteristics are potentially useful partitioning variables. We have restricted our examination to three dwelling unit attributes: structure type, physical quality and size. Location is not considered because of the somewhat undifferentiated spatial pattern of the small city and because our survey was restricted to areas within the corporate city limits. Consequently, simple distinctions, such as inner-core, outer-ring and suburban, are not meaningful. Locational differences that do exist are taken into account by the neighborhood quality and the accessibility variables included in the model. Unfortunately, sample size restrictions preclude a full three-way classification based on these dimensions. Even defining submarkets using only one or two dimensional typologies leads to uncomfortably few observations. The results presented below are, therefore, only indicative of the underlying submarket structure which characterizes the nonmetropolitan market.

Structure-Type Differentiation

The major stratification variable we considered was the type of structure in which the dwelling unit is contained. The analyses of both Blank and Winnick [1953] and Ingram et al. [1972] rely heavily on this characteristic to distinguish housing types. For our purposes, three categories were established: single family detached; two-unit structures (duplexes); and apartment buildings, defined to include all three or more unit structures. At the margin, duplex and apartment structures may be very similar for most practical purposes; however, no definition would be completely unambiguous. In large part, the classification scheme was based on sample size considerations.

The reasons for expecting the rental market to be segmented by structure type are threefold. In part, units in the various types of structures may offer different combinations and amounts of the services and attributes which housing units provide. Systematic variations in quality, size and other characteristics among the three types will result in technological heterogeneity [Lancaster, 1966:144]. Related to, and perhaps one cause of, technological differentiation are probable differences in the production possibilities function which lead to variations in supply prices. If structural quality, size and land are the major components of the output, the economics of combining them into a final product is likely to vary substantially between a detached house and a garden apartment. Scale economies in multifamily units may enable a household to purchase more in the way of structural quality for a given unit price, assuming that limited space is not a problem. Finally, on the demand side, certain household types may be restricted to a single submarket because of their particular needs. Large families, for example, may be able to find units with sufficient space only among single family houses. It is also possible that the differences among structure types reflect features we cannot measure. Single family units offer more privacy to the household, but it is often the case that the occupant is responsible for undertaking minor maintenance of the dwelling. Intangible factors such as these cannot be subjected easily to price analysis.

The homogeneity tests (Table 5–3) indicate that structure type does in fact distinguish three submarkets.[8] On average, single family units are considerably larger than duplexes or apartments in terms of both interior and exterior space. They are of lower average quality and are much less likely to have nonshelter services included in the rent. The price estimating equations for each submarket (Table 5–4) provide about the same levels of explanation and accuracy as does the full sample equation.[9] If we examine the coefficients of the individual variables, some interesting differences and similarities become apparent. In all three equations, the coefficient of quality is significant at the .01 level; a t-test comparing these values at the .05 level indicated no significant differences among them, or between them and the elasticity for the full sample.[10] Thus the response of rent to an increase in structural quality is invariant across these submarkets. Dwelling unit size, however, is statistically less significant in the duplex and apartment than in the single family equation, reflecting the fact that this partition has greatly reduced the variation in size within these two submarkets. The implication of this result is that structure type may be acting as a proxy for dwelling unit size.

The relative importance of neighborhood factors among the submarkets is difficult to assess since each of the various neighborhood indicators is significant in only one or two of the three equations; this is clearly a result of multicollinearity effects which did not emerge in the estimate for the entire sample. Single family rents are systematically affected by lot value, the population density and the incidence of plumbing deficiencies.

Table 5–3. Tests for Submarket Homogeneity

	F-ratio	Degrees of Freedom	Significance Level
Structure Type			
Single Family/Duplex	1.83	16,391	.05
Apartment/Other	2.33	16,493	.01
Dwelling Unit Size			
<800 sq.ft./800–1,100	3.08	16,326	.01
>1,100/Other	1.80	16,493	.05
Quality Level			
$QIND \leq 4.85/QIND > 4.85$	4.37	16,493	.01

Table 5–4. Estimating Equations for Submarkets Defined by Structure Type

	Single Family	Duplex	Apartment
QIND*	.452[a]	.389[a]	.558[a]
	(.033)	(.056)	(.134)
SIZE*	.282[a]	.132[c]	.280[b]
	(.048)	(.088)	(.131)
LTSIZ*	.011	.185[a]	.078
	(.031)	(.053)	(.067)
FURN	.316[a]	.089[c]	.198[a]
	(.075)	(.067)	(.068)
HEAT	−.016	.019	.117[c]
	(.045)	(.088)	(.084)
LTVAL*	.111[a']	.148[a']	.095
	(.034)	(.053)	(.076)
POPDEN	.134[b']	.217[a']	−.058
	(.052)	(.081)	(.116)
PLUM1	−.135[a]	.024	−.139
	(.045)	(.063)	(.115)
PLUM2	−.181[a]	.088	−.213
	(.077)	(.116)	(.167)
REN1	.047	.255[a]	.089
	(.062)	(.092)	(.133)
REN2	.180[b]	.320[b]	.382[b]
	(.092)	(.139)	(.196)
DSTCBD*	−.041	.063	−.184[c]
	(.046)	(.079)	(.127)
TENURE	−.112[a]	−.104[b]	−.042
	(.031)	(.050)	(.072)
LEASE	.068	−.184[b]	−.080
	(.067)	(.090)	(.111)
RESLL	−.293[a]	−.080[c]	.062
	(.101)	(.074)	(.170)
Constant	4.440	3.356	3.859
Corrected R^2	.736	.705	.631
SEE	.236	.243	.292
C_v	.036	.037	.043
F	56.68	20.42	12.52
N	300	123	102

See Notes to Table 5–2.
Figures in parentheses are standard errors of coefficients.

For duplexes, the neighborhood average rent variable takes on more importance, while the plumbing variables are not significant.

Size and Quality Differentiation

The two most important results of the above analysis are that the rent-quality relationship does not seem to vary by structure type, while size is apparently an important differentiating element in these submarkets. It is useful to consider, therefore, whether size or quality characteristics distinguish submarkets as sharply as does structure type. In the case of dwelling size, it is logical to presume that the basic household need for shelter space is strong enough to segment households of various sizes into discrete consumer groups. If the within-group demand tends to be for specific house sizes, and if members of a given household size cohort tend not to compete for housing with members of other groups, the price equilibria for submarkets based on size will be relatively independent. Quality-based submarket differentiation is more likely to be the result of income and spatial segregation in the market. As a result of market externalities, low quality housing units will tend to be located proximate to each other; submarkets defined by quality will, therefore, be comprised of housing units in geographically homogeneous clusters containing low-income households.

Three submarkets can be identified using dwelling size as the criterion[11] (Table 5–3). The estimating equations for the three subsamples based on dwelling unit size are shown on Table 5–5; in all three cases the accuracy and explanatory powers of estimators are similar to those for the composite equation. The coefficient of the quality index is highly significant in each equation and as size increases, so does the elasticity of rent with respect to quality. These differences, which are all statistically significant, indicate that while a 10 percent increase in the quality of a small unit will result in a 3.3 percent rent increase, a similar improvement for large units will produce a 5.8 percent rent increase. Looked at another way, the marginal products of quality at the means for the three submarkets are, respectively, $44, $69, and $99. Thus, as one would expect, quality is an increasing function of dwelling size, *cet. par.* The remainder of the variables generally behave as expected, although the estimators for the two submarkets containing the larger units have considerably fewer significant coefficients than does the composite equation.

Only two submarkets can be identified using the quality level as the criterion variable (Table 5–3). That we can identify only two quality submarkets but three size submarkets is a reflection of the higher degree of heterogeneity among dwellings containing different amounts of space; this provides additional evidence that households are more constrained by space requirements than by quality preferences. On average, rents are nearly twice as high for better quality housing, but dwelling unit size does not differ between the two submarkets. The neighborhood variables reveal a high degree of neighborhood homogeneity. Compared to 85 percent of the low quality units, only 41 percent of the high quality units are located in areas with a high incidence of plumbing deficiencies.

The most striking difference between the two estimating equations (Table 5–6) is that rent is more than twice as responsive to quality changes in the high quality sector of the market.[12] A 10 percent increase in

Table 5–5. Estimating Equations for Submarkets Defined by Dwelling Unit Size

	<800 sq. ft.	*800–1,100*	*>1,100*
QIND*	.333[a]	.484[a]	.583[a]
	(.036)	(.043)	(.048)
SIZE*	.255[a]	.270	.242[b]
	(.097)	(.236)	(.108)
LTSIZ*	.086[a]	−.007	−.012
	(.029)	(.040)	(.043)
FURN	.307[a]	.021	.131[c]
	(.055)	(.068)	(.091)
HEAT	.033	.149[a]	.007
	(.059)	(.056)	(.056)
LTVAL*	.096[b']	.121[a']	.137[a']
	(.041)	(.046)	(.048)
POPDEN	.029	.144[c']	.104
	(.059)	(.078)	(.077)
PLUM1	−.220[a]	.045	−.085[c]
	(.060)	(.059)	(.056)
PLUM2	−.216[b]	.237[a]	−.170[b]
	(.108)	(.106)	(.095)
REN1	.154[b]	.309[a]	−.083
	(.091)	(.078)	(.075)
REN2	.407[a]	.477[a]	−.005
	(.131)	(.115)	(.113)
DSTCBD*	−.060	.022	.018
	(.061)	(.068)	(.070)
TENURE	−.037	−.097[b]	−.116[a]
	(.043)	(.044)	(.043)
LEASE	−.243[a']	−.056	.119
	(.093)	(.079)	(.075)
RESLL	−.276[a]	.056	−.220[b]
	(.085)	(.086)	(.109)
Constant	3.963	3.824	4.459
Corrected R^2	.754	.678	.702
SEE	.237	.256	.242
C_v	.037	.039	.036
F	37.63	25.87	27.09
N	180	178	167

See notes to Table 5–2.

Figures in parentheses are standard errors of coefficients.

the quality of a low quality unit will lead to a 3.3 percent increase in rent, while for a high quality unit, the response would be 7.4 percent. At the means, these figures translate into a marginal product of $60 per year for low quality units, compared to $99 for the better dwellings. Since these results appear to indicate an increasing returns effect, they require some further elaboration. We tested the possibility that extreme values of rent were distorting the results for the high quality sector, but eliminating the four highest rent units did not noticeably alter our results. In the process

Table 5-6. Estimating Equations for Submarkets Defined by Quality

	QIND ≤ 4.85	QIND > 4.85
QIND*	.330[a]	.737[a]
	(.046)	(.068)
SIZE*	.202[a]	.358[a]
	(.052)	(.056)
LTSIZ*	.024	.067[a]
	(.030)	(.027)
FURN	.292[a]	.102[b]
	(.058)	(.047)
HEAT	−.002	.053[c]
	(.054)	(.041)
LTVAL*	.085[a']	.117[a']
	(.032)	(.041)
POPDEN	.131[a']	−.043
	(.057)	(.063)
PLUM1	−.096[b]	−.129[a]
	(.054)	(.046)
PLUM2	−.060	−.314[a]
	(.077)	(.104)
REN1	.165[a]	−.054
	(.052)	(.092)
REN2	.024	.139[c]
	(.008)	(.107)
DSTCBD*	−.017	−.141[b]
	(.052)	(.061)
TENURE	−.054[b]	−.130[a]
	(.033)	(.036)
LEASE	.026	−.025
	(.108)	(.050)
RESLL	−.099	−.103[c]
	(.086)	(.065)
Constant	4.520	3.145
Corrected R^2	.468	.584
SEE	.244	.244
C_v	.039	.036
F	16.24	32.20
N	261	264

See notes to Table 5-2.

Figures in parentheses are standard errors of coefficients.

of testing for quality-based submarket differentiation, we tested a three category breakdown. The results of that test indicated that the lower two groups did not significantly differ from each other, and we adopted the two level classification presented above. That test did reveal, however, that it is among the highest quality units that the rent-quality relationship is very elastic. For both the low and middle quality units, the elasticity is about .36, while for units in the highest third of the quality range, the elasticity is about .90. It is likely, therefore, that the highest quality dwellings constitute a unique sector of the rental markets in nonmetropolitan cities. In the lower quality sectors, both rent and quality span a relatively narrow range—reflecting a lack of housing opportunities and, likely, low levels of expressed demand. Finally, we should note that these results probably reflect the racial segmentation of the market; the limited choices available to blacks who are disproportionately represented in the low quality sector may be manifested in these estimates. While we will explore the issue of race and prices in the next chapter, it is significant that fewer than two percent of the highest quality units are located in predominantly black neighborhoods.

Quality is an increasing function of size, and here we find size to be an increasing function of quality. An additional 100 square feet in a low quality unit will add about $11 to annual rent at the mean; the same size increase will raise the rent of a high quality dwelling by about $37. Finally, it appears that while long-term residence in the dwelling unit will produce a 13 percent reduction in the rent of high quality units, only a five percent discount is available to long-term occupants of low quality units. The explanation of this difference may be that the low quality submarket is tighter, that competitive conditions do not prevail to the extent that they do elsewhere, or that landlord-tenant interactions tend to be less personal in this sector of the market.

Two-Dimensional Stratifications

The above analyses indicate that structure type, quality, and dwelling unit size define internally homogeneous rental submarkets. Since the tests for the existence of these housing clusters were performed independently of each other, it is logical to question whether these three characteristics account for overlapping phenomena, or whether stratifications based on a multidimensional typology would reveal submarket homogeneity at a finer level. Unfortunately, sample size considerations restrict our ability to develop a fully disaggregated model. Even a six-cell matrix of housing types taxes the limits of our sample. If the results are interpreted cautiously, however, we can provide additional insights into the structure of the market.

On theoretical grounds, we would expect structure type to be the basic distinguishing housing characteristic. Therefore, we tested whether clusters defined by structure type can be further disaggregated into homogeneous groupings based on size or quality; the results of these tests are summarized in Table 5–7. In general, single family housing units comprise the most heterogeneous structure type class; both size and quality provide a basis for further disaggregating the submarket. Single family rental housing in these cities includes a large segment of minimal quality, shotgun shacks as well as a considerable portion of newer units

Table 5–7. Characteristics of Housing Submarkets Based on Two-Dimensional Typology

Submarket	Mean Annual Rent	Mean Quality Score	Mean Square Feet	Corrected R^2	C_v	N
Single Family						
QIND ≤ 4.61[a]	$ 548	2.86	1,078	.468	.039	170
QIND > 4.61	995	6.89	1,194	.748	.029	130
<1,100 sq. ft.[b]	606	4.20	817	.690	.034	165
1,100 +	906	5.10	1,508	.713	.037	135
Duplex						
QIND ≤ 5.59	603	3.54	839	.553	.039	72
QIND > 5.59	1,068	8.47	990	.417	.031	51
<900 sq. ft.	623	4.52	691	.593	.040	60
900 +	961	6.60	1,102	.687	.030	63
Multifamily						
QIND ≤ 7.68[a]	674	5.38	816	.546	.038	50
QIND > 7.68	1,297	9.88	801	.297	.039	52
<810 sq. ft.	928	7.87	649	.739	.040	56
810 +	1,069	7.43	1,002	.511	.045	46

[a] Submarkets differ at .01 level.
[b] Submarkets differ at .05 level.

built to much higher standards; these two types of units provide the basic elements of the respective quality classes; for practical purposes they comprise separate markets, between which there is very little interaction.

Similarly, structural quality defines two apparently independent submarkets among units in multifamily structures. The bulk of the low quality apartment units is contained in converted buildings and older, cheaply built structures containing fewer than six units; the higher quality housing consists primarily of modern garden apartments. We would expect, and the homogeneity tests confirm, that there is little overlap between the household populations served by these types of units. Moreover, the former are located in the older, central portions of the city, while the latter are found in neighborhoods that provide much more in the way of residential amenities. Dwelling size does not contribute to further submarket differentiation among multifamily units, and neither size nor quality provides a basis for disaggregating duplexes.

Summary

The analyses presented in this section indicate that the nonmetropolitan rental market is composed of a complex array of homogeneous submarkets, a result which is consistent with studies of metropolitan housing markets. Unlike metropolitan areas, however, the small city, by virtue of its compact size, is not spatially differentiated. Meaningful analyses of SMSA markets need to account for suburban-versus-central city locations, and probably for inner-core versus outer-ring differences within the central city itself. The large geographic area included in an SMSA, the proximity of each subarea to various employment centers, and the tendency for each area to contain comparatively homogeneous housing types and population groups result in relatively independent housing submarket areas, as Straszheim [1974] has demonstrated for San Francisco. We have relied exclusively on structure-specific characteristics to identify submarkets resulting from technological differences among housing units as well as from variations in supply and demand influences. While our analyses suggest that combining the entire sample into a single market for the purposes of price estimation may involve some aggregation error, two points should be made with respect to this. The homogeneity tests performed here were based on a relatively small sample which was not designed for fine levels of disaggregation; hence the results are far from conclusive. Secondly, compared to the homogeneity tests of Straszheim [1974], those presented here show a much lower level of reduction in the equation residuals. Thus the aggregation error is likely to be considerably less than that which would result from combining a central city and its suburbs into a single market.

In the next chapter we will ignore the aggregation problem while testing a number of hypotheses related to price differences among supplier types and to price discrimination. Because of the complexity of submarket-specific analyses, the sample size, and the presumed low aggregation error, we will examine the market as a composite for this purpose. In Chapter 7 we will reconsider the issue of submarket structure in the context of rental housing investments.

NOTES TO CHAPTER 5

1. This discussion is based on Henderson and Quandt [1958:86–7].
2. Under the strictest assumptions of a Cobb-Douglas model, the coefficients are constrained to satisfy:

$$(1) \quad \sum_i b_i = 1,$$

and

$$(2) \quad 0 < b_i > 1 \text{ for all } i.$$

Condition (1) implies unitary substitution elasticities, while (2) implies negative second derivatives and positive cross partials. We have not included either condition as an explicit constraint in our estimates. (See Henderson and Quandt [1958:63–4], for a discussion of the Cobb-Douglas production function.) In a simple additive model, the coefficient of each independent variable represents the highest market bid price for that attribute under the relatively strong assumption that the price associated with each characteristic is independent of the amount of the other characteristics contained in the bundle. The linear model also assumes zero second derivatives, which implies constant returns to scale. Preliminary tests confirmed that the multiplicative model provided greater estimating accuracy and higher predictive power than the linear model.

3. The simple correlation between the log of the index and the log of rent is .73, indicating that it accounts for about 53 percent of the variation in contract rent. If the full vector of individual attributes is used, the explanatory power (i.e., the corrected coefficient of determination) has about the same value; thus without impairing our ability to explain rent, we can reduce the number of independent variables from more than a dozen to a single measure.

4. About 18 percent of the rents include water; gas and electricity are included in the rents of only six percent and four percent, respectively. In preliminary runs, dummy variables measuring the inclusion of gas, electricity, or water in rent generally had negative coefficients and/or *t* values less than 1.0. The erratic behavior of these variables, all of which should have a positive influence on rent, indicates that there was some measurement error associated with them, and they were all deleted from the final equation.

5. Since the estimated error term is *ln u*, the coefficient of variation is $ln(u)/ln(ANRENT)$. Thus, our estimates are within four percent of the actual value of the logarithm of rent 68 percent of the time. The spread around *ANRENT* is substantially greater than this.

6. This figure is the uncorrected coefficient of determination. The increment of explanatory power contributed by each variable depends, of course, on the order of inclusion in the regression procedure. The results reported here were obtained using a multiple-mode algorithm in which the variable order was: dwelling characteristics, accessibility, neighborhood features, and market factors.

7. They considered single family, owner-occupied units as another distinct submarket. Our interest here concerns only the rental market. We would expect, however, some substitutability between more expensive single family rentals and owner-occupied dwellings and between rental units and mobile homes. Our sample includes neither owner-occupied dwellings nor mobile homes; thus we can make no statements about these interactions.

8. Three-category classifications were tested by partitioning the full sample into subsets $i;j;k$ and $(i,j);k$. We first tested for $(i,j) = k$ and then for $i = j$. Under "Structure Type" on Table 5–3, for example, the first F-ratio tests single families versus duplexes; the second is the test of apartments against single family and duplex units combined.

9. These results must be viewed with care, since there may be too little variation for us to have confidence in each of the dummy variable coefficients. The results for the most part do seem reasonable and are indicative of the factors that lead to market segmentation.

10. The t-statistic was calculated from:

$$t = (b_1 - b_2)/ \sqrt{(SE_1)^2 + (SE_2)^2}$$

where the b_i and the SE_i are, respectively, the coefficients and the standard errors of corresponding variables [Blalock, 1960:172–5; Johnston, 1963:130].

11. The cutting points of 800 and 1,100 square feet were determined by examining the size distribution of the dwellings and by attempting to create clusters with roughly equal observations. While there is a correspondence between structure type and unit size, the three structure types are represented in all the size classes. Although single family units tend to be large, they constitute over 43 percent of the smallest units. Apartment units fall primarily into the lower two size groups, but they still comprise over four percent of the largest units.

12. The explanatory power of the low quality equation is considerably lower than that for the high quality submarket. Since the quality distribution is positively skewed, the division of the sample into approximately equal cell sizes substantially reduces the variation in both rent and quality at the low end of the stock. The estimating accuracies for both quality classes are, however, similar to that attained for the full sample.

✳ *Chapter 6*

Price Variations in the Rental Market

INTRODUCTION

Building on the price analysis of the last chapter, we will now examine a number of hypotheses related to systematic price variations across the rental market. We first test whether discernible price differences are associated with different landlord types, an analysis which supplements the one presented in Chapter 4. While the earlier analyses failed to uncover any systematic relationship between important owner characteristics and either housing price or quality, here we subject the same hypotheses to more rigorous examination in a multivariate analytical framework. We then consider and test the proposition that the poor pay more for equivalent housing in the rental market, but the analyses fail to support the existence of so-called class monopolies. Finally, a major portion of this chapter is devoted to an examination of price discrimination against blacks. The analyses indicate that black renter households pay a substantial discriminatory premium in the market. The potential impact of open occupancy legislation is considered from the perspectives of the coverage of the law, landlord resistance to blacks, and the likelihood that blacks would take advantage of new housing opportunities.

The general procedure for testing the price hypotheses is to add to the price equation derived in the last chapter one or more variables relevant to the respective propositions. As we have noted, the hedonic price equation represents a reduced-form model from which implicit attribute prices can be derived, although the underlying market structure is unspecified. Theoretically, the model should include only those consumption-related attributes that contribute to total rent. We have specified the hedonic model as completely as possible without using household characteristics as proxies to account for omitted housing factors, a procedure which confuses the interpretation of the results [de Leeuw, 1970a]. By using the fully-specified hedonic model as the basis and adding household or supplier characteristics, we are testing the proposition that these factors have independent, direct effects on rent. We recognize, of course, the possibility of some bias due to simultaneous determination of the endogenous dwelling unit attribute prices; however, for our purposes this bias is not likely to have a significant effect on the analysis.

SUPPLIER CHARACTERISTICS AND RENT

As we discussed in Chapter 4, a considerable portion of the nonmetropolitan rental stock is owned by nonprofessional investors. Because of the predominance of small-scale, local owners, we examined owner behavior in the context of the peasant economy model, but we were not able to establish unambiguous and consistent relationships between owner type and rent or quality. We were able to demonstrate, however, that well-defined owner types do vary in their investment motivations and in the manner in which they operate their rental properties. Our interest in this chapter is to reconsider certain relevant owner characteristics in terms of their possible impacts on market price. These analyses are designed to supplement the behaviorist approach taken earlier by estimating the magnitude of supplier-related price effects in the context of the competitive equilibrium model. Using the price model, we can control much more effectively for the characteristics of the housing unit and, thereby, test more completely for systematic price variations resulting from different landlord motivations and characteristics.

Price differences associated with producer characteristics may be the result of variations in the factor prices producers face or of technological differences in production. An additional possibility that was explored earlier is that certain owner types may be motivated by nonprice objectives and, therefore, may demand lower than normal returns on their invested capital. Finally, market imperfections and lags may lead to supplier-based price differences. Although less efficient suppliers may continue to operate, in the long run they would theoretically be forced out of the market through the price mechanism. Their continued operation would imply the existence of adjustment lags or high entry costs. Similarly, impediments in the flow of information could produce price differentials.

Earlier we hypothesized, and confirmed to a limited extent, that nonprice directed behavior is related both to the residency status and the scale of operations of the landlord. Since that examination of landlord behavior relied on nonparametric statistical analysis, we combined scale and residency status into a three category, single dimension typology. Here, since we are examining only price effects using a multivariate statistical procedure, we have considerably more latitude in terms of the owner characteristics we can consider. Specifically, we examine residency, scale, ownership form, and the summary measures of sophistication and profit orientation for their respective effects on market price.

Assuming that residency status acts as a proxy for nonprice directed behavior, we would expect residents of the neighborhood to charge lower prices in their attempt to locate tenants whose characteristics are compatible with the owner's perceptions of the neighborhood. Conversely, absentee owners would be expected to be the least concerned about tenant-neighborhood compatibility. In the earlier analysis, resident owners included landlords who lived in the building or in the same neighborhood in which their sampled property was located. The presence of a building-resident owner has been defined for the price analyses as a dwelling unit characteristic, and we have demonstrated that resident-owned units carry an 11 percent rate discount. In addition to building residents, dummy variables to designate neighborhood residents (*NEIGHLL*) and owners who live outside the county (*ABSENT*) are entered. The latter are an unusual type, and we would expect that there would be little or no price effect associated with the units they own. We would expect dwellings owned by neighborhood residents to be priced lower than those owned by landlords living in the city or county but not in the neighborhood (the suppressed category), and higher than those owned by building residents.

The other characteristic in the landlord typology analyzed earlier was scale, and it was hypothesized that an owner's professionalism and profit-motivation would increase with the size of his holdings. As the degree of professionalism increases, so would market sophistication and access to market information. Blank and Winnick [1953:198–200] also recognize the likelihood of nonrational behavior on the part of small-scale owners, but they consider the dynamic relationship between scale and price. They argue that, assuming an owner's holdings are homogeneous, the more units he owns, the less likely he is to respond to changes in vacancy rates by altering price. One would thus expect a negative coefficient when demand is falling, but since our data are cross-sectional, we cannot test this theory. Two measures of scale were tested. A dummy variable which defined large scale owners consistent with our earlier definition did not perform in the model as well as a continuous variable entered in logarithmic form (*SCALE*).

The type of ownership used for the unit was tested for its influence on price. Landlords electing a corporate ownership form (*CORP*) would be expected to display the most detachment from their dwellings; they would thus have higher profit requirements and few nonprice objectives in pricing and managing their housing units. Trusts and estates (*TRUST*) on the other hand, are generally handled by persons whose interest in rental housing is minimal and who depend very little on it for income. In the large majority of these cases, the housing portfolios are managed by the heirs of deceased persons. Except in situations in which the trusts are administered by banks, the executors of the estates and trusts tend to have little concern for the properties or the profits they generate. The suppressed category includes all individual forms of ownership.

Finally, the interviewer evaluations of landlord sophistication (*SOPH*) and profit motivation (*PROFIT*) were tested. These measures and the problems associated with them were discussed in Chapter 4. To a great extent, they may summarize characteristics measured by the residency, scale, and ownership form measures and may, therefore, introduce a degree of multicollinearity into our equation. This was not a serious problem, as we will discuss below.

The partial correlations between rent and owner characteristics (Table 6-1) indicate that once dwelling characteristics have been controlled, the

Table 6-1. Supplier Characteristics

		Correlation with Log Annual Rent	
Variable	*Mean*	*Simple*	*Partial[b]*
NEIGHLL	.115	.014	−.038
ABSENT	.059	.066	−.007
SCALE[a]	16.844	−.051	.092**
	(19.932)		
SOPH	.626	.041	.080**
PROFIT	.606	.021	.074**
CORP	.075	.070	−.006
TRUST	.048	−.175	−.105***
N	505		

[a] Variable in natural log form. Mean (Std. dev.) shown for untransformed variable.
[b] Partials computed controlling for 16 dwelling unit characteristics. One-tailed significance levels: *** .01; ** .05; * .10.

residency status of the owner (excluding building residents) is unrelated to rent. The shift in the direction of the relationships after the dwelling controls are introduced implies that both residents of the neighborhood and absentee owners underprice their units, but the lack of statistical significance makes it impossible to draw any inferences. The apparent paradox of both absentee and neighborhood resident owners displaying similar behavior was discussed in Chapter 4 and attributed to the unusual characteristics of absentee owners in the nonmetropolitan city. Neither of these variables displayed a systematic relationship with price in the estimating equation (Table 6–2).

Table 6–2. Effect of Supplier Characteristics on Rent**

Variable	Coefficients	Std. Error
NEIGHLL	x	x
ABSENT	x	x
SCALE*	.014^c	.011
SOPH	.033	.028
PROF	x	x
CORP	x	x
TRUST	−.140^a	.056
Corrected R^2	.709	
SEE	.256	
C_v	.039	
F	69.15	
N	505	

** Values shown are coefficients of variables entered into full price model (Table 5–2).
* Entered in log form.
x Not entered; t value less than 1.0.
One-tailed significance levels: (a) .01 (c) .10.

Scale is positively correlated with rent, but its coefficient in the rent equation implies that the price effect associated with increases in portfolio size is not very strong. A doubling of the number of units owned will produce only a 1.4 percent increase in rent. The correlations between scale and rent indicate that large owners tend to own lower quality units; once quality is controlled, however, a higher price is associated with large scale ownership. This at least partially confirms the hypotheses relating to the professionalism and profit motivation of large scale owners. No price effect is associated with corporate ownership, but units owned by trusts and estates are rented at 14 percent less than those owned by individual investors.

Both sophistication and profit motivation are positively correlated with rent, *cet. par.*, but both are collinear with scale and, to a lesser extent, with each other. As a result, only sophistication enters the equation with a significant coefficient, the value of which indicates that, controlling for dwelling characteristics, ownership form, and scale, units owned by "sophisticated" landlords rent at a 3.3 percent premium. In contrast, whatever price effects may be associated with profit-motivated owners are accounted for by the other objective characteristics we have identified.

These results are consistent with the earlier analysis of landlord types, from which we concluded that differences in owner behavior and motivations are not translated into significant price variations. The two important exceptions to this rule are the 11 percent discount for units owned by building residents and the 14 percent discount for units which are in the hands of trusts or estates. Together, however, these owner types control less than 10 percent of the rental stock. The eight percent of the stock which is held by corporate owners carries no price premium, and neither neighborhood residency nor absentee ownership impact on price levels.

CLASS MONOPOLIES AND MARKET DUALITY

Despite the growing body of empirical analyses on market pricing which are based on the assumption that urban housing markets are competitively organized, a parallel body of literature disputes the contention that buyers and sellers behave in accord with the presumptions of the competitive theory—particularly in the lower reaches of the market where prices are determined without direct and immediate reference to the new supply sector.[1] A body of theory has evolved which accepts the premise that, while the housing market at large may be reasonably competitively organized, the submarkets serving low income families reflect anything but the dynamics of perfect competition. The essence of these theories is that the housing choices of lower income families are so restricted that suppliers in this sector of the market behave as if they have monopoly pricing powers.

Harvey [1973:168–71], for example, argues that the urban housing market is characterized by a sharp duality which is the inevitable result of a housing allocation system based upon a competitive bidding process where there exist serious income disparities. He conceptualizes the market as being reasonably competitive at the top, with high income consumers enjoying substantial consumer surpluses which are generated by the large external benefits that attach to desirable locations in the urban complex. At the bottom of the market, however, low income households face monopolistic conditions under which most or all of their consumer surplus is extracted as producers' surplus or monopoly profit. The basis for this socially inequitable, dual market is the competitive bidding system under which successively higher income demanders need only outbid their nearest competitors for desired housing by marginal amounts in order to secure choice housing locations. Greater purchasing power, wider residential choices, and the fact that higher income households can escape the most serious effects of monopoly pricing by entering the new construction sector, places them in a superior market position relative to their poorer counterparts. At the bottom of the market, low income households are served by a class of producers whose collective operating policies are little affected by the mass of transactions taking place throughout the mainstream market. Thus the supply function is, to a great extent, discontinuous.

While competing with each other for tenants, suppliers of the low quality housing are assumed to exercise monopoly powers over the poor to the extent that they collectively set required levels of returns which if unmet would result in the withdrawal of their units from the market. Thus, while all suppliers have limited price setting powers, landlords at the bottom of the market can exercise these powers more extensively than can others. While particular market conditions determine the actual extent to which slum landlords can raise rents without reducing total revenues, Harvey [1973:171] argues that the poor pay at or very close to the maximum rents they are willing and able to pay for the housing they secure, while the rich do not; in effect, "the rich can command space while the poor are trapped in it."

Vaughn [1972], who views the inner-city housing market in much the same way, carries the dual market argument a little further. He suggests that poor people are locked into their neighborhoods and are captives of their landlords, with the result that "poor housing may be the normal, inevitable product of the social organization of the housing market as it is presently constituted" [Vaughn, 1972:78]. The housing choices of low income tenants are sufficiently limited and their need for shelter sufficiently immediate as to make them psychologically and financially dependent upon their landlords. Indeed, he views the contractual relations between landlords and tenants as part of a broader class struggle between the powerful and powerless in our society. Our social and political system-maintenance institutions are alleged to function in such a way as to suppress overt expressions of conflict, with the result that tenant dissatisfaction with housing arrangements is likely to take some "sublimated, covert form of expression" [Vaughn, 1972:79].

Perhaps the most important testable proposition that emerges from Vaughn's class-struggle concept of the market is one which relates to the nature of the pricing mechanism. He hypothesizes that rent is not a function of the flow of housing services per time period as it is in a competitive market, but that in restricted markets "landlords can use their power position in the relationship to tie rent levels to income" [Vaughn, 1972:81]. A test of this proposition in a low income neighborhood in Columbus, Ohio, revealed that the proportion of income devoted to rent was relatively constant despite variations in levels of housing consumption. Controlling for quality differences, he found that households whose incomes were above the median consistently paid higher rents than those with incomes below the median. Conversely, when income was held constant, similar rents were paid despite differences in the number of rooms contained in the dwellings.

From Vaughn's perspective, the implications of these findings are clear. The superior bargaining position of landlords in the inner-city market provides them with little economic incentive to improve or even maintain the quality of their housing. Since most of their lower income tenants are already paying substantial portions of their limited incomes for rent, landlords cannot expect to recapture in even higher rents any investments they may make in improved maintenance or renovation. The issue is joined with the tenants' recognition that they can do little to improve their own living conditions. The monopoly powers exercised by inner-city landlords prevent tenants from realizing housing gains by way of moving to other available dwellings. Thus, it is argued, the forces of neighborhood change bring about market conditions that sustain patterns of exploitive behavior by landlords and that help create an environment of tension and despair within which tenants do little to care for the houses in which they are forced to live.

Assuming that various instruments of public policy are impotent to control the macroforces that contribute to neighborhood change, Vaughn [1972] argues that policy must then deal with the institutional framework within which landlord and tenant agreements are negotiated. His view of the low income market suggests that the reform of landlord-tenant law, the possible adoption of some form of rent control in specified submarkets and the strict enforcement of housing occupancy codes are more important than more conventional efforts to improve inner-city living conditions, such as the attraction back into the area of reasonably priced mortgage capital. Although he does not comment on the likely outcome of demand side subsidy programs, it follows from his argument that inner-city market conditions are sufficiently far from being perfectly competitive that rents would likely increase more rapidly than quality under a direct cash assistance program.

One can also view the market duality problem in the more traditional economic terms of differential demand pressures and lags in the market adjustment process. Among others, Muth [1969:115–34], Olsen [1969] and Nourse [1973:123–27] exlain housing quality variations as the result of income differentials in an equilibrium market, but they do not specifically address the manner in which the market adjustment process may lead to income-based price differences. Low income households who are generally unable to compete for new construction create a strong demand for lower quality housing in older, centrally located neighborhoods. This demand can be satisfied by increasing the number of housing units through conversion, or the supply of lower quality dwellings can be augmented by the filtering down of higher quality dwellings. Price pressures in the lower quality stock will increase the returns to capital that its owners realize. This will create an incentive for the owners of slightly higher quality units to reduce maintenance outlays and rents to the point where they can compete in the lower quality sector. To the extent that the conversion and downward filtering processes are highly inelastic, long-term, seemingly permanent price differences may result [King and Mieszcowski, 1973].

The utility of this model rests on the assumption that the housing market is in, or is moving toward, a single equilibrium position given the supply and demand influences across the entire market. Our earlier analyses of submarket differentiation suggest, however, that the market may be characterized by a number of more or less independent equilibrium positions. In particular, dwelling quality appears to differentiate submarkets, thus supporting the contentions of Vaughn [1972] and Harvey [1973] that lower income families are somewhat insulated from the larger market processes.

Unfortunately, it is difficult to determine empirically whether observed price differentials are permanent market phenomena or simply manifestations of adjustment lags. We can, however, examine pricing patterns across the market and estimate the degree to which lower income households pay more for housing in the nonmetropolitan rental market. Harvey [1973] suggests that low income households are taxed close to their maximum willingness and ability to pay, while Vaughn [1972] hypothesizes that rents for low quality housing are more closely related to household income than to derived services. One would expect, therefore, to find rent-income ratios to be relatively invariant with housing quality, holding income constant. In the nonmetropolitan market this is not the case. In each quality class, the percentage of income that is devoted to rent decreases monotonically as income rises (Table 6–3). Even among the occupants of the worst quality housing, households in the second income quartile spend an average of only 13 percent of their incomes on rent, and those whose incomes are in the bottom quartile still devote less than one-quarter of their limited resources to housing. High income renters living in low quality housing spend only five percent of their incomes for rent, while those in the best units spend 13 percent. Conversely, within each income group, rent-income ratios increase with housing consumption. Indeed, the fact that substantial portions of the very low income nonmetropolitan population are able to secure relatively good quality housing at the expense of substantially higher rent-income ratios may suggest that many households suffer from serious income problems, rather than from problems of monopoly pricing.

Table 6-3. Contract Rent as a Percent of Income by Housing Quality and Income

| Housing Quality | Household Income Quartile | | | | | |
	1	2	3	4	Total	N
1 (Lowest)	23.5%	12.8%	9.1%	4.6%	14.7%	46
2	29.3	18.8	10.2	6.6	18.0	102
3	33.1	17.3	10.2	6.4	18.4	99
4	48.8	18.6	12.9	8.9	20.0	102
5	43.3	25.5	15.3	9.6	18.6	96
6 (Highest)	49.1	32.9	18.7	12.6	22.6	38
Total	34.5	19.5	12.6	8.6	18.6	
N	116	123	122	122		483

These hypotheses can be subjected to more rigorous testing in the same manner in which we examined the effect of supplier characteristics on rent. If rent is more closely tied to income than to the services provided by a dwelling, then income should have a positive coefficient if it is entered as an additional explanatory variable in the price determination equation. Essentially the test is based on the assumption that housing attributes should fully explain rent variations and, therefore, that household income should not be systematically related to rent once those factors have been controlled. The results of such a test, however, would be somewhat ambiguous. In general one would expect income and rent to be positively related, and the simple correlation between current income and rent, both in log form, is .39. Only in the unlikely event that the price equation is perfectly specified will we observe no systematic income effect. Any housing characteristics that are not controlled are likely to be picked up by the income variable.

In order to test the hypothesis more adequately, we have estimated income effects separately for high and low quality submarkets as well as for the full sample. Although income may have a positive impact on rent, the class monopoly theories imply that the effect would be stronger in the low quality submarket than in the high quality sector. Possible discontinuities in the rent-income relationship were tested by entering income in two forms. In addition to a logarithmic specification, tests in which income was grouped into four quartiles were performed. Finally, we should note that other household characteristics (such as household size, and sex and age of head) which may be correlated with income and rent have not been controlled. In preliminary tests, they did not materially affect the results; for simplicity they have been omitted from the analyses presented below.

The results of the tests are summarized in Table 6-4. When current

Table 6–4. Tests for Market Duality Based on Household Income and Housing Quality

		Coefficient of Income Variable in Price Equation[1]		
Income Variable[2]		*Full Sample (N = 457)*	*Low Quality (N = 232)*	*High Quality (N = 225)*
Log (Income)	b	.071[a]	.080[a]	.055[b]
	(SE_b)	(.018)	(.023)	(.026)
	R^2	.690	.475	.636
	C_v	.039	.038	.035
Income Quartiles[3]				
$INCQ_2$	b	.064[b]	.077[b]	−.013
	(SE_b)	(.035)	(.041)	(.060)
$INCQ_3$	b	.101[a]	.126[a]	.071
	(SE_b)	(.036)	(.046)	(.056)
$INCQ_4$	b	.130[a]	.132[a]	.087[c]
	(SE_b)	(.036)	(.048)	(.056)
	$\bar{R}^2$	.687	.468	.636
	C_v	.039	.038	.035

1. Coefficient is value when variable is entered into price equation containing dwelling attributes. The attribute coefficients are not shown since they do not vary substantially from those obtained earlier for the full equation (Table 5–2) or for the equations for each quality submarket (Table 5–6). The N's differ since these analyses are restricted to occupied units for which household income information was obtained.
2. Current income is the measure employed here.
3. $INCQ_2$ equals 1 if household income is in the second quartile; 0 otherwise.
$INCQ_3$ equals 1 if household income is in the third quartile; 0 otherwise.
$INCQ_4$ equals 1 if household income is in the top quartile; 0 otherwise. Suppressed category is household income in the lowest quartile.
Significance levels: (a) .01
                 (b) .05
                 (c) .10
All tests are one-tailed.

annual income is entered in logarithmic form, an income elasticity of .07 is obtained for the full sample. Thus, if housing quality is held constant, rent will increase less than one percent given a ten percent increase in income. For low quality units, the estimated income elasticity is eight percent, but it is less than six percent in the high quality sector. These values are not statistically different from each other and there is no strong basis for inferring that the occupants of the low quality stock are forced to pay more in relation to their incomes than are those who occupy higher quality housing.

If income is disaggregated into four quartiles, the differences in the income effects between the two submarkets are slightly more pro-nounced, but they still do not vary enough for us to establish statistical significance. For the entire market and for each submarket, the income effect increases monotonically with income. Overall, households in the second income quartile pay rents that are six percent more than those paid by the lowest income households. The rents paid by those in the third and fourth quartiles are, respectively, 10 and 13 percent greater than the rents of the lowest income families. The figures for occupants of the low quality stock are very similar to those for the whole market; in the high quality sector, on the other hand, the income effects are somewhat weaker. Statistical significance can be attached neither to differences in the income coefficients within each submarket equation nor to the differences between corresponding coefficients in the two submarket equations.

In sum, these analyses provide no unequivocal verification of the hypothesis that lower income families or the occupants of poor quality housing pay more for rental housing than do other households in the nonmetropolitan market. The possibility that the poor do pay more should not, however, be totally disregarded. That the income coefficients in the price equation are significant and positive suggests that income may be acting as a proxy for omitted housing characteristics that are positively correlated with rent. To the extent that this is the case, we would expect the error to be primarily in the direction of underestimating the amenities and positive externalities associated with higher quality housing, which would increase the income coefficients in the high quality sector. If there is some error in the measurement of housing services, the fact that the income effect is slightly weaker in the high quality sector may indicate that higher income households benefit disproportionately from the rent structure and market bidding process.

Even if this error is much larger than we think, however, income-related price discrimination in the rental market does not have any apparent market significance that would require public intervention remedies. From a pragmatic standpoint, the differences observed are too small in most cases to represent a substantial welfare loss to lower income households. Any public sector efforts to improve housing and neighborhood quality would increase the amenities and external benefits enjoyed by lower income households and would likely eliminate any observable price differences. More importantly, the results do not indicate that income-based market segmentation is severe enough to undermine important public sector housing objectives.

RACIAL DISCRIMINATION

In earlier chapters we indicated that the nonmetropolitan rental housing market is sharply segmented by race and that blacks consume housing that is of substantially lower quality than that occupied by whites. These observations taken together suggest that the rental market is structured in such a way as to enable housing suppliers to behave as if they discriminate against blacks. It may be the case, however, that the pattern of residential segregation is the result of both blacks and whites preferring to live in racially homogeneous areas, and the generally low quality of black-occupied housing may be purely a function of the low incomes of black households. In any case, market segregation does not inevitably lead to discrimination, if the latter concept is defined as a systematic price variation related to race. In order to separate and clarify the issues of discrimination and segregation, we focus here on the former by attempting to measure the price effects, if any, of racial discrimination in the nonmetropolitan market.

A substantial body of empirical evidence relating to metropolitan housing markets does indicate that blacks pay higher prices than whites for equivalent housing, although the results of the various investigations are not unanimous in this regard. Rapkin's cross-sectional study of SMSA's based on 1960 Census data led to the conclusion that "it is more than evident that Negroes spending the same rent as whites to rent the same number of rooms obtain a substantially greater proportion of substandard units" [Rapkin, 1966:338]. Bonham employed a components of difference analysis using similar data and also found strong evidence of price discrimination and "little difference in the level of racial discrimination observed in the North and the South" [Bonham, 1972:32]. Ridker and Henning's [1967] analysis of 1960 tract data indicates that the price of single family homes in St. Louis increased with the proportion of the tract that is nonwhite, while Muth [1969] estimated racial markups of from two to five percent in the Chicago ghetto.

Because of their reliance on aggregated census data, all of these studies were hampered by inadequate measures of housing consumption.[2] A number of other studies of discrimination have been carried out using detailed housing data obtained either from public records, realtor files or household interviews and dwelling unit inspections. Bailey [1966] found no evidence of price discrimination in single family home prices, but his results have been criticized since they were based on sales in areas proximate to the University of Chicago where white demand may have been unusually high [Muth, 1969:302]. The results of Kain and Quigley [1970] indicate a discrimination markup of from five to eight percent in the owner and renter submarkets, respectively, but Lapham [1971] found no evidence of price discrimination in Dallas. Since neighborhood racial composition, rather than the occupant's race, was used in both of these studies, there is some doubt as to the ability of the analyses to account for all of the complexities of price discrimination. King and Mieszcowski

[1973] estimated that rents in the New Haven ghetto are nine percent higher than those in white areas of the city and that, where whites and blacks live in close proximity, the latter pay more for equivalent housing.

Sources of Racially-Based Price Differences

If we consider the impact of race on housing prices in the context of a general equilibrium model of the market, the relationship is more complex than it first appears. Becker [1971:78] has demonstrated, for example, that whether segregated living patterns are the result of public policy or of the preference of the members of one group for living near other members of the same group, it does not necessarily follow that one group will "pay more for a dwelling of given quality." Using an equilibrium model developed by Bailey [1959] and put into a racial context by Muth [1969:107ff.], one can demonstrate that if whites have a taste for segregation they will outbid blacks for housing located in white neighborhoods. Whites will, therefore, pay a premium in order to maintain racially homogeneous neighborhoods. This model is consistent with the commonly accepted belief that racial segregation is the result of white prejudice rather than of a preference among blacks for voluntary self-segregation. This thesis is supported by Pascal's [1965:8] evidence that blacks tend to be more segregated than other ethnic groups "among whom one would expect a significant amount of voluntary self-segregation."

The resultant spatial configuration, given these assumptions, will contain a white neighborhood where price is P_w and a black area where price is P_n. The equilibrium relationship between P_n and P_w is determined by interactions at the neighborhood boundary and by tastes for segregation. In an extreme case in which the two neighborhoods are separated by an impervious boundary, P_w and P_n are completely independent. Assuming that competitive conditions exist in both areas, that the cost of providing housing is the same, and that new construction is possible in both areas, then we would expect P_w to equal P_n [King and Mieszcowski, 1973:591].

More realistically, however, there will be an interface between the two neighborhoods. Consider the situation in which whites prefer segregation, but blacks prefer living near whites (perhaps for reasons related to the provision of public services, the quality of available housing, or simply out of a taste for integration). Assume a configuration exists in which houses on streets occupied by blacks are priced at P_n and those on streets occupied by whites are priced at P_w. At the boundary, prices on a white-occupied street will be P_{wb}, which must be less than P_w to reflect white tastes for segregation. The prices on a black-occupied boundary street will be P_{nb}, which will exceed P_n by the amount equal to the black taste for integration. If in the initial situation $P_n = P_w$, then it follows that

P_{nb} exceeds P_{wb}. This boundary price inequality will be eliminated by the conversion of white-occupied units to black occupancy since owners who convert will realize a gain equal to $(P_{nb} - P_{wb})$. Owners of units on streets in the white interior which become white boundary streets due to the expansion of the black area will realize a loss of $(P_{wb} - P_w)$; similarly, owners on black boundary streets which become interior streets will lose $(P_b - P_{nb})$. The expansion of the black area will drive down P_n and cause a rise in P_w. At the equilibrium point P_{nb} and P_{wb} will be equal, thus eliminating the incentive for further expansion.

The resultant equilibrium price configuration across the market is given by:

$$P_n < P_{nb} = P_{wb} < P_w.$$

Thus, prices in the black interior are lower than prices in the white interior. This result is entirely consistent with Becker's [1971:14] assertion that, in order to satisfy their taste for segregation, whites must be willing to pay a premium to associate only with whites. As Muth [1969:107–8] argues, it is irrelevant whether blacks prefer integration or segregation, as long as they are willing to pay less in a white neighborhood than whites will bid. If blacks are indifferent to segregation, P_w will still exceed P_n, and P_{nb} will equal P_{wb}; but P_{nb} will then equal P_n. If blacks prefer segregation, the boundary prices will be less than either of the interior prices, but only in the unlikely event that black preferences for segregation are much stronger than those of whites will P_n exceed P_w.

Short-run aberrations resulting in blacks paying higher prices than whites can be explained, within the context of this model, in terms of differential growth rates and housing supply elasticities. If the black population is growing more rapidly than the white population, then any market lags which act to retard the movement of the racial boundary will result in temporary relative price increases for blacks. Becker [1971:80] suggests that these rent differentials, "although caused by an adjustment lag, would appear to be a long-run equilibrium differential." This view has been embraced by Muth [1969:110] and has been supported by the cross-sectional analysis of Haugen and Heins [1969] which showed a direct relationship between rent differences and the growth rate of the black population for SMSA's in 1960. One of the critical factors resulting in these price differences is the fact that blacks are rigidly confined to relatively small areas in their search for housing. In metropolitan areas, white household expansion generally can be satisfied through new construction and movement to outlying areas. Black housing needs are more often met by occupancy changes at neighborhood interfaces. If the conversion process has a low supply elasticity, price differentials "may be both large and persistent" [King and Mieszcowski, 1973:593].

It can be argued, however, that these price differentials are in fact evidence of noncompetitive behavior and are long-run effects. For this to be true, it must be demonstrated that whites are able to satisfy their taste for segregation through nonprice means and/or that, with the support of the white population, organized real estate interests can create permanent market restrictions on the availability of housing for blacks and, thereby, reap monopoly profits. Thompson et al., [1960:59–61] for example, describe the situation in Birmingham, Alabama, where racial zoning laws, the discriminatory behavior of the housing inspector and the threat of violence acted to freeze for 30 years the area in which blacks could reside. This is an extreme example of what Foley [1973:96] describes as the "institutional web that blocks the minority family from the main housing market." Unfortunately, the great complexity of the housing development and allocation process makes it difficult to isolate the real source of discrimination or to separate discriminatory practices as such from the larger process of decision-making [Foley, 1973:137–8].

While Muth [1969:107] contends that attempts by owners and sellers of real estate to collude would be undermined by the profit motives of those willing to deal with blacks, his argument is valid only if the price mechanism is the controlling factor in the allocation of housing to whites and blacks. With the strong support of the majority population behind it, collusion can be both possible and highly profitable. Moreover, it may be that an important role of real estate agents and brokers is to act to centralize housing transactions to prevent the losses that would accrue to owners in the white interior if black expansion does not take place in an orderly and predictable fashion [Kain, 1969]. If the restrictions imposed by organized real estate interests cause the expansion of the black neighborhoods to proceed at a slower rate than would occur naturally, the result will be higher prices in the black than in the white interior. This, of course, is counter to the equilibrium situation which follows from Bailey's model. To dismiss an observation that blacks do pay more for equivalent housing as a temporary disequilibrium may, therefore, lead to incorrect conclusions about the operations of the housing market and to inappropriate prescriptions for public sector actions. In particular, if white tastes for segregation can be satisfied through noncompetitive means, blacks will suffer a considerable welfare loss in attempting to satisfy their housing needs.

Testing for Price Variations
A simple and direct test for racially-based price variations could be performed by entering into the price determination equation a dummy variable to designate either the race of the occupant or the predominant race of the neighborhood. While such a test could provide a general insight into the problem, it would be deficient for at least two reasons.

First, our theoretical analysis suggested that certain systematic price variations would be expected given the segregated residential pattern of these cities. Secondly, price differences that appear to be the result of discrimination may in fact be related to differences in the socioeconomic characteristics of white and black households. Accordingly, a series of tests for price discrimination were performed, some of which include these factors and some of which do not. The results of these tests indicate that price discrimination against blacks is an important factor in the nonmetropolitan rental housing allocation process.

Socioeconomic Controls: In order to assure that race is not acting as a proxy for household-specific factors that may result in higher rent, a number of socioeconomic controls were introduced into the analysis. In this regard, Muth [1969:111] suggests that because of their low income, black households will consume less space than white households of the same size. The more intensive use of the dwelling will result in more rapid physical depreciation for which the landlord may require higher rent. We have therefore included in our model a continuous variable which measures the number of square feet of living space per person in the household (Table 6–5). It is also possible that owners prefer to rent to older

Table 6–5. Occupancy Characteristics Entered Into Supply Equation for Price Discrimination Tests

*SQFTPER**	Square feet of living area per person in household
YRSCTY	1 = household moved to city less than one year ago
AGEHD1	1 = head of household under 25
AGEHD2	1 = head of household 65 or over
SEX	1 = female head
*INCOME**	Current total income of household
RACE	1 = black household
BWN	1 = black occupant in white area (20% or less black)
BBN	1 = black occupant in black area (60% or more black)
WBN	1 = white occupant in black area
BMN	1 = black occupant in mixed area (25–50% black)
WMN	1 = white occupant in mixed area

* Variable entered as natural logarithm.

persons and are reluctant to rent to young families; they might also have a preference either for male or female-headed families. Accordingly, the model includes dummy variables to control for the price effects of households headed by persons 65 or over, by persons under 25, or by females.

In addition, we control for the length of time the household head has been living in the city. This variable measures an information lag among recent arrivals to the city which is likely to result in their paying higher rents. In the case of New Haven, King and Mieszcowski [1973] suggested that the relatively large numbers of black households who had been in the city only a short time are not familiar with the market and have not established themselves as good tenants. In the small cities, recent immigrants do not constitute a large proportion of the households, and they are more likely to be white. These facts do not render the variable any less important; they do suggest, however, that to omit it would produce a slight downward bias on the estimated difference between rents charged to blacks and those charged whites. In New Haven, the opposite bias would have occurred.

The final socioeconomic control is income, which, as we have noted, is positively related to rent even after the characteristics of the unit and its neighborhood are controlled. We speculated that to some extent income may be acting as a proxy for omitted dwelling unit attributes. Since white households have higher incomes, omitting an income control would produce a downward bias on the estimated race premium. On the other hand, we also noted a slight tendency for the rent of low quality housing to increase more rapidly with income. Since blacks comprise a large portion of the occupants of these dwellings, the income effect would tend to overstate racial discrimination if income is not controlled. It is impossible to determine which of these factors is more important, or what bias would result if income were not controlled.

Race and Neighborhood Composition: In order to test the equilibrium theory discussed earlier and to sort out the likely sources of the race premium, we identified three neighborhood types according to racial composition and examined the interactions between the race of the household and the dominant race of the neighborhood. The measure of the neighborhood is the census enumeration district. Because of the sizes of ED's, they may contain internal pockets which are racially homogeneous, and their boundaries may cut through large ghetto areas. The actual extent of racial segregation thus will be understated by an aggregate ED statistic. By defining neighborhoods as being predominately black (more than 60%), or mixed (28%–46% black), we can be reasonably sure that the price measures for the interior areas are consistent with those that apply in the theoretical context of the equilibrium model. While mixed areas are not boundaries in the strict sense, we would expect lower prices there since interracial contact is at a maximum. Although we cannot test the model perfectly, we can draw important inferences about the mechanism by which prices for blacks are maintained at the high levels indicated by our results.

Empirical Results: A number of insights can be developed from the information contained in Table 6–6. Among the six control variables

Table 6–6. Occupancy Characteristics

Variable	Mean	Simple Correlation with RACE	Correlation with Log Annual Rent	
			Simple	Partial[b]
SQFTPER[a]	523.414	−.311	.151	−.091**
	(332.813)			
YRSCTY	.094	−.149	.219	.130***
AGEHD1	.193	−.147	.205	.078*
AGEHD2	.158	.011	−.166	−.150***
SEX	.425	.085	−.151	−.142***
INCOME[a]	6,074.611	−.254	.390	.186***
	(3,891.023)			
RACE	.335	1.000	−.529	.090**
BWN	.022	—	−.077	−.008
BBN	.182	—	−.386	.164***
WBN	.024	—	−.136	−.138***
BMN	.131	—	−.265	−.042
WMN	.179	—	.067	−.017

N = 457
See notes to Table 6–1.

related to characteristics of the occupant, four have moderate-to-strong simple correlations with race. Black renters tend to consume less space per person than do white renters. Once all dwelling-specific characteristics are controlled, a decrease in the amount of space per person is associated with a rent premium, as we would expect. Income is negatively correlated with race and positively related to rent. The latter relationship holds true even after dwelling attributes are controlled, but the partial correlation is less than half the value of the simple correlation. Newcomers to the city, who tend to be white, pay higher rents, as we hypothesized. Finally, the heads of black households tend to be older, but the correlation between race and sex of the head is weak.

The relationships between rent and the race variables are particularly interesting. Race alone explains 28 percent of the variation in rent across the market. While black households pay lower rents in the aggregate, controlling for the attributes of the dwelling produces a positive and significant partial correlation between rent and race. The magnitude of the partial is not very large, but the shift in direction is clearly indicative of a racial premium or markup. The same phenomenon occurs for the interaction variable designating black households living in predominantly black neighborhoods. There is no significant relationship between rent and the interaction variables for black households living in predominantly white areas or for households of either race living in mixed areas. There does appear to be a rent discount for white households in black neighborhoods.

The estimates of the price effects associated with household socioeconomic characteristics and race are presented in Table 6–7, which contains the coefficients for the household characteristics when all dwelling, neighborhood and market transaction variables are controlled.[3] The first equation simply tests whether rent is related to race after we have controlled for the other occupancy characteristics. Although our partial correlation analysis revealed that the household-specific characteristics are related to rent in the predicted direction, collinearity among them produces coefficients which are not statistically significant. Since these variables are entered as controls and are not central to the hypotheses we are testing, this is not a problem. The elasticity of .06 suggests only a

Table 6–7. Effect of Race and Other Occupancy Characteristics on Rent**

	Eqn. 1	*Eqn. 2*
SQFTPER*	.013	.004
	(.023)	(.022)
INCOME*	.059[a]	.048[b]
	(.022)	(.022)
YRSCTY	.126[a]	.120[a]
	(.044)	(.044)
AGEHD1	.017	.008
	(.035)	(.034)
AGEHD2	−.054[c]	−.052[c]
	(.038)	(.037)
SEX	−.028	−.028
	(.029)	(.028)
RACE	.075[b]	—
	(.039)	
BWN	—	xx
BBN	—	.118[a]
		(.049)
WBN	—	−.127[c]
		(.084)
BMN	—	xx
WMN	—	xx
Corrected R^2	.697	.702
SEE	.249	.248
C_v	.038	.038
F	48.82	47.70
N	457	457

** Values shown are coefficients of variables in equation containing all supply characteristics (See Table 5–2). Figures in parentheses are standard errors of coefficients.
* Variable entered as natural logarithm.
xx Variable not entered; t value less than 1.0.
Significance levels for coefficients (one-tail):
  (a) .01
  (b) .05
  (c) .10

moderate price effect related to household income. Recent arrivals to the city pay premiums of nearly 13 percent, while both elderly and female-headed households enjoy moderate discounts of five and three percent, respectively. The favorable treatment received by female-headed households is the result of their being predominantly one-person, elderly households; female headship is not as strongly associated with single parent, multiple children families in the small city as it is in inner-city areas.

The test for racial discrimination embodied in the first equation suggests that black households pay a markup of 7.5 percent compared with what similar white households pay for equivalent housing. Since this test abstracts from the presumed equilibrium relationships that result from spatial segregation, it provides an incomplete picture of the phenomenon. Nonetheless, at the mean this race premium amounts to about $58 per year, a substantial welfare loss to blacks. This estimate is consistent with those obtained from two preliminary tests which were based on the price equation for the full sample. Entering the race of the occupant, or of the last occupant in the case of vacant units, produced an estimated premium of 6.3 percent. A dummy variable indicating units located in neighborhoods which are predominantly black (60%+) yielded a 10.4 percent discrimination factor. Neither of these tests included any controls for other household characteristics; the overall correspondence among these three estimates strengthens our confidence that the rental market is structured in such a way that housing suppliers act as if they discriminate against blacks.

Although these analyses do not provide any insights into the nature of price discrimination processes in the market, they are suggestive of spatial relationships between race and price. A higher premium is attached to units located in black neighborhoods than to units occupied by black households across the market area. This suggests that the 46 percent of all black households who do not live in predominately black neighborhood pay lower premiums than those located in the heart of the black community.

A more explicit test for the interaction between neighborhood composition and the race of the occupant is provided in the second estimating equation in which the race dummy is replaced by a series of interaction variables (Table 6–7). The coefficients of these variables measure the percentage increase in rent compared with the rent paid by white households living in predominately white neighborhoods. A number of striking results emerge from this refinement of the tests. Among households living in predominately black areas, there are substantial price differentials that suggest that the containment of blacks in well-defined areas has a considerable impact on the housing welfare of these families. Black households in black areas pay a 12 percent premium for housing compared to whites in white neighborhoods. This result is consistent with the equilibrium theory if we are willing to accept the argument that the pressure of black population growth produces adjustment lags. Under this pressure, black areas will experience a short-run price increase, thus inducing expansion at the periphery; if the expansion process is slow due to the reluctance of whites to move and to the amount of the time required for them to find new housing, then the price increase will be persistent [Becker, 1971:80]. But we demonstrated in Chapter 1 that, compared to northern cities, nonmetropolitan cities have not been subjected to large increases in the black population, and there has been substantial new construction within black areas. Becker [1971:81], in fact, argues that "since the relative number of Negroes in southern cities has been fairly constant," and since "one hears more about residential discrimination . . . in northern cities," the equilibrium theory is supported. Our results indicate that, while Becker is correct in terms of the stability of the relative size of the black population, the existence of measurable price discrimination in the absence of a marked increase in the size of the black population refutes Bailey's [1959] equilibrium theory.

Although segregation does not inexorably lead to discrimination, the ability of whites to maintain strict patterns of residential segregation apparently enables them both to restrict the supply of housing available to blacks and to prevent blacks from expanding into white neighborhoods. The former provides an opportunity for socially enforced collusion by the owners of black housing, while the latter enables whites to satisfy their taste for segregation through nonprice means. Together these effects result in an equilibrium configuration in which prices in black neighborhoods exceed those in white areas. King and Mieszcowski [1973] estimated a nine percent markup in the black interior of New Haven, and they attributed it to severe demand pressures in the ghetto. In the nonmetropolitan city, where this is much less of a factor, but where the discriminatory markup is somewhat higher, we are led to conclude that the market for black housing is subject to collusionary behavior.

The few black households that do manage to break the segregation barrier and find housing in white areas do not pay a premium, implying that blacks are not subjected to selective price discrimination in white areas. More surprising is the lack of any measurable difference between the prices paid by whites or blacks in mixed areas and the prices they pay in white neighborhoods. The most likely reason for this result is that our relatively coarse neighborhood measure may be masking the fact that these cities are so rigidly segregated that they contain few real racial interfaces, even in areas that we have defined as being racially mixed. Our analysis of block-by-block segregation supports this supposition. At the racial boundary in New Haven, which King and Mieszcowski [1973] were able to define more precisely than we could, they found white prices to be less than those in the white interior, while prices paid by blacks were at the same level as those in the white interior. They attribute this to pure discrimination, but it also suggests the existence of a boundary price disequilibrium which would be eliminated through further expansion of the black area.

The few whites who live in black neighborhoods pay nearly 13 percent less than do whites in white neighborhoods. We can interpret this discount as a measure of the white taste for segregation. Most likely these households are living in areas which have undergone some racial transition during recent years; in an effort to keep these families in their units, the owners apparently are willing to forgo rent increases. The magnitude of the difference between the black premium and the white discount in black neighborhoods (25%) suggests a strong prejudice on the part of white landlords.[4] In the New Haven rental market, whites living in black areas paid the same price as blacks, leading King and Mieszcowski [1973] to conclude that market separation rather than pure discriminatory pricing was leading to higher ghetto prices. Here we find further evidence of discriminatory behavior in the southern, nonmetropolitan market.

The price configuration we observe in the rental housing markets of these cities is, thus, strongly at odds with that postulated by the equilibrium model discussed earlier. Using the symbols defined above, we have found the variation in rents paid by blacks to be:

$$P_n > P_b = P_w.$$

For whites the pattern is:

$$P_n < P_b = P_w.$$

The circle is completed by the equality of prices in boundary (or mixed) areas and white neighborhoods, regardless of the race of the occupant. In contrast, the equilibrium model suggests that we should observe the following pattern:

$$P_n \leq P_{nb} = P_{wb} < P_w$$

and that neither P_n nor P_w should vary with the race of the occupant. This evidence, combined with our earlier analysis of racial segregation and relative growth rates, suggests that the confinement of blacks to well defined ghetto neighborhoods creates an environment conducive to discriminatory landlord behavior.

It can be argued that the observed price differences may be explained by differences in the cost of supplying housing to various socioeconomic groups rather than to discriminatory behavior. In the development of the price model, we have attempted to control for those factors which would be likely to lead to systematic cost variations. Since the model includes controls for the inclusion of nonshelter services in rent, the intensity of use to which the unit is subjected, and household income, it is unlikely that important variations in expenses are contributing to the observed price differences. It is particularly interesting that we could not find firm support for the hypothesis that the poor pay more, adding further evidence that it is racial prejudice per se that lies at the heart of the price discrimination we have observed. In the next chapter our analysis focuses on rental housing investment and the cash flow position of investors. We will return to the price discrimination issue in that context and consider more directly whether racially-based price differentials are cost justified. As we will demonstrate, the cash flow data provide no basis for attributing price differences to systematic cost variations.

The Potential Impact of Fair Housing Laws

In the face of strong tastes for segregation among the majority white population, it is not clear that open occupancy legislation will have a marked effect on either the pattern or process of residential segregation [Muth, 1969:109]. While such laws could make available to blacks housing in neighborhoods that would otherwise be inaccessible to them, whites in the proximate area would seek housing elsewhere as long as such alternatives remain available at an acceptable cost. If there is vigorous enforcement of such laws, and if black households take advantage of the new opportunities available to them, then over time the proportion of the housing stock located in homogeneous white neighborhoods may substantially decrease. The effect of the decrease in the supply of housing in white neighborhoods would be to increase the price of this housing and, thereby, increase the premium whites will have to pay to satisfy their taste for segregation. In the nonmetropolitan market, where the white taste for segregation can apparently be satisfied without such a premium, open occupancy legislation could have the effect of forcing this preference to be translated into a price premium.

Even if fair housing legislation could not materially reduce residential segregation, such laws could have a beneficial welfare effect that would enhance the efficiency of housing market operations. At the least, they could enable the expansion of black neighborhoods to proceed at a rate commensurate with the increase in demand among black households. By removing artificial market restrictions, they would ease the price pressures in black neighborhoods, thus improving the housing welfare of blacks. The removal of these restrictions would effectively undermine those factors that are conducive to the collusionary-like allocation system which appears to characterize the nonmetropolitan rental market. Whether the pricing patterns we have observed are the result of deliberate efforts of the real estate industry or simply represent the industry's ability to capitalize on strong social pressures that restrict the geographic mobility of blacks is irrelevant. Even moderate enforcement of open housing laws would have the potential to reduce substantially the effects of either active or passive collusionary behavior.

In general, the impact of fair housing legislation will depend on three factors: the extent to which blacks are able, given their incomes, and are likely to take advantage of new housing opportunities; the strength of owner resistance to housing desegregation; and the coverage of the law. The vigor with which the law is enforced will, of course, significantly affect its impact. Although we cannot speculate on this aspect of the problem, insights into the other three can be developed from our data.

Household Responses: If blacks do not attempt to find housing in white neighborhoods because of the threat of violence against them or because of the social relationships they have developed in their current neighborhoods, then the impact of open occupancy will not be great. It is, of course, difficult to speculate about the response of black households to aggressively administered fair housing laws; some tentative conclusions can, however, be drawn from patterns of past moving behavior, future mobility expectations, and the level of satisfaction with current housing circumstances.

In the past, blacks have tended to be considerably less mobile than whites. Not only have the former been residents of the city longer, but they have longer periods of tenure in their current dwellings. While about one-quarter of the white households have lived in their current units for five years or more, the comparable figure for blacks is nearly 46 percent (Table 6–8). That almost twice as many blacks as whites are long-term residents of their dwellings can only be the result of either higher levels of satisfaction or of a marked absence of available housing alternatives. If we consider the reasons households gave for their last move, it would appear that whites tend to be less satisfied with their housing than blacks. Dissatisfaction with their previous dwelling was the reason given by nearly 45 percent of the whites, but by only 38 percent of the blacks. Including moves made in an effort to secure better locations or neighborhoods, 72 percent of the whites compared with 53 percent of the blacks made their last move in an attempt to improve their overall housing circumstances.

Current levels of housing and neighborhood satisfaction, however,

Table 6-8. Past Household Mobility and Race

Numbers of Years in Present Dwelling Unit	White	Black	Total
<1	35.6%	24.9%	32.1%
1-4	38.4	28.2	35.0
5-9	12.9	21.5	15.8
10+	13.1	25.3	17.1
Total	100.0	100.0	100.0

Tau = .172, p < .001; Gamma = .295
N = 546

Reason for Last Move			
Dissatisfied with last house	44.6%	38.1%	42.5%
Better location or neighborhood	27.5	14.4	23.2
New household	10.2	13.8	11.3
Other voluntary move	6.1	8.8	7.0
Forced move	11.6	24.9	16.0
Total	100.0	100.0	100.0

N = 544

make it clear that blacks are far less content than whites. The reasons given for the last move reflect the considerably greater ability of whites to translate dissatisfaction into actual mobility. Only 56 percent of the black households are satisfied with their current dwellings, compared with 78 percent of the whites, and nearly two-and-a-half times as many blacks as whites think the condition of their dwellings is a "big problem" (Table 6-9). To some extent the dissatisfactions among blacks are expressed as hostility toward their landlords. Fewer than half think the owners of their units do a good job in maintaining the dwelling, while over one-third think that the rent they pay is unfair. In contrast, almost 90 percent of the whites think they pay a fair rent, and nearly three-fourths are satisfied with the maintenance efforts of their landlords.

Overall levels of neighborhood satisfaction are generally high in the nonmetropolitan city. As is the case with respect to dwelling-specific satisfactions, whites are generally more positive about their neighborhoods than are blacks, but the differences are not as strong. Approximately 95 percent of both black and white households responded that their neighborhoods are either "not bad" or "very good" places in which to live, although whites were more likely to think they were "very good" (Table 6-9).

Taken together, the pattern of past household mobility and the satisfaction levels of whites and blacks point toward severely limited housing opportunities for black households. We cannot, of course, discount the possibility that income disparities lie at the heart of the inconsistency

Table 6–9. Housing and Neighborhood Satisfactions by Race

Satisfaction with Dwelling Unit	White	Black	Total
Satisfied	77.5%	55.8%	70.3%
Not too satisfied	16.7	35.4	22.9
Very dissatisfied	5.8	8.8	6.8
Total	100.0	100.0	100.0

Tau = .211, $p < .001$; Gamma = .421
$N = 547$

Condition of Dwelling Unit	White	Black	Total
Not a problem	58.6%	37.6%	51.7%
Slight problem	32.6	41.0	35.4
Big problem	8.8	21.4	12.9
Total	100.0	100.0	100.0

Tau = .210, $p < .001$; Gamma = .388
$N = 543$

Does Landlord Do a Good Job Maintaining This Place?	White	Black	Total
Yes	73.8%	48.1%	65.2%
Not sure	22.9	45.3	30.4
No	3.3	6.6	4.4
Total	100.0	100.0	100.0

Tau = .236, $p < .001$; Gamma = .454
$N = 543$

Is the Rent You Pay Fair?	White	Black	Total
Yes	88.9%	64.4%	80.8%
No	11.1	35.6	19.2
Total	100.0	100.0	100.0

Tau = .292, $p < .001$; Gamma = .630
$N = 536$

Is This a Good Neighborhood to Live in?	White	Black	Total
Yes, very good	78.8%	63.3%	73.7%
O.K., not bad	17.0	31.7	21.9
No, not good	4.2	5.0	4.4
Total	100.0	100.0	100.0

Tau = .157, $p < .001$; Gamma = .338
$N = 539$

between housing satisfaction and mobility. Low income households, whose ability to purchase quality housing is minimal, are less than satisfied—particularly since they are likely to compare their circumstances not to what is possible for them to attain given their resources but to a probably unattainable ideal or community norm. Our purpose here, however, is not to delve deeply into the mobility process; in the context of the racial discrimination we have observed, the importance of the racial differences in mobility and housing satisfaction lies in their ability to clarify the dual nature of the rental market and the difficulties facing black households. Moreover, we have demonstrated that the sources of many of the housing problems facing blacks can be directly attributed to race, holding income constant.

The inability of blacks to secure better housing in the past suggests that restrictions on their mobility are sufficient to deter them from attempting to gain access to housing in white areas, where the bulk of the good quality housing is located. To some extent this is reflected by the absence of any correspondence between race and household plans to move in the near future (Table 6–10). In regard to prospective mobility, however, two

Table 6–10.   Prospective Household Mobility and Race

Plan to Move in Next Year or Two?	*White*	*Black*	*Total*
Yes	32.1%	28.7%	31.0%
Not sure	9.4	15.5	11.4
No	58.5	55.8	57.6
Total	100.0	100.0	100.0

Tau = −.004, NS; Gamma = −.008
N = 545

Are You Looking for Another Place Now?	*White*	*Black*	*Total*
Yes	29.6%	42.9%	35.4%
No	70.4	57.1	64.6
Total	100.0	100.0	100.0

Tau = .153, $p < .05$; Gamma = .312
N = 175

Do You Want to Stay in This Neighborhood?	*White*	*Black*	*Total*
Yes	21.9%	43.8%	29.4%
Not sure	12.6	15.0	13.4
No	65.5	41.2	57.2
Total	100.0	100.0	100.0

Tau = −.237, $p < .001$; Gamma = .431
N = 231

factors do differ significantly by race. First, among those households who indicated that they plan to move, blacks were considerably more likely than whites to be looking currently for another place. While this provides some evidence that prospective black movers may be more likely actually to move, the mobility history suggests that many of their plans will be thwarted by the lack of attractive and available alternatives. Perhaps more relevant from the perspective of desegregation, potential black movers indicated that they preferred to remain in the same neighborhood twice as often as did their white counterparts. Given that blacks tend to be less happy with their neighborhood, this suggests feelings of resignation to being confined to the ghetto, a general fear or reluctance to cross the racial boundary or, in a more positive sense, an attachment to a familiar area and a social network of friends and relatives. In any case, the available evidence provides no basis for being sanguine about the prospects for widespread desegregation or for general improvement of the housing conditions of blacks through the enforcement of open occupancy laws in nonmetropolitan cities.

Landlord Resistance: If owners are unwilling to rent to blacks, either because of their own prejudice or out of the fear that the demand among whites for housing in the area will fall, the impact of open occupancy laws will be diluted. Not only will owners with a strong resistance to desegregation attempt to circumvent the law, but the incentive among blacks to locate housing in white areas will diminish if they encounter antagonism and hostility in their search for housing. As we noted in Chapter 4, nearly 70 percent of all owners are opposed to renting to blacks. This includes 47 percent who stated that they definitely would not rent to blacks or that they would do so only in a black neighborhood and about 22 percent who preferred not to rent to blacks. Together these owners control about 44 percent of the rental stock.[5] Given the severity of segregation in these cities, this relatively low figure probably reflects some reluctance among owners to state their feelings openly. It is also likely that owners who have never had to make the choice in the past and who do not expect to face the situation in the future would not express their prejudice against blacks.

More important than the marketwide landlord resistance is the manner in which the reluctance to rent to blacks is distributed across the market. Among units which are currently white-occupied, 55 percent are not available to blacks because of expressed owner prejudice (Table 6–11). As the proportion of the neighborhood population that is black decreases, owner resistance to black tenants increases. Where blacks constitute less than 20 percent of the population, about 55 percent of the rental stock is inaccessible to them; where they comprise 60 percent or more of the households, owner resistance falls to less than 20 percent. Finally, as housing quality increases, so too does owner resistance to blacks, although the relationship is relatively weak. Even among low quality housing, the owners of nearly 40 percent of the units are unwilling to rent to blacks; the corresponding statistic for high quality housing is 52 percent. That such a large proportion of owners of low quality housing expressed racial prejudice is consistent with the price analysis which clearly indicated that race per se, rather than income or other socioeconomic correlates of income, leads to discriminatory pricing. Were the problems of

Table 6–11. Owner Resistance to Black Renters

	Percent Who Would Not Rent to Blacks[a]	Gamma	Tau[b]
Race of Occupant			
White	55.1%		
Black	9.8	.837	.389***
Neighborhood Composition			
0–20% Black	54.9		
21–60% Black	34.7		
61–100% Black	19.3	.471	.254***
Quality Level			
Low	39.6		
Medium	41.4		
High	51.7	.165	.095**
Total	44.3		

[a] Includes responses: definitely would not; would prefer not; and only in black neighborhoods.
[b] Significance levels for tau: *** .001
                              ** .05

segregation and discrimination more a function of income than race, we would expect to find much less prejudice among the owners of the low quality stock.

No firm conclusions can be drawn from this analysis. In all likelihood, the extent of prejudice among owners against blacks is understated by their responses to our questions. Indeed, the owners of only about three-quarters of the stock responded at all. If the majority of those who did not respond did so because of their unwillingness to express their prejudice, then the data may contain a considerable downward bias. Even ignoring this possible bias, it is clear that blacks will face considerable antagonism should they attempt to locate housing outside of well defined existing black neighborhoods.

Fair Housing Coverage: At the heart of the open occupancy issue lies a basic conflict of rights. The right of minority households to have free and open access to the housing market cannot be enforced without limiting the freedom of choice and personal property rights of landlords. It is beyond the scope of this work to engage in a philosophical or legal debate on this issue; it is relevant, however, to consider the way in which these conflicting issues are likely to be resolved in the legislative arena. The Federal Fair Housing Act of 1968 attempts to achieve a balance by exempting from coverage those dwellings whose owners are likely to have a higher than normal amount of direct contact with their tenants and who do not have a great influence on the market. Specifically, Section 803(2)(b) of Title VIII of the Act exempts single family houses provided that the owner does not own more than three such single family homes at any one time and that the home is not rented through a real estate agent, broker, salesman or through advertising. Also exempted are dwellings in structures occupied by four or fewer families if the owner resides in the building. While future legislation may be more inclusive, the passage of new and more stringent local or federal laws does not seem imminent. Using the federal exemptions as a basis, we can examine the coverage rates that are likely to be in existence for the foreseeable future.

In the nonmetropolitan market, where nearly two-thirds of the rental housing is in single family structures and where one-third of the stock is owned by landlords who own three or fewer dwellings, the federal exemptions apply to 31 percent of the stock (Table 6–12). That the coverage is even this high is a function of the relatively large proportion of the stock that is professionally managed. The exemptions are highest (36%) in the middle quality reaches of the stock where the law could be most useful to blacks. While only 30 percent of the worst housing is exempt, the bulk of it is already available to and occupied by blacks. At the other end of the quality range, 22 percent of the best housing, much of which is comprised of new garden apartments, is exempt, but these units are generally inaccessible to blacks by virtue of their low incomes.

Table 6–12. Coverage of the Federal Fair Housing Act[a]

	Percentage of Units Exempt	Gamma	Tau[b]
Quality Level			
Low	29.5%		
Medium	36.2		
High	22.5	.105	.055*
Race of Occupant			
White	36.8		
Black	17.7	.460	.194***
Neighborhood Composition			
0–20% Black	37.5		
21–60% Black	27.3		
61–100% Black	17.7	.312	.158***
Owner Preference			
Willing to Rent to Blacks	22.7		
Would Not Rent to Blacks	42.3	.429	.210***
Total	30.6		

[a] Based on exemptions under: Federal Fair Housing Act of 1968, Title VIII, Sec. 803(2)(b).
[b] Significance levels for tau: *** .001
               *   .05

Similarly, exemption rates are lowest for housing which is already occupied by blacks or which is in predominantly black neighborhoods. While 38 percent of the units in predominantly white neighborhoods are exempt, the exemption rate in black neighborhoods is only 18 percent. In mixed neighborhoods, which are the areas where blacks are most likely to search for better housing, more than one-quarter of the stock is exempt. Finally, it is noteworthy that the coverage rate for units of owners who expressed racial prejudice is only 58 percent, compared to the 77 percent rate for units of owners willing to rent to blacks. The former category includes 14 percent of the total stock; this represents the minimum proportion of the stock that is virtually inaccessible to black households.

Currently existing legislation not only exempts a considerable portion of the stock, but coverage rates tend to be lower than average in those segments of the stock where open occupancy is most needed. Fair housing is clearly irrelevant in predominantly black neighborhoods, yet coverage is least extensive in mixed and predominantly white areas. Similarly the medium quality housing stock, for which black demand is potentially highest, is subject to the least fair housing control. These factors, combined with an understandable reluctance among blacks to venture into potentially hostile neighborhoods or to confront strongly prejudiced landlords, are likely to result in the indefinite perpetuation of residential segregation.

NOTES TO CHAPTER 6

1. See, for example Mollenkopf and Pynoos [1973]; Nevitt [1969]; Krohn and Tiller [1969]; and Vaughn [1972].

2. For a candid discussion of the difficulty in using variables defined from census data, see Wihry [1969:86], who makes the following statement about his regression equations attempting to measure price discrimination: "Whether the above analysis indicates price discrimination against blacks is a matter of interpretation."

3. For each equation, the coefficients of the dwelling variables which are presented in Table 5–2 are essentially invariant, and they are not repeated. It should also be noted that the earlier analysis included all rental units, whereas we are restricted here to occupied units only. In addition, nonresponses to the income question result in a further sample size reduction. Since the coefficients of the dwelling attributes are essentially unchanged, we are confident that there is no bias created by these adjustments.

4. Although a small portion of the housing in these cities is owned by blacks, in no case does a black landlord own a white-occupied dwelling.

5. A 1960 study of vacant housing in Schenectady, New York, revealed that 65 percent of the owners "were opposed to renting to Negroes." The figure had been 75 percent in 1951 [Mercer, 1962:49]. Since the study was not based on a random sample of either dwelling units or landlords, we cannot draw a direct comparison with our results.

✱ *Chapter 7*

The Rental Housing Investment Market

INTRODUCTION

Preceding chapters have examined important characteristics of housing suppliers, consumers, and dwelling units in an effort to develop an understanding of the rent determination process in the nonmetropolitan market. Here we assess the state of the investment climate in order to provide insights into the equally important matter of how capital values are determined. Although the consumption and investment sides of the housing market are intimately related, we focus exclusively on the latter in this chapter by taking as given the market rents for housing of various types. Judgments about the state of the investment environment are based on a conceptually and analytically simple gross rent multiplier (GRM) investment model.

We begin the presentation with a discussion of the concept of gross rent multipliers and their use in testing theories about housing market structure. Throughout the chapter, we focus on two analytically distinct components of gross rent multipliers which were critical elements of the seminal work of Grebler et al. [1956] on long-run changes in residential capital formation rates: namely, net-to-gross income ratios associated with different dwelling classes and the respective rates at which incomes are capitalized. We attempt in the first section to link this early analysis of market structure with more recent, cross-sectional studies of inner-city housing market dynamics undertaken by, among others, Rapkin [1959], Sternlieb [1966; 1970], and Stegman [1972]. Here, we indicate the different issues with which more contemporary GRM analysis deals and suggest that the low multipliers noted by the above analysts are due to factors qualitatively different from those identified in Grebler's prior work.

In order to compare the relative vitalities of metropolitan and nonmetropolitan rental investment markets, we delineate a series of nonmetropolitan submarkets by building upon the submarket structure developed in the earlier chapter on the rent determination process. This assures that the comparative analysis is not affected by differences in the structural composition or in the quality distributions of the respective inventories. We then evaluate the performance of rental housing investments across the nonmetropolitan submarkets through a comparative cash flow analysis. One of the implications of the analyses presented thus far is that the prevailing rent structure may be too low to generate sufficient investment benefits to owners of high quality housing to induce any substantial increase in new supply. To pursue this possibility further, we present a cash flow analysis of recently built rental housing properties where we examine their respective abilities to withstand reasonable debt service requirements at rates that are likely to prevail in the short to intermediate future.

In the final sections, we return to the issue of race, exploring its relationship to housing quality and investment experiences. The economics of shotgun houses, which provide minimal housing services almost exclusively to low income blacks, is an important dimension of the nonmetropolitan rental market. These units are qualitatively different from any housing type found in the inner-city, and their income-generating characteristics are, therefore, of particular interest. Finally, we employ cash flow data to test further the price discrimination hypothesis that was supported by our analyses in the last chapter; essentially we focus on the issue of whether racially-based price differentials may be cost-justified.

THE USE OF GROSS RENT MULTIPLIERS IN INVESTMENT ANALYSIS

It is important to note that we are not concerned here with the use of gross rent multipliers in the appraisal context. Rather than applying multipliers to determine market value, we are interested in the use of GRM's to test various hypotheses about the structure of investment markets or changes in these markets over time. The gross rent multiplier is defined as the ratio of current market value to gross annual rent. Ignoring for the moment certain of its inherent deficiencies as a measure of investment worth, the GRM is elegant in its simplicity and embodies useful relationships from which insights into the investment climate of the rental housing market can be derived.[1] The inverse of the GRM is the gross capitalization rate for an investment which is assumed to return a constant, perpetual income stream. Under these restrictive assumptions, variations in the capitalization rate across dwelling types reflect differential risk assessments; other things equal, a greater risk results in a lower GRM. Thus we would expect older and/or lower quality structures and those in transitional neighborhoods to be characterized by lower GRM's. While the use of gross rather than net rent weakens the GRM as an investment criterion, one can make some general statements about net rent using GRM. Specifically, since it is the net rent that is of interest to the investor, in a given submarket (i.e., a cluster of buildings having a common GRM) we would expect to find a constant ratio of net to gross rent for all structures. Furthermore, if two submarkets are subject to the same risk, dwellings in the one having a higher GRM would have higher net to gross income ratios; that is, expenses would absorb lower proportions of gross income.

As implied above, changes in gross rent multipliers are functions of two analytically distinct, but empirically interrelated, investment phenomena. The first is a change in the ratio of net to gross income and, the second, a change in the rate at which incomes are capitalized. Within particular submarkets, changes in the former can be measured and verified, but evidence of changes in capitalization rates is "supportable more by qualitative judgments than by actual data" [Grebler et al., 1956:410]. The effects of risk and net to gross ratios on GRM's within submarkets may operate in either the same or opposite directions. For example, a sector subjected to increasing risk over a given time span would experience a reduction in the GRM unless the net to gross ratio were increasing at a rate sufficient to offset the GRM decline. On the other hand, if expenses were increasing relative to rent concurrently with the increase in risk, the GRM decline would be accentuated. These interactions are critical to a cross-sectional analysis such as the one presented here. That two structures have the same gross multipliers is not sufficient reason for placing them in the same submarket. The risk and expense factors could be acting in opposite directions for each property, thus yielding equal GRM's even though the structures are similar neither from an investment nor a demand-side perspective. For this reason, we not only examine variations in gross multipliers across the nonmetropolitan market but also compute net to gross income ratios, net rent multipliers and capitalization rates for each market segment. By controlling for relative expense levels, we are able to assess the risk associated with various investment possibilities.

Secular Changes in Gross Rent Multipliers: 1890–1940

Observed changes in gross rent multipliers within various submarkets, or across the market as a whole, provide insights into changes in important market relationships within the residential investment sector. In the study of Grebler et al. [1956:409], sufficient longitudinal data were collected on gross rents, expense ratios, and values in several submarkets to enable them to conclude that "available evidence points to a long-run decline in the gross rent multiplier." Tracing trends in GRM's between 1890 and the 1940s, they noted a decline for single family houses from about 14 to 10. For tenements, the GRM fell from 9.5 to less than 5; and for apartment houses, from about 10 to less than 6 [Grebler et al., 1956:409]. Although these secular declines in GRM's could possibly be explained by alterations in either one or both of the investment parameters discussed above, they concluded that the fall in multipliers was apparently related to a long-run decline in the ratio of net to gross income. Although gross rent multipliers had suffered declines that were greater than the declines in net to gross income ratios, which suggested that some upward adjustment in capitalization rates had occurred, they concluded further that a change in the concept of housing from a flow of shelter services to one of a more broadly defined class of housing services was chiefly responsible for the secular decline:

> The stock of residential real estate is no longer merely a producer of the service of shelter; it also produces many additional consumer utilities, which add to the value both of its output and of the resources embodied in its capital [Grebler et al., 1956:419].

It is important to recognize that the changes in GRM's observed by Grebler et al. do not necessarily reflect significant problems in the residential investment sector or any downward adjustments in the quality of the occupied stock. Rather, the declines can be attributed to an increase in the relative quantity of nonresidential capital (i.e., appliances, etc.) per dwelling, and to the rise of noncapital inputs (i.e., utility and heating costs) associated with rental housing investments and the delivery of housing services [Grebler et al., 1956:419]. To the extent that returns to nonresidential capital are higher than those associated with residential capital, capitalization rates will increase even though market risks remain unchanged. Similarly, an increase in the proportion of gross rent consumed by the noncapital costs of residential housing services, *cet. par.*, will depress net to gross income ratios and, hence, gross rent multipliers.

Metropolitan Market Dynamics and Gross Rent Multipliers

One might expect, a priori, that the expansion of the function of the housing stock from the mere provision of shelter to a more inclusively defined flow of housing services would have completely run its course by the end of the 1950s. Any subsequent declines in net to gross income ratios would likely be functions of supplier inabilities to pass through capital or noncapital costs, of declines in net incomes due to shifts in demand, and of other problems such as rising rent delinquencies and related income losses. To the extent that continuing declines in the net to gross income ratios could not further explain continued downward drifts in gross rent multipliers into the 1960s and seventies, one might surmise, on the basis of related market information, that there has continued to be an upward drift in capitalization rates. Indeed, a review of more recent studies, particularly those centering upon market dynamics in declining metropolitan centers, indicates that further declines in GRM's may be attributable to continued declines in net to gross incomes, to the downward adjustments in the expected period over which incomes can be earned, and to heightened concern over the increasing instability of annual income flows.

Recent empirical studies involving gross rent multiplier analysis seek answers to different questions and attempt to address different market issues from those that concerned Grebler et al. [1956]. The recent work is largely cross-sectional and place-specific and is cast more in a microeconomic framework. It seeks a better understanding of how suppliers in particular submarkets operate within an environment where they are buffeted by a variety of social, economic, and political forces which are beyond their individual or collective control. Among the important issues dealt with here are determining housing quality and maintenance levels, estimating rehabilitation potentials, understanding management processes, and identifying the relationships among investor characteristics, cash flows, rates of returns and other measures of profitability. Accompanying this shift in the focus of research questions are, necessarily, changes in research methods. The work of Grebler et al. [1956] centered around the systematic analysis of aggregate time series data obtained from secondary sources, while the later studies of metropolitan core city housing markets are built around survey research techniques and the systematic sampling of investors, consumers, and related market actors.

Rapkin's [1959] study of the housing market in Manhattan's West Side Urban Renewal Area in the late 1950s represents an important link between the early work of Grebler et al. [1956] and Sternlieb's [1966] subsequent study of the Newark tenement market in the mid-sixties. According to Rapkin [1959], housing and investment conditions in the 20-block West Side Area were on the decline in 1956. Significant shifts in the use and occupancy of the physical stock were continuing unabated; turnover rates were on the rise; holding periods and rates of resident ownership were on the decline, and institutional sources of mortgage capital were drying up. In 1958, one-third of all West Side households were overcrowded and over one-third of the total stock of dwelling units lacked adequate sanitary facilities. Within this declining market context, Rapkin [1959:82] found gross rent multipliers exhibiting two distinct characteristics: "First, they appear to be quite low, and second, they reveal an extremely narrow range of variation. For all properties combined, the multipliers equaled slightly less than five." Although expense ratios on the West Side were on the rise during the period covered by his work, Rapkin [1959:83] concluded that the low multipliers were due primarily to the high discounting of future incomes by potential investors:

> Of all the aspects of the renewal program, attempts to rehabilitate existing buildings . . . will undoubtedly encounter the most difficulty. Among those properties where the need for such activity is greatest, an increasing proportion of the property owners are interested in high short-term returns rather than long-term investment earnings.

The adverse market forces which Rapkin [1959] identified in the soon-to-be-renewed West Side Area were, according to Sternlieb [1966], running rampant in Newark's central core during the mid-sixties. Sternlieb [1966:106] concluded that, due primarily to low capital gains potential, gross rent multipliers for slum tenements had fallen to no more than three-and-one-half to four times gross rent: "In essence then, the very weakness of the whole market produces a requirement for higher rates of return on new investment." Although the demand for higher rates of current return in Newark could be viewed as a continued rise in the capitalization rates being applied to inner-city properties, the weakness of the whole market and the weak rent structure suggest that the declining multipliers may also be related to reduced ratios of net to gross incomes. The latter hypothesis was not tested since Sternlieb [1966] did not gather primary data on operating expenses or expense ratios.

In subsequent investigations of New York City's rent controlled inventory [Sternlieb, 1970], of New York's stock of housing occupied by welfare tenants [Sternlieb and Indik, 1973], and in Stegman's [1972] study of the market dynamics of Baltimore's inner-city, special efforts were made to obtain more data on the expense side and to relate these data to net income ratios and the resulting price structures in these markets. In essence, the three studies emphasize the importance of declining net to gross income ratios in the continued plunge in gross rent multipliers in core city housing markets in the late 1960s. Indeed, the rapid decline in multipliers may be attributed to the fact that declining net to gross income ratios continue to accompany upward shifts in capitalization rates.

One source of the decline in net to gross income ratios among inner-city properties has been high vacancy rates. In Sternlieb's [1966:88] judgment, the 1960 vacancy rate of four percent in Newark's inner-city had substantially increased by the middle of the decade, while Stegman

[1972:76] found a 13 percent average vacancy rate in 1968 within the predominantly single family, marginal quality rental stock in Baltimore. In the latter case, it was not atypical to find fixed and variable expenses averaging upwards of 85 percent of gross collectibles, with substantial numbers of parcels showing expense levels, including debt service, greater than net rents received. In New York's welfare-occupied housing, Sternlieb and Indik [1973:185] indicated that expense levels varied with the proportion of the building's tenantry receiving public assistance; as a percent of net rents received, mean expense levels, excluding debt service, ranged between 57 and 67 percent. They found too that "for each of the building categories with over 30 percent of the tenants on welfare, the mean cash flow is negative" [Sternlieb and Indik, 1973:195].

The phenomenon of declining net to gross income ratios in the inner-city markets of the late sixties was due not to the inclusion of additional services in shelter transactions, but to spiraling operating and maintenance costs which could not be passed on to consumers in the form of higher rents. Should rents be increased, net rental income would remain relatively unchanged as vacancy and arrearage problems intensified. In short, not only are gross returns to residential capital continuing the secular decline first noted by Grebler et al. [1956], but in metropolitan core markets the pace of the decline in multipliers has probably intensified over the past decade. Indeed, it would appear that the phenomenon of residential abandonment, which has become a problem of serious national concern, represents a culmination of these adverse market forces. Were high capitalization rates accompanied by high net to gross ratios, present owners would be realizing high rates of return relative to the current depressed market values of their parcels. Even in a deteriorating investment climate, these high current returns would encourage holders of marginal properties to continue operations. What appears to have occurred in the inner-city, however, is that, increasingly, net to gross ratios are declining beyond the critical point after which rational investor behavior leads to abandonment.

THE NONMETROPOLITAN INVESTMENT MARKET

Having established the metropolitan benchmarks, we turn now to an analysis of the nonmetropolitan rental investment market where poor quality properties continue to command relatively high prices and where residential abandonment is virtually unknown. Our earlier effort to define a series of rental submarkets was related to hypothesized differences in rent determination processes across dwelling clusters which are distinguished by different supply and demand interactions in the consumption market. Our present interest concerns hypothesized differences in important investment parameters across submarkets. To maintain consistency with the earlier analysis and to facilitate metropolitan comparisons, the nonmetropolitan rental inventory was segmented into six submarkets defined by structure type and quality. The basic hypothesis is that these clusters constitute independent investment submarkets which can be distinguished from each other by their respective GRM values. In the context of the consumption market, submarket differentiation was presumed to be the result of varying substitution effects within and among clusters.

In an analogous manner, we would expect that, from the investment perspective, the mobility of capital among various dwelling types would be the primary source of submarket differentiation. In particular, independent clusters would be characterized by differences in requisite management skills and capital commitment and by varying risk levels, operating experiences and capital appreciation rates. It is unlikely that GRM alone is a sufficiently sensitive measure for unambiguously identifying investment submarkets. Similar GRM values may mask differences in risk and net to gross ratios, while submarkets with different GRM's may in fact be similar with respect to either of these parameters. Nonetheless, noting significant differences in gross multipliers across market sectors is an important step in building a better understanding of the nonmetropolitan investment environment.

Before considering the rent multipliers that characterize each submarket, it is useful to analyze the underlying value and rent distributions across the market (Table 7–1). If quality is ignored, the mean values of single family, duplex and multifamily dwellings vary by less than $1,000 per unit, but within structure types, there is a large variation in value.[2] The relationship between rent and structure type is considerably stronger, but here too the respective distributions are characterized by relatively large standard deviations which reflect principally the quality differences within each structure type. When quality is introduced as a further differentiating variable, both rent and value are strongly and consistently related to the rental submarkets. Both rent and value tend to be around twice as large for high quality units as for low quality housing within the same structure type class.

The distribution of gross rent multipliers displays expected trends (Table 7–2). Although the GRM variation is statistically significant across structure types, the relationship is much stronger when quality differences are also taken into account. Across structure types, the GRM increases as the number of units in the structure decreases.[3] The single family multiplier of 11.0 is 25 percent larger than the GRM of 8.8 which

Table 7-1. Market Value and Rent by Rental Housing Submarkets

Submarket	Mean Market Value per Unit	Mean Annual Gross Rent	N
Single Family	$ 8,759	$ 774	212
High Quality	13,334	1,082	88
Low Quality	5,513	555	124
Duplex	8,471	831	64
High Quality	11,847	1,062	35
Low Quality	4,397	551	29
Multifamily	7,944	992	70
High Quality	9,908	1,160	46
Low Quality	4,178	669	24
Total	8,541	828	346
Analysis of Variance: By Structure Type Only	$F = 0.43$ NS	$F = 6.33$ $p < .01$	
By Structure Type and Quality	$F = 33.04$ $p < .01$	$F = 37.04$ $p < .01$	

Table 7-2. Summary Investment Parameters for Rental Housing Submarkets

Submarket	GRM[a]	Net:Gross[b]	NRM[c]	Net Capitalization Rate[d]
Single Family	11.14	.4602	23.99	.042
High Quality	12.25	.5074	24.14	.041
Low Quality	10.19	.4129	24.68	.042
Duplex	9.97	.5993	16.64	.060
High Quality	11.62	.6277	18.51	.054
Low Quality	7.98	.5356	14.90	.067
Multi-Family	8.84	.5841	15.13	.066
High Quality	9.95	.5345	18.62	.054
Low Quality	6.71	.6699	10.01	.100
Total	10.40	.5071	20.51	.049
N	346	195		

[a] Analysis of Variance: by Structure Type only $F = 3.40, p < .05$
by Structure Type and Quality, $F = 4.53, p < .01$
[b] Analysis of Variance: by Structure Type only $F = 4.42, p < .01$
by Structure Type and Quality, $F = 2.88, p < .05$
[c] Derived by dividing GRM by net to gross ratio
[d] Inverse of NRM

characterizes multifamily housing. Within each structure type class, quality distinctions reveal GRM differences that are generally stronger than those between structure types. Single family units are characterized by the least within-class variation; the high quality multiplier of 12.3 is about 20 percent larger than that for low quality units. Among multifamily dwellings the high quality submarket has a GRM value which is nearly 50 percent greater than that for low quality units.

This latter submarket, which contains single family conversions and cheaply built, relatively small apartment buildings, has the lowest GRM of any submarket. Its value of 6.7, when compared to estimates that metropolitan inner-city rental housing units are traded at three to five times gross annual income [Rapkin, 1959:82; Sternlieb, 1966:103], suggests the existence of significant differences in the two market types. Clearly, nonmetropolitan rental markets have not suffered from the kind of trauma and depression that characterize metropolitan core city rental housing markets.

Although the GRM analysis provides clear evidence of the strength of the nonmetropolitan rental investment market, it does not offer any clues as to the source of that strength. Either very high net to gross ratios or low assessments of risk as reflected in low capitalization rates could be the controlling factor. In order to assess which of these is the more important and how expense ratios and capitalization rates vary across the submarkets, we computed net to gross ratios for 195 rental units for which detailed operating cost statements were obtained. This information enables us to suppress GRM variations that are the result of differences in costs and thereby to consider directly the way in which the investment community evaluates the risks associated with different kinds of rental properties.

The net to gross ratios are exclusive of debt service requirements, if any, and they include an imputed management cost whether or not the services of a professional manager are employed by the owner. The imputed costs were based upon the prevailing fees charged by professional management firms—ten percent of actual collections for weekly rentals, and eight percent for dwellings renting by the month. Since the use of managers varies both by structure type and quality, the expense levels will deviate from the actual cash expenditures according to the extent to which the rate of professional management is more common in certain submarkets than in others. In particular, expenses will be overstated in the high quality sectors where professional management is less common. The imputation of management fees is intended to account for the opportunity costs associated with the owner's day-to-day involvement in running his operations; in this sense, therefore, the expense ratios more nearly reflect the true economic costs of providing rental housing services. Even if a considerable proportion of the owners who manage their own investments attach a very low value to their time and effort, it would be unreasonable to draw policy inferences from analyses which presume that management is an essentially free resource. Although the influence of nonprofessional owners is likely to remain strong in these markets, intervention strategies may require the attraction of professional investors to the rental market. For them, effective management will be accomplished only by incurring an out-of-pocket expense or by making an investment in time and effort that will carry a significant opportunity cost.

If differences in quality are ignored, net to gross ratios across structure types do not vary as expected (Table 7–2). Relative expenses are higher than expected in single family dwellings given the extent to which tenants are generally responsible for routine maintenance, but expense ratios are lower than would seem reasonable in multifamily dwellings where both maintenance and utilities are typically landlord responsibilities. If the structure types are partitioned into quality classes, however, net to gross ratios behave more systematically, although not entirely consistently with a priori expectations.[4] Multifamily net to gross ratios are buoyed by very low expense ratios in older converted structures. Nearly 50 cents of every rental dollar is available to meet debt service and profit requirements in the high quality submarket, while among lower quality multifamily properties, the investor nets 67 cents of every gross rental dollar. Within the single family submarket this pattern is reversed. Low quality houses return only 41 cents on the dollar, while 51 cents is netted for high quality houses.

Net rent multipliers (NRM) were derived by dividing the average GRM by the net to gross ratio for each submarket.[5] On a cash basis, single family dwellings in the nonmetropolitan market enjoy the highest net rent multipliers and, therefore, the lowest capitalization rates; on average, these properties are priced at around 24 times net income. Multifamily structures are typically traded at 15 times net income and duplexes at a net multiplier of around 17. For even the poorest quality houses in the rental market, net capitalization rates are extremely low and payback periods correspondingly large. Net income earned on the worst quality single family dwellings is only capitalized at a four percent rate, which translates into a lengthy 24-year payback period. For low quality apartments, which are predominantly conversions, the cash payback period is still a relatively long 10 years.

The nonmetropolitan market is thus characterized by a narrow range of risk variation and investment returns across submarkets. The spread between the demand for a cash return is only from four percent in the high quality single family submarket to ten percent on investments in the lowest quality multifamily stock; this suggests that commonly assumed risks associated with holding poor quality housing are virtually nonexistent in the smaller cities. Low capitalization rates at the bottom of the market imply a stability that is unmatched in the metropolitan core city rental market. However, the long payback periods and relatively low net to gross ratios characteristic of the higher quality nonmetropolitan stock suggest that the prevailing rent structure may be unable to support debt service requirements for new rental construction, since these requirements are likely to remain substantially higher than those associated with the existing high quality inventory. The analyses also imply that good capital gains potential still exists within the better quality nonmetropolitan stock, and not just with respect to the better single family inventory. The problem here, as above, is whether the demand side of the market is sufficiently strong to pay the higher rental necessary for the conversion of paper gains into cash. In the single family sector the conversion of gains can be accomplished through sale in the fee simple market, but this is not a realistic possibility for multifamily housing.

One final implication of our review of gross and net rent multipliers and corresponding capitalization rates should be pointed out. The housing stock in nonmetropolitan cities remains principally a producer of shelter services rather than a provider of a more inclusively defined flow of housing and housing-related services. Returns to owners are predominantly returns to residential capital, while expenses are generally not weighted heavily toward residential amenities. To the extent that this is the case, the nonmetropolitan market, particularly within its lower quality reaches, may be more properly characterized by terms which Grebler et al. [1956] applied to the central cities of 50 or more years ago. Then, rental housing owners were described with reason as lords of the land, providers of shelter space pure and simple, with little obligation or incentive to maintain the quality of their dwellings in core city markets swelled by immigrant populations. Although the populations of nonmetropolitan cities are not growing rapidly, the institutional context within which rental housing owners function may not differ substantially from that associated with core cities of a generation or more ago.

THE INVESTMENT ENVIRONMENT

The apparent strength of the nonmetropolitan market, compared with its inner-city counterparts, partially can be explained by a number of factors relating to investor characteristics and to the investment climate (Table 7–3). At least some of the explanation lies in the differences among the respective inventories. Sternlieb's [1966] work in Newark focused entirely on tenement buildings, and in Rapkin's [1959:6] New York study area the structures were primarily brownstones and multifamily tene-

Table 7–3. Selected Investment Characteristics by Rental Housing Submarket

Submarket	Percent of Units Which Are:		Percent of Units Whose Owners:	
	Professionally Managed	*Mortgaged*	*Anticipate Mortgage Problems*	*Acquired Property for Capital Gains Potential*
Single Family	*34.2%*	*20.4%*	*20.5%*	*21.9%*
High Quality	22.6	27.7	8.8	21.1
Low Quality	43.2	13.7	30.8	21.4
Duplex	*28.0*	*36.7*	*14.6*	*24.1*
High Quality	15.7	53.2	13.0	28.3
Low Quality	38.2	20.0	17.1	15.6
Multifamily	*30.2*	*56.3*	*17.4*	*37.6*
High Quality	22.7	63.3	13.8	47.5
Low Quality	45.9	42.4	28.0	8.7
Total	*32.3*	*30.3*	*18.8*	*25.7*
Number Responding	545	495	420	386

Table 7–3   continued

Submarket	Percent of Units Whose Owners:			
	Expect Value Increased in Next 5 Years	*Perceive Neighborhood Decline in Last 5 Years*	*Have Never Evicted a Tenant*	*Complain of Problems with Current Tenant*
Single-Family	*64.8%*	*14.9%*	*89.9%*	*10.6%*
High Quality	68.2	5.3 ˙	90.6	6.8
Low Quality	59.5	21.8	89.6	13.9
Duplex	*65.5*	*12.6*	*84.1*	*6.7*
High Quality	66.7	4.5	88.1	6.4
Low Quality	63.4	21.4	79.5	7.1
Multifamily	*60.5*	*15.9*	*85.9*	*4.6*
High Quality	68.7	7.0	94.0	3.6
Low Quality	40.7	32.1	68.0	6.9
Total	*63.5*	*14.7*	*88.0*	*8.7*
Number Responding	414	431	405	449

ments, 90 percent of which were built prior to 1901. In small cities, on the other hand, over 50 percent of the lowest quality units are in single family structures, and only one-quarter are in multifamily buildings. Even here, the average age is much lower than the 70 or more years in the New York renewal area. Other things equal, a lower average age will translate into a higher GRM. Management is, furthermore, a less severe problem in one and two unit structures. While a few bad tenants in a large multifamily building can have a deleterious effect on the entire investment, the occupant of a single family unit is isolated, and tenant control is thus more directly and easily handled.

Stock factors cannot, however, provide the entire answer. Converted single family buildings are among the most marginal residential uses in any city. They have suffered severe physical depreciation due not only to their change from owner to rental tenure, but also from the intensification of their use. In addition, the process of conversion is often accomplished as cheaply as possible and represents a last ditch effort to milk whatever returns are possible from obsolete structures. Still, in the small city, the submarket comprised almost entirely of conversions displays a net capitalization rate of only eight percent.

There is a high degree of investor confidence in the future of the rental market in nonmetropolitan cities. These cities were not affected by the urban riots of the late 1960s to the extent that the metropolitan core cities were, nor have they experienced a comparable influx of low income, minority populations. One measure of this stability is that the owners of only nine percent of the stock feel that their tenants create problems (Table 7–3). These owners' complaints were equally divided between charges of careless or deliberate property damage and of late rent payments. Consistent with this, 88 percent of the rental units have never had a tenant evicted from them. In addition to having very few complaints about their own tenants, the overwhelming majority of owners expressed no concern about the neighborhood in which their parcels are located. The owners of 85 percent of the dwellings felt that during the last five years the neighborhoods had either improved or not changed at all, while the highest incidence of perceived neighborhood decline (32%) was among the owners of the poorest quality multifamily units.

This stability has its counterpart on the investment side of the market, where remarkably little trading of rental properties occurs. More than two-thirds of the rental units have been owned by the current owner for six years or more, compared with 57 percent in Newark. Only about 22 percent of the small city units have been acquired within the last four years, while in Newark the comparable figure is over one-third [Sternlieb and Burchell, 1973:57]. Perhaps the most telling statistics are that 26 percent of the units were acquired primarily in expectation of future capital gains, while the owners of a large majority (64%) of the units expect their properties to increase in value over the next five years; in only 10 percent of the cases were value declines anticipated in the near future. Sternlieb and Burchell [1973:57] found that fewer than one percent of their Newark sampled properties were bought in the expectation of future gains.

A generally sensitive barometer of the future of the housing market is the availability of mortgage money. Because of the predominance of single family structures in the smaller city, and due to the fact that rental units are traded infrequently, relatively few properties are mortgaged (30%). Among those nonmetropolitan mortgages that were obtained within the last five years, however, nearly 90 percent were financed by banks, insurance companies, or other traditional financial institutions. There is no evidence, as there was in Newark, where nearly half the mortgage capital was provided by noninstitutional sources, that "institutions are fleeing the market" [Sternlieb and Burchell, 1973:238-9]. Rapkin [1959:51] similarly found that during 1950-1955, 83 percent of the mortgages in the West Side Area were secured from noninstitutional sources.

Furthermore, the owners of only 19 percent of the nonmetropolitan stock feel that they would have difficulty getting mortgages on their properties today. Owners in the low quality single family and multifamily submarkets express substantially greater doubt about their ability to obtain mortgages for their properties. But the owners of fewer than one-third of even these properties think they would have difficulty, compared to the 52 percent of all Newark owners who said either that they could not get a mortgage or that they could get one only with some difficulty [Sternlieb and Burchell, 1973:240].

The final market factor that is relevant to the investment climate is the activity of the public sector. Stated simply, the owners of the most marginal residential dwellings in the nonmetropolitan city have little concern that their investments are endangered by the possibility of forced withdrawal due to the enforcement of housing codes. Fewer than two percent of the owners reported having received code violation notices during the past year. In none of these cases was the cited infraction severe enough to require substantial repair costs, much less to force withdrawal. Related to code enforcement, of course, is the issue of residential abandonment, which was pursued in detail in our landlord survey. While the abandonment problem provided the organizing framework for Sternlieb and Burchell's [1973] revisit to the Newark tenement markets, there is no evidence that this phenomenon exists at all in the nonmetropolitan city. Only about seven percent of the owners have taken a rental unit off the market in the last five years. Although some demolition has occurred for purposes of renewal, public housing and highway construction, the impact on the market has been barely perceptible. As a rule, structures that were voluntarily removed from the market were dilapidated to the extreme and were of no further economic value. Most of these were torn down, so that no further blight to the neighborhood occurred; in all cases the owners have retained rights to the land and continue to meet their tax obligations. In only two cases was the reported removal the result of severe vandalism damage.

CASH FLOW AND OPERATING EXPERIENCES

Expense Levels Across the Market.

In this section we focus our attention on the components of the investor's operating statement in order to isolate those expenditures which are unusually low and which contribute to the low expense ratios across the market. Compared with the ten percent vacancy rate in Newark [Sternlieb, 1966:47] and the 13 percent combined vacancy and arrearage rate in the Baltimore inner-city [Stegman, 1972:76], rental occupancy levels in the nonmetropolitan market remain quite high across all structure types and quality levels (Table 7–4). Overall, vacancy losses average 4.9 percent. Only in the low quality single family submarket does the average vacancy rate exceed eight percent, but that average masks wide variations within the group. Fully 74 percent of these units realized an effective income of 100 percent of collectibles, the 8.2 percent average being the result of a few units standing vacant for virtually the entire year. Across the entire market, nearly 75 percent of the dwellings experienced full occupancy during the year. Among high quality single family and duplex units, 89 and 84 percent respectively had no vacancy loss at all. Although high quality multifamily units experienced an average 5.4 percent vacancy loss, that submarket is subject to the highest turnover rate, with nearly 62 percent of the units having had at least some vacancy loss during the year. Although the poorer quality sectors of the market are

Table 7–4. Cash Flow Statement for Rental Housing Submarkets[a]

	Total Market	Single Family Low Quality	Single Family High Quality
Gross Collectibles ($)	818	559	1,020
Less: Vacancy and arrears (%)[b]	4.9	8.2	1.5
Property Taxes (%)	11.4	10.9	13.6
Insurance (%)	4.3	4.8	4.8
Maintenance and Repair (%)	20.9	27.0	21.4
Management[c] (%)	7.9	7.7	8.0
Net Cash Flow before Debt Service ($)	431	227	536
(%)	50.7	41.3	50.7
N	195	63	63

Table 7-4   continued

	Duplex		Multi-Family	
	Low Quality	High Quality	Low Quality	High Quality
Gross Collectibles ($)	472	1,029	638	1,033
Less: Vacancy and Areas (%)	7.5	3.3	5.2	5.4
Property Taxes (%)	8.0	11.7	7.6	9.9
Insurance (%)	4.6	3.5	3.1	2.5
Maintenance and Repair (%)	18.6	10.9	8.8	21.2
Management[c] (%)	7.7	8.0	8.3	7.7
Net Cash Flow before				
Debt Service ($)	251	655	420	559
(%)	53.6	62.8	67.0	53.4
N	12	27	11	19

[a] All figures are per dwelling unit.
[b] Percentage figures are percent of gross collectible.
[c] Imputed to all units. See text for computation.

decidedly softer than the better quality submarkets, the nonmetropolitan investor loses less than half as much potential income off the top as does an inner-city owner.

With respect to fixed costs, the small city landlord has an even greater competitive advantage. In total, fixed costs, exclusive of debt service, average around 16 percent of gross collectibles in the smaller cities, roughly half the proportion of rental income that is consumed by such outlays in metropolitan centers. Not only is fire and liability insurance routinely available, while in the inner-city it is not, but, on average, it accounts for only four percent of gross collectibles compared with nine percent in both Newark and Baltimore. More important, however, is the substantial difference between the two market classes in the proportion of gross rental income consumed by real estate taxes. While Sternlieb and Burchell's [1973:232] typical operating statement for a two unit parcel in Newark indicates that real estate taxes absorb almost 36 percent of gross collectibles, in Baltimore in 1969 they accounted for a lower, but still significant, 14 percent of gross income [Stegman, 1972:76]. In nonmetropolitan cities, real estate taxes account for just 11 percent of gross rent across the entire rental inventory and are highest (14%) for high quality single family units. Of course, since vacancy and arrearage rates are lower in the smaller city, taxes also consume smaller percentages of effective rental income. Furthermore, as a consequence of rapidly declining values, the effective tax rate in Baltimore's blighted inner-city neighborhoods is 15 percent of market value, compared with less than two percent in stable areas of the city [Arthur D. Little, Inc., 1973, Pt.I:2]. In contrast, nonmetropolitan effective tax rates range from a high of 1.4 percent within the poorest quality stock to less than one-half of one percent for high quality single family units.

Variable expenses account for 21 percent of gross income in the nonmetropolitan market compared to 28 percent and 36 percent in Newark and Baltimore, respectively. Moreover, while virtually all of the variable costs in the small city are devoted to repair and maintenance, utility costs absorb nearly 80 percent of the variable expenses in Newark, leaving only seven percent of gross available for normal maintenance and repairs [Sternlieb and Burchell, 1973:232; Stegman, 1972:76]. In fewer than 20 percent of the nonmetropolitan units are any utilities included in the rent. In single family units, 94 percent of the tenants are responsible for paying utilities; in duplexes, over 80 percent pay them. Only in apartments do a substantial number of the owners (64%) provide utilities. As the energy shortage continues to cause higher utility costs, housing quality is likely to suffer relatively greater declines in market areas where, by either law or tradition, landlords must directly bear these costs. Currently, small city investors thus are better able to provide the necessary maintenance and repairs that will prolong the economic lives of their properties, because larger proportions of their variable expenses relate directly to physical quality; this advantage over their metropolitan counterparts is likely to increase in the years ahead.

These expenditure patterns provide some insights into the more important differences in net to gross ratios which we discussed earlier. Proportionately, around four times as much expense in the low quality sector is income foregone due to vacancy loss, while around one-half of this savings to owners of high quality dwellings is consumed by higher taxes. Similar variable expense rates also reflect different types of costs in the various submarkets. Outlays in the high quality sector tend to be preventative in nature, while in the low quality stock, they are necessary for continued operations. Nowhere is the variation in operating patterns within a structure class more striking than in the multifamily submarket. The substantial difference is a function of high variable expenses among good quality units and virtually no outlays in the poor quality stock. On a relative basis, two-and-one-half times the proportion of gross rent is spent for maintenance outlays and utility services in high quality, multifamily units.

Mean cash flow, after management, averages 51 percent of gross collectibles in the nonmetropolitan city, or around $431 a year per unit. The cash throw-off ranges from $227 for low quality single family units to $655 for high quality duplexes. Although these figures are exclusive of debt service, it is important to recognize that the data reflect neither the atypical situation, nor only the experiences of exceptional managers and certain large scale professionals. Most small city owners are earning several hundred dollars a year on each unit they own. In comparison, the typical Baltimore investor earned slightly less than $120 a unit per year in 1969 despite the fact that gross rents there averaged some 20 percent higher than in the nonmetropolitan market [Stegman, 1972:76]. Substantial losses are frequently incurred by Baltimore investors, with the smaller scale owner very likely to be operating in the red. This is likewise the case in Newark and in the older segment of New York City's inventory that is heavily dominated by households receiving public assistance. In buildings where over 30 percent of the tenants received welfare assistance, in 1971, net cash flow as a percent of net rent received was, on average, negative and ranged between −3 percent and −31 percent, depending upon the proportion of the tenantry on welfare [Sternlieb and Indik, 1973:194].

The typical smaller city rental property throws off sufficient cash to meet reasonable debt service obligations. Even the lowest quality units could support maximum mortgages of between $1,900 and $4,000, assuming a mortgage constant of around 10 percent. Substantially higher constants would result in negative cash flows while lower constants would, of course, increase leverage and permit the economical carrying of larger debts. In comparison one would not likely find many mortgaged properties in the inner-city throwing off any cash flow; most encumbered units in Baltimore, for example, show large negative returns [Stegman, 1972:84-85].

Although the average nonmetropolitan owner of rental housing is better off than the typical inner-city landlord, the former's smaller scale of ownership militates against his exercising any significant economic leverage in the market. With a mean rental housing portfolio of only 2.4 dwellings, the average nonmetropolitan landlord nets only around $1,000 a year from his properties. Indeed, it would take between 15 and 20 high quality, and around twice that many poor quality, dwellings to produce an aggregate cash flow of around $10,000 a year. Fewer than three percent of all nonmetropolitan landlords own more than 20 dwellings.

It is not so much the fact that the average small city landlord owns far fewer houses than his core city counterpart that distinguishes the respective roles each might play in local market improvement efforts. Rather, from an investment standpoint, the difference between the two markets is that the core city is characterized by a sizable nucleus of large scale, well capitalized investors who are highly visible, and whose substantial net worth, although eroding with market conditions, is still sufficiently great to make it worth their while to become actively involved in market improvement efforts. Whether these landlords will contribute ultimately to a complete market reversal in the core city is not the relevant issue. What is important is the fact that such a potential resource is lacking in the smaller city.

Indeed, because the fewer than one percent of all nonmetropolitan landlords who own at least 30 dwellings are more than likely to hold eithe₁ low quality, single family dwellings or new multifamily garden apartment developments, it is unlikely that this small investor group would become a force for local housing improvement. On the other hand, shotguns are performing well because of the absence of local efforts to enforce minimum occupancy standards, while the performance of new garden apartment developments is unrelated to municipal ordinances and actions concerning minimum occupancy standards. The relationship between rent levels at the top and the prevailing charges for the lower quality stock is, at best, too subtle and tenuous to transform the multifamily investor into an agent of local housing reform.

The New Construction Market

The nonmetropolitan rental inventory will have to be expanded substantially beyond the level required to accommodate net household growth if overall housing conditions are to be improved to any significant degree. The possibility of such expansion is a function of current investment outcomes at the margin of the market in the relatively thin new construction sector. We therefore turn our attention to investor cash flow experiences with new single family, duplex and garden apartment developments. While the ability of typical nonmetropolitan rental units to throw off sufficient cash flow to withstand reasonable debt service demands is an indication of general market vigor, the capital costs and the corresponding debt service requirements are relatively higher for the newer stock than for typical market dwellings. From these analyses, we hope to gain some insights into the cost-income squeeze characteristic of the more recently built stock.

Single Family Detached Rental Housing: Perhaps the most noteworthy operating characteristic of comparatively new single family detached dwellings in the smaller city is that annual rentals are sufficiently low to preclude any cash throw-off if the properties are mortgaged (Table 7–5). Despite virtually full occupancy and low insurance costs and real estate taxes, which together consume less than 20 percent of gross collectibles, and variable expenses which average less than $11 a month, net cash available for debt service is around $700 less than actual mortgage payments on encumbered properties.

This should not, however, be interpreted as an indication of a weak market. Of the four percent of all nonmetropolitan rental dwellings that

Table 7–5. Cash Flow Statement for New Construction

	Single Family	Duplex	Multifamily Garden Apartments
Gross Collectibles	$1,220	$1,113	$1,209
Vacancy and bad debt	19 (1.5%)	7 (0.0%)	79 (6.5%)
Taxes	180 (14.8%)	126 (11.3%)	108 (8.9%)
Insurance	53 (4.3%)	42 (3.8%)	30 (2.5%)
Variable Expenses	128 (10.4%)	114 (10.2%)	220 (18.2%)
Net Cash Flow	719 (58.9%)	713 (64.1%)	659 (54.5%)
N	7	13	5
Current Market Value	$17,740	$11,632	$9,378
Net Cash as Percent of Value	4.1%	6.1%	7.0%
Debt Service (if any)	1,930	747	530
Net Cash After Debt Service	$-710	$34	$129
N	4	11	7

See notes to Table 7-4.

are new single family detached dwellings, a relatively substantial portion was not built originally for rental occupancy and, indeed, may not remain in the rental inventory over the long term. Although capital gains opportunities may help explain the relatively high gross rent multipliers of these properties, the comparatively low rent structure for this portion of the high quality single family submarket is as much a function of nonmarket pricing as of any other factor. Typically, the owners of these dwellings are not real estate investors in the traditional sense of the term and are more interested in protecting their properties while they are being rented than they are in maximizing cash flow.

In addition to the nonmarket-oriented owners of high quality single family dwellings is a group of professional investors whose primary motivation is the accrual of long-term capital gains. Typically not large-scale holders of rental properties, these investors earn relatively substantial livelihoods from nonhousing business endeavors which afford them the opportunity of contributing out-of-pocket costs to the monthly support of their housing investments. To these landlords, the ownership of new rental housing, like raw land, is not a cash flow enterprise; the windfall comes later on down the line. A not atypical illustration of the problems involved in generating positive cash flows on comparatively new mortgaged single family dwellings is shown in Exhibit 7–1, which is a combined cash flow statement for two high quality single family units

Exhibit 7–1.   Operating Statement for Two High Quality Single Family Dwellings—1972

Gross Collectibles (rent: $135/mo.):		$3,240.00
Less: Vacancy/Bad debt	$135.00 (4%)	
Gross Rent Collected:		3,105.00
Less: Taxes	370.02	
Insurance	122.00	
Total fixed expenses:		492.02 (15%)
Less: Maintenance/Repair		
Painting	300.00	
Total variable expenses:		300.00 (9%)
Net Income Available for Debt Service:		2,312.98 (71%)
Less: Debt Service*	2,244.00 (69%)	
Net Cash Flow:		$68.98 (2%)

* Mortgage data: 1) $15,500 total cost: $10,000 face value, 7%, 15 year;
2) $15,500 total cost: $6,500 face value, 7%, 10 year.

owned by an investor whose primary occupation is retailing. Between 1968 and 1972, he built seven single family dwellings and purchased an eighth, which represent his total rental portfolio.

The operating statement exhibited is for calendar year 1972, at which time one of the dwellings was five years old, and the other four years old. Because long term capital gains is the most important investment objective of this and similarly situated owners, their properties, when encumbered, typically are strapped with shorter term mortgages than would have been dictated by market conditions which prevailed at the time of acquisition or construction. Consequently, the properties are likely to operate in the red while the owners accrue equity at a more rapid rate than would otherwise be the case.

In the present example, net cash flow on the two sampled dwellings amounts to $2,313, or around 7.5 percent on total development costs of $31,000. Because of the short terms of the first mortgages on the two dwellings, however, the properties show a negative cash flow of around $240 after management. At the time of construction, had the investor secured a longer term first mortgage for around two-thirds of the combined cost of the houses, together the properties would currently be showing a small but positive cash flow. Before management, net cash flow on the two properties would be around $560 a year, were the respective mortgages written for 25-year terms rather than for 10 and 15 years. On an equity basis, this would have amounted to an annual return of around 5.5 percent before taxes.

In today's market, going rents on new single family dwellings, which average only $102 a month, are not able to support mortgage constants much greater than five or six if the properties are to show any positive cash flow after debt service and management requirements have been met. Typical constants on mortgaged, new single family dwellings, however, are in the neighborhood of 9–12. In order to make new single family construction feasible for rental occupancy, mortgage capital would have to be available at a 25 to 30-year term and at interest rates no higher than four or five percent. Overall, then, we can conclude that current price levels are not supportive of an expansion of this thin sector of the market over the long run. Construction costs and market values in the existing stock may, however, still be low enough in the smaller city so that a moderately subsidized mortgage program could generate a potentially significant increase in the effective demand for owner-occupied single family housing affordable by families of modest means.

Duplexes: The most striking operating characteristics of newly constructed duplex units are that they command monthly rentals only nine percent lower than do recently built single family detached dwellings, while they have average values which are 34 percent lower (Table 7–5). Together, these findings imply that the feasibility of producing new duplexes for renter occupancy is substantially greater than that for detached dwellings. Indeed, after management and before debt service, new duplexes throw off the same amount of cash as do new single family houses. The former's lower rents are offset by slightly lower insurance and real estate taxes than characterize the single family submarket, with the result that net cash flow before debt service amounts to almost two-thirds of gross collectibles.

Despite the fact that most new duplexes were built for rental occupancy, few, if any, produce positive cash flows at current interest rates and mortgage terms. Assuming a 25-year mortgage term, an eight percent interest rate and 75 percent financing, annual debt service requirements on a typical new duplex unit would be approximately $805 a year, producing a negative cash flow before taxes and after debt service of around $100. For an average investor in the 40 percent marginal income tax bracket, after-tax returns would amount to around $111, or a rate of return on initial equity of less than four percent. Somewhat surprisingly, then, new duplex construction currently represents a rather poor option for equity investors in the nonmetropolitan rental market. That around four percent of the inventory is composed of such structures is likely a function of the fact that original construction costs were lower than current values (which are the basis of our analysis), that debt service requirements were substantially below current or anticipated levels likely to prevail in the years ahead, and that many investors built their units on a cash basis. For the latter, average cash flow relative to current value produces before-tax returns of around six percent.

What is suggested by this analysis is that current rents for high quality, low density rental housing are insufficient to support the substantial growth of these housing alternatives. Inasmuch as fixed and variable expense rates are exceptionally low, while occupancy levels remain high, one cannot point to poor management or spiraling costs as the principal problem confronting investors who may be considering the development of low density rental housing. With the growing demands in the long-term capital markets resulting in a need for the mortgaged portion of a new single family or duplex unit to return 10 percent or more on borrowed capital, including amortization, the return to equity must grow accordingly if supply is to be materially increased. It is interesting to note that most smaller city landlords, who are not dissatisfied with the operations of their newer investments and whose properties are either not mortgaged or are not heavily mortgaged, demand lower returns on their cash than do lenders who finance their properties. While this helps explain the relatively high proportion of newer developments which are unencumbered or only lightly so, it is not a factor upon which hopes for the future expansion of low density rental submarkets can be based.

Multifamily Housing: Unquestionably, comparatively new, low-rise garden apartment developments, built between 8 and 14 units to the acre, fare almost as well as their lower density counterparts on a cash basis and enjoy a substantially stronger cash flow position after debt service requirements have been met. The reason for their favorable showing is that average rents for newer garden apartments are virtually identical to new single family rental charges, while average per unit values are around 47 percent lower (Table 7–5). Though multifamily vacancy rates are higher, taxes consume a smaller proportion of gross collectibles, with the result that cash flow before debt service is less than $50 a year lower per garden apartment dwelling than for single family units. This is true despite the fact that variable expenses are substantially higher in new multifamily complexes because utility costs are paid for by the landlord and are reflected in contract rents.

Because of unit costs of construction which are relatively low compared with those for duplex and single family units, mortgaged developments tend to throw off positive cash after debt service requirements and management costs have been met. Overall, encumbered, newer garden apartment units show a positive cash flow before taxes of around $130 a year, or 11 percent of gross collectibles. In general, the before-tax cash picture is more encouraging than the above figures imply because of the general tendency of the owners of newer mortgaged multifamily complexes to hold short-term permanent loans.

Exhibit 7–2 illustrates the cash flow status of a 17 unit brick veneer complex built in 1969 at a total development cost of $127,000. Net of vacancies, which amounted to around six percent of collectibles, the 17 unit development grossed around $24,000 in 1972, or around $118 per month per dwelling. Insurance and taxes absorbed about 9 percent of potential collections, while variable outlays amounted to 24 percent of potential gross. The largest variable cost is for utilities, while the general maintenance and repair expense represents the prorated costs of maintenance and related direct labor costs attributed by the investor to this particular development in his portfolio. Though the operating statement is only for one year, the relative absence of any major maintenance outlay reflects the general experience with new, modern residential developments in the smaller city.

Based upon original development costs, debt service requirements and equity considerations, the 17 unit complex returned around 12 percent on a cash basis and 19 percent on initial equity, after debt service. Although

Exhibit 7–2. Operating Statement for High Quality 17 Unit Structure—1972

Gross Collectibles: (Average rent: $126/mo.)		$25,620.00
Less: Vacancy/Bad debt	$1,643.00 (6%)	
Gross Rent Collected:		23,977.00
Less: Taxes	1,575.00	
Insurance	791.00	
Total fixed expenses:		2,366.00 (9%)
Less: Maintenance/Repair		
Wages and Salaries	1,500.00	
Plumbing/heating	215.00	
Painting	140.00	
Cleaning	376.00	
General repairs	330.00	
Misc.	475.00	
Total:	3,036.00 (12%)	
Less: Fuel and Utilities		
Fuel oil	988.28	
Electricity/water	2,150.00	
Total:	3,138.28 (12%)	
Total variable expenses:		6,174.28 (24%)
Net Income Available for Debt Service:		15,436.72 (60%)
Less: Debt Service*	12,236.40 (51%)	
Net Cash Flow:		$3,200.32 (13%)

* Mortgage data: $127,000 total cost: $110,000 face value, 7½%, 15 year.

in this case relatively restrictive financing terms did not prevent the earning of fairly high net returns, the point made earlier about stringent debt service requirements can be elaborated by reference to the 15-year mortgage term secured for this particular development. Were the mortgage constant lowered from 11 to 10, which could be achieved by extending the mortgage term to 20 years, before-tax cash would increase to around 26 percent of initial equity. Tax savings, which would be some portion of the amount by which depreciation deductions exceed mortgage amortization payments, would further enhance this already desirable investment.

To explore further the proposition that moderate density multifamily housing can be developed feasibly in the nonmetropolitan market, even at existing rent levels, reference is made to Exhibit 7–3, a combined three-year operating statement for a high quality, 12 unit, brick veneer development also built in 1969. Constructed by a wealthy individual without the aid of any permanent financing, the property returns around nine percent a year on a cash basis. Consistent with the earlier exhibits, low fixed costs and minimum maintenance requirements result in a substantial cash flow, which is further enhanced by virtually no vacancy loss. In part, full occupancy and low turnover are accomplished by virtue of the low rents on these dwellings, which average just $90 a month.

Exhibit 7–3.   Combined Operating Statement for High Quality 12 Unit Structure for Three Years, 1970–1972

Gross Collectibles (average rent: $90.42/mo.):		$39,060.00
Less: Vacancy/Bad debt	$976.95 (3%)	
Gross Rent Collected:		38,083.05
Less: Taxes	3,756.64	
Insurance	902.00	
Total fixed expenses:		4,658.64 (12%)
Less: Maintenance/Repair		
Plumbing/Heating	445.68	
Painting	349.10	
Cleaning	250.00	
Lawn care	243.54	
Misc.	245.83	
Total:	1,534.15 (4%)	
Less: Fuel and Utilities		
Gas for heating	3,311.12	
Electricity/water	2,026.25	
Total:	5,337.37 (14%)	
Total variable expenses:		6,871.52 (18%)
Net Income Available for Debt Service:		26,552.89
Less Debt Service		-0-
Net Cash Flow:		$26,552.89 (68%)

Our particular purpose in evaluating this exhibit is to explore the cash flow and return implications of this development under alternative, hypothetical debt service requirements. With a net operating income of almost $9,000 for each of its three years of operation, this project could withstand relatively stringent debt service requirements and still remain a viable, if not overwhelmingly desirable, investment. Seventy percent financing ($70,000), for example, over a 20-year term at an eight percent rate of interest would cost $7,026 a year, or around $21,000 over the three-year period covered by the operating statement. Net cash flow after debt service would be reduced to about $5,500, or to around 18 percent on initial equity before taxes, over the three year operating period. Assuming a depreciable base of $90,000, a 30-year building life, and a 50 percent tax bracket for the owner, annual tax savings of approximately $750 would produce an annual after-tax return to initial equity of nine percent.

In order for developments of this type to withstand reasonable debt service requirements and still return between 12 and 15 percent on initial equity after taxes, rents would have to be nudged up to market levels, or to around $100 a month, while mortgage terms would have to be extended to no less than 25 years. Under these two conditions, average annual cash flow after debt service would amount to nearly $3,600, or 12 percent on initial equity. Tax savings due to depreciation deductions would boost net after-tax cash to around 15 percent of initial equity.

A substantial portion of all newer, moderate density, multifamily developments in the smaller city generate substantial cash flows for their owners. Neither on a cash nor equity basis, however, do before or after-tax returns appear to be very high relative to less risky, nonhousing forms of investments. But multifamily developments can support reasonable restrictive debt service requirements without operating in the red and are inherently capable of producing rather desirable returns with very moderate upward rental adjustments. Extremely low maintenance and service demands enhance their potential as income producers, but rising costs, particularly utility services, suggest that upward rental pressures will grow more rapidly than would otherwise be the case. Indeed, the growth potential of this submarket is substantially greater than that for new single family detached rental dwellings and better than that for new duplexes. The key to the expansion of the duplex and multifamily submarkets will probably lie in the capital markets. To the extent that permanent financing can be found within a mortgage constant range of 6–9, a reasonable expansion in both submarkets would be facilitated.

Shotgun Shacks

To the extent that the relative size of the rental stock does not increase substantially in the years ahead, that the market remains rigidly segregated along racial lines, and that the worst quality housing is not replaced directly by deeply subsidized new construction, the shotgun shack will maintain its present prominent position in the nonmetropolitan rental market. While this fundamentally inhumane shelter form is virtually independent of the new construction submarkets, some of the same factors that militate against new construction contribute to the lengthening of the economic lives of the shotguns. Beyond this tentative relationship, the economics of shanties is important because they represent around eight percent of the small city rental stock and are a constant reminder of the inevitable consequence of direct, private construction for poor blacks in cities in which minimum building codes have only recently arrived.

We experienced greater difficulty in securing comprehensive operating data for sampled units in the shotgun submarket than in any of the others. In part, the problem was one of landlord failure to maintain systematic records for what might be referred to as "nickel and dime-type" operations. In part, too, the deplorable condition of this housing and its obvious inability to meet even minimal code standards likely discouraged some landlords from discussing the relative profitability of their shotgun houses, many of which are handled by professional managers who will not divulge financial data without express owner consent. We did, however, manage to secure a good deal of operating data on shotgun shacks from several management firms; unlike the earlier submarket discussions, these data are not drawn entirely from sampled dwellings, but from the total inventories of large-scale holders. Because the operating data is not derived from the sample, we cannot vouch for its representativeness, but since the set of properties is relatively large, it should provide reasonable insights into the operating characteristics of the shotgun submarket as a whole. Exhibits 7–4 to 7–7 each reflect the operating experiences of shotgun portfolios that are handled by different professional management firms.

Aside from their renting for substantially less than other housing types in the smaller city, the most interesting performance characteristic of shotguns is their proven ability to throw off positive cash flows under widely varying operating conditions. In this market sector, which serves the basic housing needs of an essentially captive population, investors tend to minimize the revenue impacts of higher than average vacancy losses by reducing variable outlays on their already dilapidated dwellings. Consequently, bottom-line performance does not necessarily vary with occupancy levels to the same degree it does in the larger nonmetropolitan rental market. This phenomenon is reflected in Exhibits 7–4 and 7–5 where net cash flow averages 59 percent of gross collectibles for each group of shotguns, despite the fact that the average vacancy loss in the latter case is five times that reflected in the former. Offsetting the 15

Exhibit 7–4. Operating Statement for Four Shotgun Dwellings—1971

Gross Collectibles (average rent: $38.25/mo.):		$1,836.00
Less: Vacancy/Bad debt	$46.00 (3%)	
Gross Rent Collected:		1,790.00
Less: Taxes	131.09	
Insurance	91.80	
Total fixed expenses:		222.89 (12%)
Less: Maintenance/Repair		
Plumbing	70.13	
Painting	55.05	
Carpentry	157.21	
Electrical	20.00	
Total:	302.39 (16%)	
Less: Management Fee	179.00 (10%)	
Total variable expenses:		481.39 (26%)
Net Income Available for Debt Service:		1,085.72 (59%)
Less: Debt Service		-0-
Net Cash Flow:		$1,085.72 (59%)

Exhibit 7–5. Operating Statement for 11 Shotgun Dwellings—1972

Gross Collectibles (average rent: $31.12/mo.)		$4,108.00
Less: Vacancy/Bad debt	$622.80 (15%)	
Gross Rent Collected:		3,485.20
Less: Taxes	291.67	
Insurance	205.40	
Total fixed expenses:		497.07 (12%)
Less: Maintenance/Repair		
Plumbing	55.85	
Carpentry	136.31	
Misc.	18.45	
Total:	210.61 (5%)	
Less: Management Fee	348.52 (9%)	
Total variable expenses:		559.13 (14%)
Net Income Available for Debt Service:		2,429.00 (59%)
Less: Debt Service		-0-
Net Cash Flow:		$2,429.00 (59%)

percent vacancy loss in Exhibit 7–5 is a variable expense rate, exclusive of management fee, of only five percent of collectibles, compared with a 16 percent rate for the houses with above-average occupancy levels. Even in the situation reflected in Exhibit 7–6, where both vacancy and variable expense rates are unusually high, the combination of a 27 percent

Exhibit 7–6. Operating Statement for Six Shotgun Dwellings—1971

Gross Collectibles (average rent: $44/mo.):		$3,168.00
Less: Vacancy/Bad debt	$863.78 (27%)	
Gross Rent Collected:		2,304.22
Less: Taxes	226.20	
Insurance	158.40	
Total fixed expenses:		384.60 (12%)
Less: Maintenance/Repair		
Plumbing	121.38	
Painting	76.12	
Carpentry, hardware	161.33	
Roof	41.61	
Glass	8.41	
Misc.	38.14	
Total:	446.99 (14%)	
Less: Management Fee	230.42 (7%)	
Total variable expenses:		677.41 (21%)
Net Income Available for Debt Service:		1,242.21 (39%)
Less: Debt Service		-0-
Net Cash Flow:		$1,242.21 (39%)

income loss off the top and a 14 percent maintenance expense rate still produced annual net cash flows exceeding $200 per dwelling, or 39 percent of collectibles.

When variable expenses on these seriously substandard dwellings represent a substantial proportion of gross collectibles, it is not because the landlords maintain them adequately, but because the most minimum of repairs has a base cost in terms of labor and material that approaches the average weekly rental charge of $9. In general, the base rentals cannot possibly support the service costs of such professional tradesmen as the plumbers, electricians, and carpenters. As a result, shotguns are typically managed by professional firms whose work crews include skilled tradesmen, and whose costs can be amortized over the large number of housing units in their management portfolios. This explains, for example, the cost phenomenon illustrated in Exhibits 7–7 and 7–8. For these 45 shotguns, variable expenses represent 23 percent of gross collectibles, but the average monthly costs per dwelling for plumbing, electrical, carpentry and related maintenance work range from $1.61 to eight cents. The combination of scale and professional management helps to keep monthly servicing costs to an absolute minimum.

Because the absolute level of cash flow earnings is low, small-scale owners can scarcely earn a livelihood from this form of real estate; volume business is necessary to generate any sizable income stream. The

Exhibit 7–7. Operating Statement for 45 Shotgun Dwellings—1971

Gross Collectibles (average rent: $34/mo.):		$19,170.03
Less: Vacancy/Bad debt	$1,693.12 (9%)	
Gross Rent Collected:		17,476.91
Less: Taxes	2,491.00	
Insurance	940.00	
Total fixed expenses:		3,431.00 (18%)
Less: Maintenance/Repair	2,641.86 (14%)	
Less: Management Fee	1,747.65 (9%)	
Total variable expenses:		4,389.51 (23%)
Net Income Available for Debt Service:		9,656.40 (50%)
Less: Debt Service		-0-
Net Cash Flow:		$9,656.40 (50%)

Exhibit 7–8. Breakdown of Maintenance and Repair Costs for 45 Shotgun Dwellings—1971

	Total Annual Cost	Average Monthly Cost Per Unit
Plumbing	$909.62	$1.61
Carpentry	828.44	1.47
Electrical	104.81	.19
Roofing	68.87	.12
Exterior Masonry	43.55	.08
Glass	40.69	.07
Painting	198.71	.35
Evictions	17.00	.03
Misc.	430.17	.76
Total	2,641.86	4.68

larger portfolio described in Exhibit 7–7 contains 45 shotgun houses whose average monthly rental is $34. For the period covered by the statement, overall vacancy and bad debt losses averaged some nine percent of collectibles. Over the period, some $17,500 in rents was received, out of which less than $3,000 was expended in repairs. As Exhibit 7–8 indicates, plumbing and carpentry outlays head the variable expense budget, the former mainly representing the costs of unclogging toilets, and the latter, essential patch-up of floors, stairs and doors. Strikingly, even in housing of this deplorable type, total eviction costs amounted to just $17 over the period. In this submarket, tenants expect and, indeed, receive very few services in exchange for their rents. If rents are paid, even somewhat irregularly, landlords will not evict. Overall, then, the owners of these 45 shanties cleared close to $10,000 during the year covered by the statement.

Because their inconsequential capital costs are sunk, and since no shotguns are mortgaged, relating cash flows to cost or equity has little meaning. More than for any other shelter form, returns in this market may be reasonable viewed in terms of markups over base costs. For the 45 shotguns in Exhibit 7–7, for example, the average out-of-pocket cost per unit is $174 and net income is $214, a markup over direct costs of 123 percent. With such substantial markups and capital costs that have been returned severalfold over their period of operations, the profitability of these dwellings seems to be assured for the foreseeable future, despite rising costs.

Aside from any direct public effort to force these units off the market, the issue of residual land value and reuse potential becomes an important element in assessing the future of shotgun housing. Because many shotguns are built on lots which are substandard under present zoning requirements, some portion of the land upon which they are built has virtually no reuse potential. For that segment of the stock situated on larger parcels or on adjoining lots which are under single ownership, the residential reuse potential of the land must be gauged against other relevant supply and demand side factors. On the demand side, new duplex or multifamily development would have to be oriented to a substantially higher income and, most likely, a different racial cohort than the housing it replaces. Currently, this sector of the market is almost exclusively occupied by black households whose incomes average about $3,400 per year. The need that is satisfied by the shotguns is implied by the fact that these households devote only about 16 percent of their incomes to rent. Were these units to be removed from the market, the only viable housing alternatives for these families would be in the public sector. No privately constructed replacement housing could be produced at a cost that would enable it to serve this market, nor is it likely that any filtering process initiated by new construction would reach these families at the low end of the income distribution.

The feasibility of new duplex and multifamily construction is a function of mortgage credit factors and of prevailing rents in the high quality sectors of the market. To the extent that tight money would force rents above current market levels, the reuse potential of land now occupied by shotguns is minimal given the generally inferior environmental quality of the surrounding areas. It may in fact be the case that these parcels would be best employed in commercial uses. The forced removal of the shotguns would, therefore, further reduce the housing supply available to blacks in these cities. Given the history of housing code enforcement, the most likely prospect is that the shotguns will disappear through a process of attrition as units become absolutely uninhabitable and unsalvageable. This will probably take many years, and land reuse will not occur until sufficiently large parcels have become available for development. What forms that development will take will depend on the environmental conditions and demand factors at the time, particularly given the ability of the units to generate a relatively sizable and stable cash flow.

Supply Costs and Race

We estimated in Chapter 6 that the rents charged to blacks are about ten percent higher than those paid by whites for equivalent housing, and we attributed this price differential primarily to racial discrimination in the market. Although our tests were designed to control for important factors that would be expected to contribute to differences in costs, the cash flow data enable us to consider more directly whether supplier costs vary systematically with race. In order to test for cost differences, we dichotomized the market according to dwelling quality. Although this is an imperfect control, it at least partially standardizes for income and other socioeconomic characteristics that may impact on cost.

Our purpose here is to assess the validity of the oft-cited argument that even if blacks do pay more than whites for comparable housing, the price markups may be justified by costs associated with providing housing to a population group of relatively low socioeconomic status. As we have already noted, Muth [1969:111], for example, suggests that because of their lower incomes, blacks may consume less space per person, thus causing more rapid physical deterioration of the dwelling. Higher rents would be required to compensate owners for large maintenance expenditures or shorter economic lives of the building. Furthermore, if minority households are more likely than others to occupy housing in slum areas characterized by severe externalities, it is possible that rentals there may be higher than "in better neighborhoods because of greater operating and/or depreciation costs, a more rapid turnover of tenants, or because of higher rental collection costs and/or delinquencies"; alternatively, "the higher rentals might merely reflect the greater risks inherent in slum properties, such as the possible losses of income from sporadic occupancy and building code enforcement" [Muth, 1969:123]. Stegman [1972:91-2] provided some confirmation of these arguments in his work in Baltimore where he observed that "taxes, insurance and management expenses account for a smaller percentage of the rental dollar in better neighborhoods, while expenses such as those associated with water charges, turnover and vandalism are smaller in an absolute sense as well."

Across the entire market the rents of black-occupied dwellings are 44 percent lower than those for white-occupied (Table 7–6). Segmenting the market into two sectors based on the physical quality of the dwelling does not fully eliminate this difference. Among low quality units, blacks still

Table 7-6. Income and Expenses by Housing Quality and Race[a]

	Low Quality		High Quality		All Units	
	White Occupied	Black Occupied	White Occupied	Black Occupied	White Occupied	Black Occupied
Gross Collectibles ($)	604	490*	1,053	584*	931	519*
Less: Vacancy and Bad Debt (%)[b]	6.3	10.3	3.1	1.4	3.9	7.6
Insurance (%)	4.5	4.8	4.0	4.5	4.1	4.7
Taxes (%)	12.1	8.9	12.3	11.5	12.2	9.7*
Variable Expenses (%)	26.3	22.5	18.0	23.2	20.2	22.7
Net Cash Flow[c] before Debt Service ($)	251	227	592	287*	499	245*
(%)	43.2	45.6	55.0	50.6	51.8	47.1
N	39	42	105	18	144	60

a See notes to Table 7-4.

* Difference significant at .001 level. No other items significantly different at .05 level.

pay rents that are nearly 20 percent lower than those paid by whites. In the high quality submarket there are very few black-occupied dwellings, and they rent for nearly 45 percent less than those occupied by whites. Within each quality sector, therefore, blacks consume less housing than whites. If, as Muth [1969] argues, the relative cost of supplying housing increases as quality declines, then we should observe higher costs for the black-occupied units in each sector. The analysis is, therefore, biased toward overestimating the expenses for black-occupied dwellings.

Rather than compare expenses in absolute dollar amounts, we focus primarily on the proportion of rent that is absorbed by each expense item in order to standardize for the rent differences between units occupied by blacks and whites. Whether we consider the entire market or each quality-defined sector, there are very few expenses that vary systematically with race. On a percentage basis there are no statistically significant differences in the expenses incurred by the owners of white versus black-occupied housing units in the low quality submarket. Vacancy and bad debt losses are higher in the black-occupied sector, but this difference is offset by the lower tax liabilities. The latter observation reflects the generally lower capital values among the poorer quality units and the fact that, relative to collectible rents, they are not being overtaxed by the city. Maintenance and repair costs are slightly higher for the white-occupied units. Net cash before debt service—either as a percentage of gross or as an absolute amount—does not differ significantly with race. On average, black-occupied, low quality units return $227 a year—about 10 percent less than white-occupied units. Although the individual expense items are not significantly different, the $114 difference in gross collectibles produces a cash flow only $24 a year more in the white-occupied sector. As a proportion of gross, the owners of white-occupied units earn an average 43 percent compared to the 46 percent earned in the black-occupied sector.

Similar comparisons for high quality units are difficult to make since the housing consumption of blacks within this sector of the market is substantially below that of whites. As was the case among low quality units, however, there are no significant differences between the proportion of rent devoted to the various expenditure items, and the net cash flow of 55 percent for white-occupied housing is not significantly different from the 51 percent earned in the black-occupied sector. Even if the entire market is considered, virtually no significant differences exist between cost items for the two racially-defined submarkets; this is true despite the fact that the black-occupied sector is comprised of housing units which are of considerably lower quality and in much poorer neighborhoods.

These data thus provide no basis for inferring that the race premium we identified in our earlier price analysis is cost-justified to any measurable degree. On the other hand, neither can we infer that the owners of black-occupied housing units are earning excess profits of the magnitude that would be expected given the size of the discriminatory markup. To some extent the inconclusiveness of the analysis may be inherent in the data. Since each cost item is characterized by a fairly high standard deviation, a considerably larger sample size would be required to test adequately hypotheses related to rental housing costs which are subject to wide variation even within reasonably well-defined sectors of the market. For example, in the low quality sector the average net to gross ratio is about .44, but the coefficient of variation is .83. Assuming a normal distribution, the data indicate that two-thirds of the time the net to gross ratio will lie between .08 and .80. Given the unambiguous results of the price discrimination tests (Chapter 6), which included multiple controls for various cost-related factors, and the inability of the cash flow analysis to support the existence of cost differences, our conclusion that blacks are forced to pay a racial markup for equivalent housing in the nonmetropolitan rental market remains unchanged.

NOTES TO CHAPTER 7

1. For detailed discussions of the use of gross rent multipliers in investment analysis, see: Winnick [1952]; Ratcliff [1967]; Wendt and Cerf [1969].

2. We have no way to test the accuracy of a landlord's value estimate, since the only real market value is the actual transaction price. Studies of the accuracy of homeowner estimates of value, however, have demonstrated that while there is substantial error in the data, it tends to average out within value classes. See: Kish and Lansing [1954] and Kain and Quigley [1972].

3. In addition to analysis of variance tests across all submarkets, pair-wise difference of means tests were performed for each of the 15 pairs in the six-cell typology. For eight pairs the mean GRM's are significantly different at the 95 percent confidence level or better. Within structure type classes, all GRM differences are significant; in each of these cases, lower GRM's are associated with poorer quality units.

4. Pairwise difference of means tests revealed that NRM's are significantly different for six pairs in the typology. For single family and duplex units, NRM's are not statistically different for the two quality classes.

5. Since only 195 complete operating statements were obtained, and since for some of these buildings value estimates were not available, the direct computation of NRM would have resulted in an uncomfortably small sample size. While computing NRM from submarket averages for GRM and net to gross ratios reduces the variation, it does enable us to examine trends across submarkets more meaningfully.

✻ *Chapter 8*

A Nonmetropolitan Housing
Policy Perspective

INTRODUCTION

Before considering nonmetropolitan housing policy and program alternatives, it may be useful to present our view of the
relationship between this discussion and the preceding empirical analysis of market operations. First, a substantial amount of our
analytical effort was directed toward the problem of estimating the size
and composition of the housing-deprived population, a task which is
necessary to lay the groundwork for developing housing assistance programs. Second, since it enables us to identify the nature of various market
disabilities and assess the contribution of each to housing deprivations,
our empirical work may be used to estimate the potential utility of various
kinds of market intervention efforts. Policy and market analyses are also
closely related to the extent that price, quality and other market factors
are important inputs for program evaluations. Where particular programs
cannot be appraised without some best estimates of the likely range of key
supply and demand parameters, an empirical market grounding is an essential element of useful policy analyses. In short, our empirical studies
enable us to gauge the magnitude of public sector efforts that would be
required to eliminate housing deprivations, to narrow the range of policy
alternatives that should receive serious consideration, and to evaluate the
relative strengths of specific program alternatives.

Importantly too, place-specific analyses of housing deprivations and
market structure can demonstrate a continuing need for particular programs that have not performed satisfactorily in other markets and consequently have fallen from national political favor. Finally, the grounding

of policy and program recommendations on empirical market data reduces the likelihood that a particular approach will be promoted primarily for ideological reasons. At either extreme of the ideological spectrum, program proposals must bear some relationship to the profile of problems that exist across the market and be capable of performing as they were intended. It is no more valid to approach policy analysis under the assumption that regardless of cost the federal government should be the houser of last resort, than it is to impose the constraint that the public presence should be minimized.

MARKET DYNAMICS AND HOUSING POLICY

Because an important element of our analytical work and policy studies is to relate the smaller city experience to that of the metropolitan core city, it is appropriate to cast the discussion of nonmetropolitan program alternatives within this comparative framework. Although we have previously referenced several evaluations of inner-city housing strategies, the most relevant empirically based core city policy study was completed recently by Grigsby and Rosenburg [1975] for Baltimore. This study provides a useful comparative base, first, because Baltimore's rental stock is dominated by one and two family dwellings and thus more closely resembles the lower density nonmetropolitan stock than does the medium density tenement inventory of Newark or Manhattan's rent-controlled high rise market. More importantly, the prescriptions for the Baltimore inner-city are so strikingly different from those which seem appropriate for the smaller city that an understanding of the causes of these program variations will give insights into the relationships between market dynamics and housing policy. Where Grigsby and Rosenburg's [1975:214–20] proposed set of remedial actions centers around the creation of market stabilizing institutions and the rehabilitation of the currently substandard inventory, our recommendations for the smaller city focus on income support and an expansion of new supply. That the major reasons for this divergence of program strategies lie in basic differences in the nature of housing deprivations and market operations in the respective cities lends support to the proposition that national housing policy must provide sufficient flexibility for the tailoring of program approaches to local market conditions.

Housing Deprivations
More than one-half of nonmetropolitan renters are housing deprived. Contrary to the Baltimore experience, the overwhelming housing problem in the nonmetropolitan community is physically inadequate shelter, which accounts for more than 70 percent of all housing deprivatons. More

importantly, while three out of every four inadequate dwellings in the smaller city are not rehabilitatable, Grigsby and Rosenburg [1975:212] estimate that all but about 8,000 of Baltimore's 65,000 occupied substandard units are basically sound and could be upgraded to at least code level for a fairly modest sum of money. In Baltimore, the worst housing problem is the very high proportion of income that low income families must allocate to expenses for shelter; fully seven out of every ten lower income households spend more than one-quarter of their total resources for rent [Grigsby and Rosenburg, 1975:214,79]. While excessive housing expenses are also a problem in the smaller city, only 23 percent of all renters and 37 percent of those with incomes of less than $6,000 have rent-income ratios greater than .25.

Compared to the situation in Baltimore, the housing expenses of deprived families in the nonmetropolitan city are typically lower, relative both to their incomes and to the cost of standard housing. Because few poorer families in Baltimore pay rents that are so low as to preclude adequate maintenance under ordinary market circumstances, Grigsby and Rosenburg [1975:175] concluded that low income per se was not the critical cause of inner-city decline. In the nonmetropolitan city, where housing expenses tend to be more in line with household incomes, it does appear that low income is a major cause of substandard occupancy. That inadequate housing is available at very low rents in the smaller city suggests that landlords do not exercise the monopoly powers that are alleged to exist in the inner-city and that cost-increasing market imperfections and externalities that plague investors in Baltimore and elsewhere are not as serious in nonmetropolitan markets.

Market Instabilities

Despite generally low rents, the smaller city rental market is characterized by high gross rent multipliers and cash flows, the virtual absence of abandoned residential properties and high levels of investor confidence. In stark contrast, gross rent multipliers in Baltimore, as in other core cities, average between 2 and 3, and a substantial portion of investors operate in the red, largely because of excessive operating costs rather than low rents [Grigsby and Rosenburg, 1975:173]. Given the anomaly in Baltimore of a basically sound housing stock in a market environment where soaring operating costs have led to a rapidly declining housing services-to-rent ratio and high rates of abandonment even for the standard quality stock, Grigsby and Rosenburg [1975:215–16] argue that before the city can concentrate its attention on longer range residential goals and programs, the negative market trends in the inner-city must first be halted and then reversed. Among the market-shoring efforts suggested by them to improve the Baltimore housing climate are: a large scale ownership transfer program which would place the unwanted inventory in the hands of individuals and organizations who have the existing or potential capability of managing it properly; an insurance program to cover the equity losses caused by vandalism and neighborhood deterioration; and programs to create new management skills in the inner-city. If necessary, ownership transfer efforts would be supported by city acquisition, rehabilitation and resale of properties whose current owners cannot or will not upgrade to city standards [Grigsby and Rosenburg, 1975:216–17]. Grigsby and Rosenburg [1975:228–31] staunchly defend the viability of a rehabilitation program that would improve to minimum code standards all salvageable rental dwellings in the city, and they develop cogent arguments against the counter thesis that a modest rehab program would be insufficient to alter the basic attitudes of landlords and tenants and thus would fail to turn the inner-city market around.

Unlike Baltimore, the nonmetropolitan city is characterized by a basically unrehabilitatable inventory in a stable market environment. If operating costs do bear a disproportionate relationship to rent, it is not because costs are too high but because rents are too low. Indeed, the combination of an extensive inventory of shotgun houses and the low rent structure for standard housing is chiefly responsible for our concluding that a major rehabilitation effort would be an inappropriate approach to the nonmetropolitan housing problem; even a modest rehab effort would require postrenewal rentals substantially greater than going market rates in the smaller city. The nine percent of the existing stock that was deemed rehabilitatable is characterized by below average market rents and above average quantities of living area. In our estimation, the owners of this housing could amortize modest rehabilitation investments with postrenewal rent increments based on going market rates for larger dwellings. That the vast majority of otherwise seemingly salvageable houses are already renting at market rate levels and contain relatively small quantities of living space implies that for this stock even moderate investments in rehabilitation would not be recoverable without an upward adjustment to the marketwide rent structure for standard housing. Indeed, the failure of market rents to increase with quality at a sufficiently rapid rate is evidenced by the fact that, in today's market, most new construction could not throw off positive cash after debt service without a relatively substantial increase in monthly rental.

From a practical standpoint, it is fortunate that the host of market supporting interventions and large-scale rehabilitation efforts called for in Baltimore is not warranted in the nonmetropolitan market. Against a background of a long and impressive history of city initiatives on the housing front, the creation of potentially costly and innovative programs does not seem out of character in Baltimore [Grigsby and Rosenburg,

1975:143–51]. In contrast, the issue of the proper city role in solving housing problems remains very much alive in the smaller city, with sentiment still running high that housing is a private responsibility. Minimum building and housing codes have only recently arrived; concentrated efforts to enforce occupancy standards in the existing stock have scarcely begun; and virtually no local revenues are allocated to improving housing conditions. Thus, to think in terms of large-scale intervention efforts would be highly impractical and politically naive, even if conditions so warranted.

The smaller city problems of inadequate supply, while serious and potentially costly to solve, can be dealt with both through market and nonmarket means. While there is no simple or inexpensive solution to the severe income problem in the smaller city, the stable market helps hold down operating costs and rents in the existing stock, which in turn enhances the potential benefits of such demand side assistance efforts as housing allowances. Because rents are lower than they would be under less stable market conditions, a given pool of allowance funds could be distributed among a relatively large group of families. In addition, those families who would be eligible are currently paying rents which are not sufficiently high to access standard housing; allowances would, therefore, expand the sector of supply from which participating families can choose housing. Finally and most importantly, because the primary purpose of housing allowances is to improve the quality of the occupied stock, it is more likely that increased rents will be translated into higher levels of housing services in stable than in unstable markets.

Given the chaotic state of core markets such as Baltimore's, it is difficult to see how a realistically budgeted direct cash assistance program would expand housing choices or improve housing quality. Although such a program could reduce relative housing costs for thousands of families who are burdened by extremely high rent-income ratios, Grigsby and Rosenburg [1975:252] estimate this cost to be substantially greater than the aggregate of all current housing subsidies in Baltimore. While it is not certain that better housing would accompany higher rent paying abilities in the smaller city, the fact that excessive housing cost burdens are less of a problem indicates that relatively greater portions of the cash transfers would be funneled into the housing market. While severe supply restrictions would likely place an upper limit on the benefits of a housing allowance program in the smaller city, its potential is likely greater than in Baltimore or other severely troubled markets.

To oversimplify somewhat, the unique complex of interrelated efforts required to stem Baltimore's precipitous market decline can be contrasted to the relatively straightforward approach that seems warranted in the smaller city. In lieu of ownership transfer, equity insurance and other interventions which focus on the existing stock and require highly skilled manpower at the local level to design, implement and administer, the major elements of a smaller city effort should combine a demand side program, such as housing allowances, with a companion supply expanding program. Both of these programs would be administered in accord with federal guidelines and financed almost entirely out of federal funds. Contrary to the skilled manpower requirements of Grigsby and Rosenburg's [1975] proposed Baltimore program, the effective administration of a housing allowance program in a smoothly funtioning smaller city market should not require a comparable pool of specialized talent. With respect to expanding supply, adequate expertise is currently available in local housing authorities.

Causes of Policy Differences

The major differences in the program prescriptions for inner-city and nonmetropolitan areas are, in part, functions of the markedly different social, economic, and political forces to which these cities have been exposed over the recent past, and to basic differences in their form and spatial structure. While no consensus exists on the fundamental causes of inner-city decay, there is at least general agreement that it is in part the outgrowth of such phenomena as: preferences for suburban living and the rise in incomes which permit these preferences to be realized; the perverse effects of the filtering process which sufficiently destabilize the market and plant the seeds of eventual decay; and racial change which contributes to market destabilizing tenure changes, altered maintenance policies and relative or absolute declines in municipal services [Grigsby and Rosenburg, 1975:195–210]. Although these and related forces have contributed to the high incidence of core city housing problems, we must look elsewhere for the roots of nonmetropolitan deprivations. Assuming that the desire for newness, greenery, low density living and whatever else is embedded in the suburban dream is held by nonmetropolitan families as well as central city dwellers, the spatial structure of the smaller city is such that these desires need not be actualized in an outward movement from the central core. Greater land availability and lower relative land costs permit the development of new housing in established neighborhoods, or the construction of new, low density subdivisions in areas close to older neighborhoods. Whole areas are not abandoned in the smaller city as a result of the achievement by more affluent families of new homes.

Furthermore, while it appears that the relatively thin sector of almost exclusively white-occupied single family conversions has filtered down to poorer families, the worst quality stock has not filtered at all. This housing was built originally to very low standards for low income black occupany.

Unlike conversions, many of which are held by their owners in the hope that the commercially zoned land can be sold at substantial gains, the shotguns are held for current income purposes, the land having little reuse potential. The nonmetropolitan city has experienced little in the way of racially changing neighborhoods. Not only does market discrimination effectively restrict blacks to the poorest quality stock, but the incomes of most blacks are so low that they could not afford better quality housing even if it were to become available.

Although many investors in the metropolitan city had to rent to blacks because of the overwhelming market forces that swept their communities during the mid-sixties, it is unlikely that similar forces will affect the nonmetropolitan market in the foreseeable future. In addition, the smaller city is not characterized by high levels of community organization among blacks, local efforts to open the housing market have been lax, and the coverage of the nonmetropolitan rental stock by federal fair housing laws is light. The combination of all these factors suggests that the market will remain sharply segmented along racial lines for some time to come.

AN INTERVENTION STRATEGY

Housing Allowances
Given our understanding of the problems of the nonmetropolitan rental housing market, our policy studies focus on a series of demand and supply side interventions. To a large extent, housing deficiencies in these markets are a direct result of low income and could be alleviated substantially through a demand side program that would increase the purchasing power of the poor. The majority of the lowest income families, who occupy clearly substandard dwellings, would thus be afforded greater access to the better quality stock. The poor who already consume standard housing at the expense of seriously overtaxing their household budgets would be able to satisfy their other needs more adequately.

Accordingly, in the following chapter we examine the potential of a restricted income transfer program which would maximize the utilization of the existing standard and rehabilitatable rental stock. The primary objectives are to estimate the costs of such a program, the extent to which it is capable of alleviating housing problems, its likely price effects and its equity features. The logic of initiating the policy analysis with an income transfer effort lies in the potential of such a program to serve the lowest income families in a more cost-efficient manner than can a new construction program. If eligibility is defined according to a household's ability to secure existing standard housing, the neediest population can be served by a transfer equal to the difference between its ability to pay and the cost of existing standard housing. The subsidy, as we demonstrate, is considerably less than that required for new construction. Moreover, the increasing federal interest in housing allowances, as well as the existing housing provisions of the new Section 8 program, make this analysis particularly timely.

We embark upon our analysis of a direct cash assistance effort with the foreknowledge that serious questions of the efficacy of housing allowances have already been raised by observers of the housing market. Noting that allowances are "the 'in' idea of the 1970s," Hartman [1975:153], for one, seriously questions the value of cash housing supplements in markets that are riddled with serious defects. If collateral programs to improve market operations are not implemented simultaneously, Hartman [1975:159] believes that housing allowances at best will not improve the housing conditions of the poor and, at worst, will have the effect of postponing "the basic changes that are needed in the housing system if all Americans are to be decently housed."

While not concurring that allowances are a backwards policy step, Grigsby and Rosenburg [1975] raise equally serious questions about their effect on market dynamics. After dismissing as overemphasized the potential problem of price inflation, which they believe can be controlled through a phasing-in of allowances over time, they suggest that a substantial program of cash transfers could destabilize many inner-city neighborhoods, causing the decline both of "marginal neighborhoods tottering at preservation's edge" and of "many reception areas that are now in good health" [Grigsby and Rosenburg, 1975:255,257]. They thus view allowances as a supplement to existing housing programs rather than as a substitute for them, believing that where "market failure and social disorganization are widespread, subsidies that are welded directly to institutional reforms would also be necessary" [Grigsby and Rosenburg, 1975:259]. Former HUD Secretary Weaver [1975:248] notes further that direct cash grants "will do little to provide access of lower income families to suburbs which have neither loose moderate-cost housing markets nor a supply of housing that the less affluent could afford even with reasonably liberal housing allowances." Inasmuch as allowances would not open up the suburbs to the poor, would not "provide construction of lower income housing in urban renewal sites, nor facilitate redevelopment of central city areas," Weaver [1975:248] also believes that housing allowances can, at best, play only a supportive role in housing improvement strategies.

To a great extent, Weaver [1975], as well as Grigsby and Rosenburg [1975], believes that by enhancing consumer mobility, a program of housing allowances will destabilize inner-city neighborhoods, thus perpetuating the cycle of vacancy increases, disinvestment and abandonment.

"People, if they have a choice today," notes Weaver [1975:249], "look for neighborhood first and shelter second." To the extent that allowances are funneled into the older housing stock, one would expect cash flows to be buoyed and maintenance possibilities enhanced. If, however, neighborhood quality is more important than the quality of the physical dwelling, it may be that allowances, by expanding the options available to recipients, will contain "a built-in impetus toward walking away from [undesirable] neighborhoods" [Weaver, 1975:250].

From the standpoint of national policy considerations, it is worth noting that these and related precautionary observations about housing allowances are decidedly core city oriented, focusing almost exclusively on serious market instabilities and problems of neighborhood decline. We have already demonstrated that the nonmetropolitan rental market does not suffer from serious decline, disinvestment, and abandonment, with the result that even the most serious concern yet voiced about the potential impacts of allowances might not be particularly relevant to the smaller city. Even Grigsby and Rosenburg [1975:259] believe that "where the market is functioning with acceptable efficiency and where the problem of low income is not aggrevated by other difficulties," a program of housing allowances might "encourage improved maintenance and minor rehabilitation, if not major upgrading."

No grave market instabilities characterize the nonmetropolitan market, and serious complaints about housing far exceed dissatisfactions with neighborhood, even among the lowest income blacks. Rather than neighborhood instabilities, in the smaller city severe racial restrictions and supply inelasticities in certain submarkets affect the potential of allowances for improving housing conditions. These two market characteristics combined could make price inflation a far more important problem in the nonmetropolitan market than Grigsby and Rosenburg [1975:255] predict it would be in the central city, a relatively long phase-in period notwithstanding. Some upward price pressures on the currently depressed rent structure would not be entirely unwelcome from a policy standpoint if such pressures narrowed the gap between rents in the older and newer inventories sufficiently to induce households to move into the higher quality stock. Increased demand at the top of the market would ultimately permit the owners of this housing to raise rents to levels above those required to attract additional capital into the new construction sector. Overall, however, in the smaller city as in metropolitan centers, it is unlikely that allowances alone can do the trick. Where companion programs to stabilize the inner-city market are required, in the smaller city allowances must be supplemented by programs which directly subsidize new construction.

Production Subsidies

The concept of demand side housing assistance is not new, there having been almost 8 million households in 1972 who received shelter allocations via the leased public housing, public welfare, military housing and rent supplement programs and through the replacement housing provisions of the Uniform Relocation and Real Property Assistance Act of 1970 [Weaver, 1975:248]. As importantly, the notion that parallel demand and supply side assistance efforts should be implemented simultaneously has been long advocated by such analysts as Weaver [1972], Welfeld [1973], Downs [1974] and others. According to Welfeld [1973:3], the need for separate but coordinated approaches is obvious:

> First there must be enough housing units so that decent housing exists for every family. If there are not enough units, it will be necessary to produce more. Second, every household must be able to afford decent housing. If this is not the case, it will be necessary to provide financial assistance to some households.

Downs [1974:44] further specifies the complementary relationship between the two approaches: allowances should be used to stimulate a greater use of the existing inventory of older housing by lower income households, while production subsidies should be used to expand supply and "thereby avoid inflationary effects of just increasing demand." Supply side assistance efforts should also attempt to "create certain types of units not provided by private builders" and to influence the spatial location of new construction [Downs, 1974:44]. In short, production assistance should be used as a "means of attracting developers into markets they would otherwise avoid" [Weaver, 1975:255].

Despite the relatively large number of households currently receiving demand side assistance, our national housing effort may be characterized as overwhelmingly supply side oriented. Indeed, most of our production subsidies are so deep as to suggest that current policy fails to grasp the distinctions between the respective purposes of supply and demand side assistance. Rather than attempting merely to expand supply via production subsidies and the separate provision of financial assistance to lower income families who cannot otherwise access standard housing, we have tied both forms of assistance into one large supply side subsidy that is attached to the dwelling rather than the family. Tying household assistance to the production subsidy raises serious political problems because "the few often get a new home while many other families—including those who pay the taxes to support these programs—must make do with inferior older housing" [*Message from the President*, 1973:7]. Such programs are also vulnerable to attack on equity grounds. The deeper the per unit subsidy, the fewer the families that can be assisted out of any given appropriation.

More important than the equity issue, which is as much a function of budgetary limitations and the temporal scheduling of production goals as it is of program design, is the problem of maintaining the financial viability of deeply subsidized housing projects during periods of steeply rising operating costs. Essentially, the problem boils down to the fact that, despite the deep subsidies attached to federally subsidized developments, most lower income residents are paying as much rent as they can possibly afford to pay for their housing. Consequently, it has not been possible to increase rents at a rate consonant with increased costs of maintenance, utilities and related operating expenditures. Neither nonprofit nor limited dividend developments have sufficient operating reserves to continue functioning for very long under conditions of a severe cost-revenue squeeze. Although unsubsidized developers likewise suffer during periods of rapidly rising costs, the public sector is all but obligated to address the problems of subsidized housing sponsors. As of July 1, 1974, for example, fully seven percent of all outstanding Section 236 moderate income project mortgages were in default, as well as 11 percent of all outstanding mortgages on projects financed under the older Section 221(d)(3) subsidy program [*Housing and Development Reporter*: 1974:193]. Overall, by year end 1974, HUD had acquired more than 141 subsidized housing projects through the foreclosure route, and FHA insured mortgages on another 578 subsidized projects had been assigned to HUD by lenders who had placed the original loans which were not being paid off by the project sponsor [*Housing Affairs Newsletter*, 1975h:3].

To help alleviate some of these problems, in 1974 Congress authorized HUD to make operating subsidies available to sponsors of subsidized projects if by so doing further foreclosure could be averted. Based on its own estimates that it would take in excess of $58 million just to offset recent increases in utility costs, taxes and related operating expenses in Section 236 housing, HUD has been loath to initiate this new operating subsidy program because of its "budget-busting" potential [*Housing Affairs Newsletter*, 1974b:4]. Of course, the Department has no such choice with respect to assisting local housing authorities counter the erosinary effects of inflation, since public housing is owned and operated by the federal government. To ensure the continuation of the low income character of the public housing program HUD has requested more than $525 million in operating subsidies for fiscal 1976, up from $450 million budgeted a year earlier [*Housing Affairs Newsletter*, 1975a:3]. Estimates presently call for HUD's public housing operating subsidy requests to increase from around $572 million in fiscal 1977 to almost $800 million in fiscal year 1980 [*Housing Affairs Newsletter*, 1975a:3]. At that time, the average public housing unit will be receiving, in addition to the subsidy based upon government payment of all debt service, operating assistance amounting to around $600 a year.

The cost-revenue squeeze and related problems confronting the nation's subsidized housing sector are relevant to our work in that the supply side options currently available to the nonmetropolitan city are limited to the array of existing programs. Should these production assistance efforts prove to be as nonviable financially in the smaller city as in many core cities, then the principal planning problem of coordinating the use of these programs with a new income transfer effort would be reduced to a meaningless exercise. Fortunately, however, as we will detail in Chapter 10, neither public housing authorities nor existing subsidized developments in our study cities have suffered the kind of financial hardship that characterizes the national experience with these programs. As of June, 1975, no subsidized housing project mortgage in the entire state of North Carolina had been foreclosed or assigned to HUD. While local authorities were beginning to feel the bite of inflation at the time of our survey (1972), annual operating expenditures for the average public housing unit were just two-thirds those in the national program as a whole. Even today, it is undoubtedly the case that net operating revenues of local authorities in the smaller city are relatively more substantial than in the nation's largest public housing programs.

Summary

We view the purpose of public and government assisted new construction as being the expansion of supply in those market sectors where serious restrictions preclude the effective functioning of the market-oriented income transfer program. The continued viability of production-oriented programs is more important to the nonmetropolitan city than to some metropolitan centers because of the unsalvageable character of the existing nonmetropolitan rental housing stock. Should a demand side program not materialize in the short to intermediate run, the need for substantial levels of deeply subsidized new construction could be moderated somewhat through traditional supply side programs which concentrate on rehabilitating the substandard stock, the creative use of general revenue sharing and community development block grants, and through city participation in the new leased housing program enacted into law as Section 8 of the Housing and Community Development Act of 1974. Accomplishing the rehabilitation of the estimated nine percent of the substandard stock which is salvageable without the assistance of a housing allowance would require the provision of low interest loans and rehabilitation grants such as those that have been available under the old urban renewal and neighborhood development programs. Because these supply side programs do not enhance tenant rent-paying abilities, it is questionable whether postrenewal rents would approach market levels. If tenants are not willing or able to pay the higher costs of standard housing, rehab of these below code properties may still be warranted if the only practical alternative for their owners is withdrawal from the market. Withdrawal could be mandated if the city were to declare target neighborhoods as concentrated code enforcement areas.

Whether this course of action makes sense depends on the spatial pattern of rehabilitatable houses. The nonmetropolitan cities do not have a history of aggressive code enforcement programs and are not likely to initiate any in the near future without substantial financial inducements from the federal government. Moreover, the national experience suggests that neither general nor community development revenue sharing monies are likely to be directed toward improving the quality of the occupied rental stock. Given the relatively small portion of the rental stock which is capable of being upgraded, we do not examine the potential of such efforts apart from their role in an allowance strategy. Rather, in the two concluding chapters we attempt to specify more precisely how demand and new construction programs might be coordinated and what the costs and potential market impacts of such an approach to the nonmetropolitan housing problem might be.

Despite these efforts, however, we should note that for several reasons we stop short of designing a comprehensive strategy for ridding these cities of all housing deprivations over some given time. First, our study deals only with the rental market, and a comprehensive housing strategy would require consideration of the ownership sector. Second, while any significant public intervention in the nonmetropolitan rental market has the potential to alter the market parameters we estimated, given the extent of the existing deprivations, a program to eliminate all housing problems would surely affect market dynamics in ways we could not predict. Because we can, with some caution, evaluate the likely market impacts of individual programs but not the interaction effects among various combinations of programs, we have limited the policy analyses to the former.

Finally, as Donnison [1969:23] has noted, the "field of housing—taken as a whole—is too big, too complex and too central to the culture and character of society for its problems to be 'solved' " in any definitive sense. In the small cities of our nation, as in large metropolitan centers, housing standards are relative and highly elastic over the long run. It is all but a truism that "as long as our families continue to change in size and structure, acquire new possessions, take up new activities and new social roles, so they will seek new or better or different housing" [Donnison, 1969:23]. In this sense, then, there can be no ceiling to housing needs.

❋ *Chapter 9*

Potential Market Effects of
a Housing Allowance Program

INTRODUCTION

Since supply programs are typically tied to new production and benefits are received only as long as the family remains in the assisted dwelling, relatively few of the income-eligible families are able to receive program benefits. Demand programs, under which housing assistance remains with the family as it moves through the stock, are considered more equitable in that, theoretically, all income eligible families may receive direct program benefits.

Although by design a housing allowance program is intended to treat identically all similarly circumstanced families, thus more nearly satisfying the objective of horizontal equity than would a supply side program, we recognize the limitations inherent in the pursuit of a narrow equity objective in the development of housing programs. First, as Weaver [1975:252] notes, "providing equitable benefits to all in prescribed income groups" will not necessarily be an effective means of improving neighborhood quality or revitalizing living environments. This problem, however, is not as potentially serious for nonmetropolitan areas as it might be in central cities, where severe negative externalities and extensive abandonment have led to neighborhood deterioration. While an allowance may encourage increased flight from declining inner-city neighborhoods, nonmetropolitan neighborhoods tend to be far more stable.

Second, the theoretical equity of housing allowances could be diluted substantially by the need for extended phase-in periods or the existence of market imperfections and immobilities. Although market imperfections are less pronounced in nonmetropolitan cities, the pervasive problem of racial discrimination could have serious equity implications. Finally, regardless of program design, the ability to achieve equity will be directly related to the level of program funding [Weaver, 1975:253]. In fact, as we demonstrate below, the average transfer cost of an allowance in nonmetropolitan cities is relatively low. The correspondingly low aggregate resource commitment required to ensure broad-based coverage, and thus to enhance equity, is one of the program's more attractive features.

The metropolitan-oriented housing allowance experiment currently being conducted by HUD [U.S. Department of Housing and Urban Development, 1975a] is designed to provide actual market tests of responses to the allowance among recipient households and housing suppliers. Particular emphasis is being placed on the degree to which the transfer program will stimulate an increase in the consumption of housing by low income families, an upgrading of existing dwellings, and inflationary increases in housing prices. These issues, which have also been explored using a market simulation model developed at the Urban Institute [de Leeuw et al., 1974; Carlton and Ferreira, 1975], are central to an understanding of the market effects and potential costs and benefits of a housing allowance program (HAP).

In this chapter we examine the potential for an allowance program to improve the housing circumstances of nonmetropolitan renters. In the absence of experimental data or a simulation model calibrated with longitudinal data, we cannot present as detailed an analysis as we might wish. By specifying a number of fairly restrictive assumptions about the nature of HAP responses and by imposing certain constraints on the design of the program, however, we can use our cross-sectional data to provide insights into the likely market effects of an allowance in these rental markets. The pattern of market responses that we assume for housing suppliers and demanders constitutes an analytically simple simulation model which reflects our understanding of the market dynamics as they have been revealed through the preceding empirical analyses.

This model and the program design are described after we define the income-eligible population that potentially, at least, would participate in supply or demand side nonmetropolitan housing assistance programs. The third section of this chapter contains a market analysis of the program in which we estimate participation rates, transfer amounts and price effects which are likely to result from increased housing consumption and from excess demand pressures. Finally, we explore a number of market phenomena which will impact on the success of a HAP, including potential for the upward movement of ineligible households and the effects of racial discrimination.

THE POTENTIAL CLIENT POPULATION

Supply side recommendations will be discussed in the following chapter, but because both demand and supply side programs embody income-conditioned eligibility criteria, in this section we identify potential client populations for each program type. For an allowance program, which is intended to foster a more efficient utilization of the existing stock, maximum income limits are defined with respect to the cost of standard housing presently available. Supply side program income limits are necessarily higher because the costs of new housing, even with deep mortgage interest subsidies, are higher than the prevailing rents for minimum standard housing.

The Cost of Existing Standard Housing

If housing allowances are to encourage a more efficient use of the existing stock and make program benefits available to large numbers of families by limiting the lize of individual transfers, the cost of standard housing (C^*) must be defined with reference to prevailing rent levels for minimally adequate housing. Determining C^* involves estimating the rent per square foot (RSF^*) for a standard dwelling and the amount of space (S^*) that would be required by households of various sizes. Thus

$$C^* = RSF^* \times S^* \qquad (9\text{-}1)$$

In Chapter 2 we identified a minimum quality standard which was priced in the market at an annual square foot rental of around $.70, the figure we employ here to estimate C^*. Since this quality level is based on the community norm of housing adequacy, the rental rate represents the unit cost of standard housing, given existing market conditions and the resultant distribution of housing services across the market.

The minimum amount of space required by various household sizes, which we also derived with reference to community norms, reflects the size distribution of dwellings which are currently available in the market. These space requirements are not minimum standards per se but, in conjunction with RSF^*, they produce standard costs that reflect what households would have to spend to purchase standard quality housing of adequate size in the private market. Based on the distributions of household and dwelling unit sizes, we employ values of S^* ranging from 800 square feet for one-person households to 1,600 square feet for households with seven or more persons. Increments of 150 square feet are added for each additional person through four, and increments of 100 square feet are added for each person beyond four (Table 9–1). These consumption standards require annual housing costs that range from about $560 per year for single person households to $1,160 for the largest families.[1]

Table 9-1. Income Limits and Eligibility Rates by Household Size

Household Size No. Persons	Existing Standard Housing Requirements		Low-Income Eligibility		Moderate Income Eligibility		Total Eligible
	Dwelling Size (sq.ft.)	Annual Standard Rent (C*)	Maximum Income	Eligible as % of Size Class	Maximum Income	Eligible as % of Size Class	
1	800	$ 562	$2,808	42.1%	$4,593	26.2%	68.3%
2	950	667	3,335	23.0	5,879	30.4	53.4
3	1100	772	3,861	20.2	6,614	21.2	41.4
4	1250	878	4,388	13.6	7,349	13.6	27.2
5	1350	948	4,739	27.0	7,808	24.3	51.3
6	1450	1,018	5,090	32.0	8,267	36.0	68.0
7+	1650	1,158	5,792	40.0	9,186	25.0	65.0
Total				28.9		26.1	55.0

Income Eligibility

The incomes (Y) that are necessary to support these costs are a function of the proportion of income (b) that a household is expected to devote to housing consumption. The minimum income is determined from:

$$C^* = bY. \tag{9-2}$$

This procedure for identifying potential housing program clients is equivalent to the "housing gap" concept that has been employed in housing allowance experiments and simulations [Carlton and Ferriera, 1975:4; U.S. Department of Housing and Urban Development, 1975a:11]. The determination of the parameter, b, is a somewhat subjective procedure that depends, to a certain extent, on how income and rent are defined. By law, public housing occupants, for example, can pay no more than 25 percent of their incomes for rent [Housing and Urban Development Act of 1969, Sec.213]. The determination of the appropriate rent under this program employs net income adjusted for the number of minors and certain household expenses; in addition, the rent includes payment for utilities as well as basic shelter services. Under Section 8 of the Housing and Community Development Act of 1974, a similar procedure is employed; the 25 percent figure is applied to all families except the most disadvantaged, who are required to devote only 15 percent of their incomes to rent and utilities. Our analysis is based on contract rent which, in the vast majority of cases, does not include utilities and, therefore, represents basic shelter costs only. Moreover, no adjustments to income are made. For these reasons, we calculate income eligibility by specifying that no more than 20 percent of gross household income should be devoted to rent. The resultant income limits range from $2,800 for one-person households to $5,800 for the largest families (Table 9–1). The families with incomes below these levels constitute the "low income" program-eligible population. In total, they account for about 29 percent of all renters.

In order to provide some perspective on these eligibility requirements, it is useful to examine their correspondence to those which apply under existing housing programs. A smaller portion of the renter population is eligible for assistance according to our criteria than is the case using new construction program guidelines. Compared to the 29 percent eligibility rate derived from the cost of existing standard housing, nearly 43 percent of the nonmetropolitan renter population is eligible for low rent public housing, and another 16 percent would qualify for occupancy under the Section 236 moderate income program.[2]

Under Section 8 of the 1974 Housing Act, which is intended to supplement these new construction programs, eligibility is based on the median income for a housing market area. Adjusting for family sizes, low income eligible housholds are those with incomes below 80 percent of the area-wide median, and very low income families have incomes less than 50 percent of the median.[3] According to our estimates, about 32 percent of the renters in these cities would be classified as very low income, and another 23 percent would fall into the low income category. The housing gap criterion based on the cost of existing standard housing thus corresponds to the "very low income" criterion as defined by Section 8 guidelines.

The most efficient way in which to satisfy the housing needs of these families is through an allowance program in which subsidy levels are determined by the rents of existing housing. The gap between these households' ability to pay and new construction rents is much too great to justify the provision of subsidized new housing for all of them. Direct construction for moderate income families is, however, much less costly and is, as we shall demonstrate, necessary, if a significant reduction in substandard occupancy is to be achieved. Because of the anticipated future reliance on Section 8 or a similar supply side variant, we define moderate income households as those whose incomes exceed our low income definition but fall within the current Section 8 limits. Depending on family size, these limits range from $4,600 to $9,200 and add another 26 percent of the renter population to the pool of housing program eligibles (Table 9–1).

Characteristics of the Eligible Populations

The income criteria we have employed to identify the potential client populations of nonmetropolitan housing programs isolate renter households which are disadvantaged in more than just income terms. With respect to income, however, the neediest category averages only about $2,100 a year, while moderate income households average about $4,800 (Table 9–2). Of the former, nearly all have incomes below $4,000, and about 80 percent of the moderate income families have annual incomes below $6,000. Those households who would not qualify for any program have an average income in excess of $9,300, with 87 percent being above the $6,000 level.

Although the moderate income cohort tends to mirror the total renter population in terms of its demographic characteristics, the lowest income group is characterized by a number of disadvantages that are likely to compound its income deprivation. Black households, who must compete for housing in a severely restricted market, are considerably overrepresented among the low income population; about one-third of all renters but over half the low income renters are black. Although blacks are proportionately represented among moderate income families, they con-

Table 9–2. Household Characteristics and Housing Consumption by Eligibility Level

		Low Income Eligible	*Moderate Income Eligible*	*Over Income (Ineligible)*	*All Renters*
Demographic					
Black	(%)	53.1	37.4	18.7	33.5
Female Head	(%)	69.0	42.0	27.6	43.3
One Person	(%)	42.1	29.0	20.4	28.9
Six or More Persons	(%)	11.0	10.7	6.7	9.0
Elderly Head	(%)	40.3	17.6	12.1	21.6
Income					
Average Income	($)	2,129	4,794	9,346	6,067
< $4,000	(%)	97.2	35.9	—	37.6
$4,000–5,999	(%)	2.8	44.3	12.9	18.2
Housing Consumption					
Monthly Rent	($)	49	63	75	64
Rent-Income Ratio	(%)	32.5	17.0	10.6	18.6
Dwelling Size	(Sq.ft.)	959	970	1,075	1,014
Housing Deficiencies					
Substandard Occupancy	(%)	62.7	43.5	23.8	40.1
Excess Rent Burden	(%)	30.3	15.3	1.3	13.3
Overcrowded	(%)	2.1	4.6	3.6	3.4
Total Deficient	(%)	95.1	63.4	28.7	56.9
N		145	131	225	501

stitute fewer than 20 percent of the over-income families. Three characteristics that tend to be intercorrelated—female and elderly headship and one-person households—all occur with considerably more frequency among low income renters than among moderate income households or all renters. Nearly 70 percent of the low income households are headed by women, while 40 percent have heads who are 62 years or older. One person households constitute 42 percent of the low income families. These family types occur only one-third to one-half as often among over-income families.

These socioeconomic differences are clearly reflected in housing consumption differences among the various population groups. Low income renters pay average rents of only $49 per month while moderate income households pay $63, approximately the city-wide average. Even given their low rents, however, the low income group allocates an average of nearly 33 percent of its income to rent. No other group averages as much as 20 percent, and over-income households spend less than 11 percent. Space consumption increases with income, but the differences are not very great; less than 120 square feet separates the averages for the low income and the over-income groups.

The problems faced by the low income class are even more dramatically reflected in their 95 percent rate of housing deprivations. Nearly two-thirds occupy substandard dwellings, and another 30 percent live in standard units for which they pay more than 25 percent of their incomes in rent. Surprisingly, moderate income households experience an above average 63 percent incidence of deprivations. While nearly 30 percent of the over-income households have one or more housing problems, the bulk of the latter are accounted for by substandard occupancy.

A MODEL OF HAP RESPONSES

Program Design

The design of the housing allowance plan we analyze flows from two basic program objectives discussed earlier. First and foremost, the assistance effort should increase housing consumption and/or reduce the burden of housing costs for poor families. While it is not our purpose here to design a broad-based attack on poverty, the importance of basic shelter services and the large portion of the low income family's budget that is typically consumed by housing outlays suggest that the overall welfare of poor families can be significantly improved by reducing their real costs of housing. Although its achievement will be constrained by certain market realities, the second objective is horizontal equity; accordingly, all households who fall below the previously defined income limits are eligible to receive a subsidy which is equal to the magnitude of their housing gap and which is unaffected by their current housing circumstances and actual rent paid.

Eligible households are those for whom minimally standard housing costs more than one-fifth of total income:

$$C^* > .20Y. \tag{9-3}$$

Each eligible household would receive a direct cash transfer (T) equal to the difference between C^* and 20 percent of its income:

$$T = C^* - .20Y. \tag{9-4}$$

The segment of the nonmetropolitan renter population that would be eligible is composed of the nearly 30 percent of the households who constitute the "low-income" program eligibles as they were defined in the preceding section.

Without any restrictions on the amount of housing consumed by participating households, an income-conditioned allowance program would be equivalent to a pure income transfer. Since increases in the quality of the occupied housing stock would be a function of the income elasticity of demand for housing and of the supply side response to the demand increase, there would be no inherent guarantee that substantial improvements in housing quality would occur. In fact, as was demonstrated in Chapter 3, nonmetropolitan renters are not likely to allocate a significant proportion of an unrestricted income transfer to housing. The HAP program design, therefore, incorporates a "minimum condition" requirement under which all recipient households must occupy standard quality dwellings. Since those families who cannot access a standard dwelling will lose their HAP eligibility, there is a built-in program incentive for households in substandard dwellings to increase their housing consumption at least to the minimum standard level. Since the subsidy does not vary with rent, however, there is no incentive to consume higher quality dwellings, and households will be encouraged to shop for bargains within the standard quality stock.[4]

Expected Market Responses to an Allowance Program

While our evaluation of the performance of a HAP will be a function of our program design, it will also depend to a large extent on assumptions regarding likely market responses. In this section we discuss these assumptions, which derive from our understanding of the market and which are partially dictated by our analytical technique. The specific issues which we address concern the behavior of recipient households and supply side responses. In addition, we provide operational definitions of a number of concepts which are employed in the analysis.

It is useful to classify HAP recipients into five categories according to their current levels of housing consumption. First, households occupying standard quality dwellings are distinguished from those in substandard units. The former are further grouped into those who are overcrowded and those who are not. Although the uncrowded occupants of standard dwellings are consuming adequate housing, they generally can do so only by over-taxing their budgets. The occupants of substandard dwellings fall into three categories: those whose units are incapable of being upgraded; those who occupy overcrowded, rehabilitable units; and those who consume adequate space in rehabilitable units.

Because of the conceptual similarity between the HAP design and an unrestricted income transfer, the responses we assume for participants in each of the five housing need classes are strongly influenced by the low income elasticities we have observed for nonmetropolitan renters. The HAP transfer shifts the household budget line to the right without altering the relative price of housing, but the decision space of participants is attenuated at the minimum housing consumption level [de Leeuw et al., 1970]. For recipients currently occupying uncrowded, standard dwellings, the subsidy is equivalent to an unrestricted income transfer which shifts their budget line to the right (from AB to CD in Figure 9–1) and thereby induces an increase in housing consumption from Q_1 to Q_2 at the new

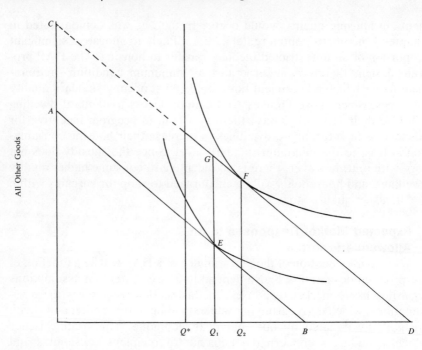

Figure 9–1. Response to Housing Allowance Transfer: Recipient in Standard Housing

equilibrium position (*F*). Given the low income elasticities and the fact that these households are already spending excessive portions of their incomes to secure adequate housing, we would expect Q_2 to be at most only marginally greater than Q_1. We will assume for simplicity that these households will remain in their present housing (i.e., that $Q_2 = Q_1$). This will produce only a slight underestimate of the portion of the transfer that enters the housing market and of the demand pressures that will contribute to inflationary price increases. The subsidy received by these families will be devoted entirely to the reduction of rent burdens, an outcome which Grigsby and Rosenburg [1975:254] suggest may be a "principal benefit" of an allowance program. In the nonmetropolitan market, even though low quality housing is the most important source of housing deprivations, the problem of excessive rent expenditures plagues a large portion of the low income population. The allowance could be a useful mechanism through which the economic circumstances of these families are stabilized and enhanced.

The situation confronting a recipient in substandard housing is depicted in Figure 9–2. Since the household must increase its consumption

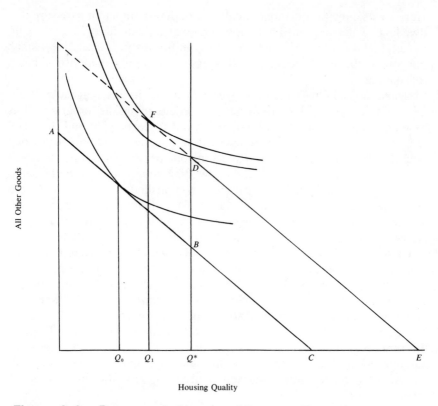

Figure 9–2. Response to Housing Allowance Transfer:
Household in Substandard Housing

of housing at least to Q^* in order to receive a subsidy, the transfer restricts the relevant budget line to *ABDE*. Without the subsidy, the household consumes Q_0 units of housing; given a low income elasticity, a pure income transfer would likely induce an expansion only to Q_1, with the new household equilibrium at point F. This position, however, is unattainable under the minimum standards restriction; the household must locate at point D, where its housing consumption is Q^*. While this is not an optimal position, the recipient household is still at a higher indifference level than it was before the transfer. Although some households may actually increase their housing consumption to a level beyond Q^*, we will assume that all will locate at point D.

Accordingly, it is assumed that all families living in substandard, rehabilitable dwellings which are not overcrowded will prefer, and will be allowed, to continue occupancy during the rehabilitation period. Standard quality dwellings and those which are capable of supporting rehabilitation capital under an exogenous rent increase were identified in Chapter 2.

Here we assume that the analytical time period is sufficient to assure that dwellings which are feasible to upgrade given a postrehab rent of C^* will, in fact, be brought up to standard. These units constitute a relatively small portion of the total stock, and this assumed supply response appears reasonable.

Those households which are overcrowded or in unsalvageable dwellings will be required to relocate to participate in the program. It is assumed that all such households will want to participate and that they will, therefore, search for replacement housing. Since overcrowded households—those at densities exceeding one person per room—will each release a standard or rehabilitatable dwelling when they move, the satisfaction of their housing needs can be accomplished without reducing the available supply of standard dwellings. The eligibles who occupy substandard units which could not be brought up to standard following an allowance-induced rent increase to C^*, on the other hand, will not release an eligible unit. For each of these households which locates a replacement unit, the available supply of vacant, standard housing will be diminished. Accordingly, the participation of these families will be determined by the current supply of vacant units which are standard or rehabilitatable. All mover households are assumed to pay postallowance rents of C^* and to confine their housing search to the market sector containing dwellings in this rent range (the HAP submarket). That some of these families may find bargains is ignored, as is the possibility that, once in the market, they will choose to acquire more than minimally standard housing renting at greater than C^*

Allocation of the Subsidy

The subsidy received by participating households, regardless of their current housing circumstances, can contribute either to a reduction in the family's rent burden or to expenditures for increased housing consumption. Those households currently in standard, uncrowded units will allocate all of their transfers to reductions in their rent-income ratios (R/Y savings). Those spending in excess of 20 percent of their incomes to secure adequate housing are paying rents of C^* or greater, and their postallowance rent-income ratios will be .20 or greater. For those who are fortunate enough to have secured standard housing at below market rates ($<C^*$), the post-allowance rent burden will be below .20. While the portion of the transfer that contributes to rent-income ratio reductions will not lead to increases in housing consumption, relieving excess rent burdens is considered a justifiable objective of the allowance program. Those transfers that reduce the burdens below .20, however, do not serve any program objective and represent pure transfer leakage.

All recipient households who must increase their housing consumption to maintain their eligibility are assumed to pay postallowance rents of C^*

and, therefore, to have rent burdens of 20 percent. Those households who currently spend more than 20 percent will, however, be able to use some portion of the transfer to reduce their excessive rent-income ratios. In other words, we assume that households paying more than 20 percent will actually reduce their own contribution to rent, at least initially. For those paying 20 percent or less there will be no R/Y savings, and the household's share of the rent will increase or remain the same.[5]

Allowance-induced rent changes will take the form of either consumption effects which will result from an expansion of the flow of housing services or inflationary effects produced by excess demand pressures. As we will demonstrate, the primary source of the inflationary price increase lies in that portion of the transfer that is devoted to R/Y savings. Our estimates of these rent changes presume that a full market adjustment has taken place within the HAP submarket. As we already indicated, Grigsby and Rosenburg [1975:255] argue that the problem of inflationary price increases can be controlled relatively easily by phasing-in the allowance at whatever rate is judged to be necessary to avoid such a problem. Inflationary effects, or a tightening of the rent structure, will ultimately provide the incentive for the bumping of higher income households out of the HAP submarket, an effect of the allowance which has the potential to be a significant stimulus to new construction. Our intent, therefore, is to estimate the magnitude of the pressures which are likely to induce movement out of the HAP submarket into higher quality rental housing or into the owner stock.

PRICE EFFECTS OF AN ALLOWANCE PROGRAM

Transfer Costs and Subsidy Levels

The renter households eligible for an allowance based on the housing gap criterion were identified in the first section. Here, for purposes of the cost and price analyses, we present figures for the full sampling universe of 25 nonmetropolitan cities in North Carolina, which contain about 69,000 rental dwellings. Of the nearly 20,000 income-eligible households in these cities, about 85 percent would have to pay standard rents of less than $900. We therefore define the HAP submarket as the sector containing dwellings renting for $900 per year or less. Although this includes about two-thirds of the rental stock (46,000 dwellings), the allowance will concentrate demand pressures on the 25,000 units which are standard or feasible to rehabilitate; our estimates of the HAP induced price pressures are confined to these units.

Overall, the average annual transfer is about $280 per year, or about $23 per month (Table 9–3). Clearly, the lower cost structure in nonmetropolitan cities produces average transfer payments substantially below

Table 9–3. Transfer Costs and Subsidy Levels Under a Housing Allowance Program

Subsidy as a Proportion of Standard Annual Rent	Percent of Eligibles	Average Annual Subsidy	Total Annual Subsidy*	Percent of Total Subsidy
< 1 month	10.1%	$ 24	$ 47,600	0.9%
1–3 months	18.2	109	381,700	7.1
4–6 months	36.5	263	1,842,300	34.4
7–12 months	35.2	457	3,081,100	57.6
Total Eligible	100.0	279	5,352,700	100.0
Total Expected Participants	89.9	308	5,305,100	99.1

* Rounded to nearest $100

those that would be required to bring the rent-paying abilities of poor families up to community standards in metropolitan cities. In the Kansas City demonstration, for example, participants received an average of $104 per month [Solomon and Fenton, 1974:214]. The dramatically lower cost in smaller southern cities is also indicated by the aggregate direct transfer of $5.3 million in North Carolina's nonmetropolitan cities.

Although we have no way of estimating administrative program costs, it is reasonable to assume that such outlays will not vary with the size of the transfers received by participating families, but will vary with the size of the participating population. The disproportionate relationship between subsidy levels and overhead expenses suggests that overall program efficiency would be enhanced by restricting participation to those households eligible for transfers above some minimum level, but equity considerations militate against this approach. On the other hand, it is very likely that many households for whom the transfer would be very small would elect not to participate in the program. In one of the experiments being conducted by HUD, for example, 30 percent of the families who were contacted declined to participate, with a substantial portion expressing the feeling that it would be too much bother [U.S. Department of Housing and Urban Development, 1975a:19]. In part, the short-term nature of the experiment may have contributed to some of this reluctance, but, in general, we would expect families to be less enthusiastic the smaller the subsidy they would receive.

About 92 percent of the total transfer to nonmetropolitan renters will be funneled to about 72 percent of the recipients, while 10 percent of the eligibles, who are in the highest income group, will qualify for less than one percent of the subsidies. There is strong evidence of relatively low housing preferences among the families who would be eligible for a transfer amounting to less than one month's standard rent. While these families have incomes which average $1,100 more than those for all eligibles, they spend an average of $90 less per year for rent. This translates to a mean rent-income ratio of .15, less than half that for the total eligible population. Compared to an overall 62 percent rate of sub-standard occupancy among eligibles, 73 percent of this group occupy units which are below standard. It does not appear that the low level of housing consumption among these households is a result of their being subjected to greater rates of market discrimination. Demographically, they tend to mirror the total eligible population and, in fact, are less likely to be black or to contain a large number of persons. Accordingly, we assume that all households eligible for transfers of less than one month's standard rent will not participate, thus reducing the total transfer by about $44,000 per year, or by less than one percent. At the same time, however, the 10 percent reduction in recipient households would lead to substantial savings in administrative program costs.

An Unrestricted Income Transfer

Having estimated the magnitude of the aggregate and average HAP transfer and the probable voluntary participation rate under a minimum standards type of allowance program, it may be useful to digress for a moment and examine the housing market implications of an unrestricted income transfer. The importance of our HAP minimum quality require-ment on housing consumption patterns can be gauged by comparing the resulting earmarking rate with that which is likely to occur under a program of unrestricted income transfer. By so doing, we can also gain a feeling for the magnitude of the error that will result from our assumptions that eligibles who are at present adequately housed will not increase their post-HAP levels of housing consumption and that families who have to move in order to maintain program eligibility will not consume housing at any cost higher than C^*.

The amount of the transfer that each household would devote to housing consumption is estimated from the income elasticity of demand which was derived in Chapter 3. For simplicity, we assume that the response of each recipient is determined by the market-wide average elasticity of .374, although our earlier analysis indicated that there are substantial variations in the rent response to income changes across various household cohorts.[6] Accordingly, for every recipient, the in-crease in rent following the implementation of the transfer system and the achievement of the new market equilibrium is given by:

$$\Delta R = .374 \ (\Delta Y/Y_p)R, \qquad (9\text{-}5)$$

where Y_p is the estimate of the household's permanent income[7] and R is its current rent. The transfer amount (ΔY) averages $308 per household, or about 15 percent of current household income (Table 9–4). Of this

Table 9–4.   Housing Consumption Effects of an Unrestricted Income Transfer

Housing Need Class	Subsidy as a Percent of Current Income	Average Annual Rent Increase	Portion of Transfer Allocated to Rent	Average Rent-Current Income Ratios		Post-Transfer Rent Deficit	
				Pre-Transfer	Post-Transfer	Average Amount	Percent of Households
Standard Housing							
Not Crowded	14.6%	$24	8.9%	.462	.375	$137	40.0%
Crowded	17.5	13	3.4	.230	.195	374	100.0
Substandard Housing							
Not Crowded	19.7	24	6.9	.278	.237	224	100.0
Crowded	21.6	19	3.1	.174	.148	619	100.0
Unrehabilitatable	14.6	19	5.8	.287	.244	195	77.8
Total	15.3	21	6.9	.344	.288	89	68.3

amount, about $21 per year, or less than $2 per month, will be allocated to rent expenditures, producing a housing earmarking ratio of only 7 percent.

With the bulk of the transfer being devoted to non-housing needs, recipient households are also able to lower their relative rent burdens, but the subsidy is too small to produce very substantial reductions (Table 9–4). On average, the rent burden drops from 34 to 29 percent of income. Those recipients who are currently consuming adequate housing will increase their housing consumption by an average of $24 per year, which amounts to less than a 3 percent increase over their current expenditure level. Their average rent burden remains at a very high 38 percent of their incomes. For all the other need categories, the post-transfer rent-income ratios range from about 15 to 24 percent; the average 4 percent increase in rent expenditures amounts to about $13–24 per year.

If we define the rent-deficit as the difference between C^* and the post-transfer rent paid by each household, the marginal effect of the subsidy on the rental market becomes even more clear. Following the full implementation of the transfer, over two-thirds of the recipients would be spending less for rent than we have estimated to be necessary to obtain standard housing (Table 9–4). Even among those already consuming adequate housing, only 40 percent would spend C^* or more—an indication of the number of households which have been able to secure standard dwellings at rentals that are below the prevailing market rate. On average, these households would spend $163 per year more than C^*, while for all other need classes, recipients will be paying rents which average from $170–600 below C^*.

The increased aggregate housing expenditures of about $362,500, representing less than a one percent increase in aggregate rental expenditures, are not likely to contribute to an improvement in the overall quality of the nonmetropolitan rental housing stock. Rather than the program's inducing increases in mobility, it is likely that changes in housing consumption will occur over time in conjunction with normal turnover and moving activity. Consequently, we would expect an unrestricted income transfer to be accompanied by little price inflation.

Somewhat similar results were obtained by de Leeuw et al. [1974] in their program simulations for prototypical metropolitan markets. In the "high minority, slow growth, inelastic supply" prototype, which approximates most closely the characteristics of nonmetropolitan cities, the earmarking ratio under a pure income transfer program was estimated at 12 percent. The transfer induced a nine percent increase in the unit cost of housing services and an aggregate increase of seven percent in total rent expenditures. In stark contrast, a minimum condition, restricted housing allowance program in those same cities was estimated to produce a 94 percent earmarking ratio, a 40 percent inflationary increase in the price per unit of housing and a 59 percent increase in aggregate rental expenditures. The much greater market impact of a restricted income transfer is clear from these simulations; our estimates of their effect in the nonmetropolitan context are presented in the remainder of this chapter.

If the unrestricted transfer were large enough, of course, it would have a greater impact on the housing market, but a pure income transfer is an inefficient way to achieve a housing objective per se. On average, for example, it would take a transfer of nearly $300 per month to stimulate an increase in rent expenditures to the current market average of about $65. At this subsidy level, the total transfer cost would be increased six-fold to $60 million and would be likely to result in considerable price inflation in the absence of substantial supply-side assistance.

HAP-Induced Price Effects

R/Y Savings: Returning to the earmarked housing allowance approach, the first task is to estimate the portion of the transfer that would be devoted to reduction in rent-income ratios by participants (R/Y savings). More than one-third of the expected program participants, who would receive about 31 percent of the total transfers, are currently consuming adequate levels of housing. On average these families spend more than 46 percent of their incomes for rent, with nearly 96 percent incurring rent-income ratios in excess of .20. Rather than increasing their housing consumption, these recipients will use $1.2 million of their transfer to lower their rent burdens to 20 percent and another $400,000 to reduce them below this program target level (Table 9–5). The latter figure represents a pure transfer leakage amounting to 7.5 percent of the aggregate subsidy.

Among the remaining recipients, 71 percent are currently allocating in excess of 20 percent of their incomes for housing that is physically deficient and/or overcrowded. The HAP will enable these families both to improve their housing circumstances and to reduce their out of pocket contributions to rent. In total these families are eligible for $3.6 million in transfers, of which $1.2 million would be used to reduce excessive rent burdens. Somewhat surprisingly then, about 54 percent of the total HAP transfer would be used initially to reduce relative housing outlays to 20 percent or less of income. This substantial portion of the aggregate subsidy represents a resource available to recipient households should they ultimately have to compete among themselves and with the HAP ineligible population for standard quality housing.

Consumption Effects: Increases in housing output and consumption within the HAP submarket will be stimulated by the portion of the total transfer that is not allocated to reductions in rent-income ratios. Deleting the R/Y savings first is consistent with our observation of low housing preferences among nonmetropolitan renters. The amount of the transfer that is available to each household after subtracting the R/Y savings is sufficient to assure a postallowance rent expenditure of C^*.

Approximately \$2.5 million, or 46 percent of the total transfer, is available for housing-deficient recipients to spend on increased consumption (Table 9–5). Over \$800,000 of this amount will be spent by the occupants of overcrowded and/or rehabilitatable, substandard dwellings. We have assumed that overcrowding will be relieved by a reallocation of households and dwellings within the HAP submarket and that rehabilitation can be accomplished while the current occupant remains in the dwelling. The total of nearly 2,100 dwellings that will be upgraded represents 12 percent of all recipient households.[8]

All additional consumption effects will occur as the result of increased demand among the more than 8,000 occupants of unrehabilitatable housing. Standard and rehabilitatable vacant units will be absorbed by these recipient households, who will leave behind unsalvageable vacant dwellings. The net number of vacancies will not change, but the utilization of housing services will increase since standard dwellings will replace below standard dwellings in the occupied sector. In other words, the average rent for occupied housing will increase by the difference between C^* and the current rent for low quality housing. The potential aggregate increase is equal to the \$1.6 million available to recipients in the unsalvageable stock.

The available vacant dwellings, however, are far outnumbered by the unrehabilitatable, occupied units in the market. The overall vacancy rate is 5.6 percent across the rental market, but of the nearly 3,900 vacant units, only about 2,100 are potentially available to HAP participants. The rents of over 1,100 place them outside the HAP submarket, and the remainder are substandard and not capable of being upgraded. Although the absorption of the full complement of available standard vacancies by these families would be certain to induce price effects, we cannot estimate the magnitude of this pressure. It is unlikely, however, that a normal five percent vacancy rate will be maintained as recipient households compete for higher quality housing in order to maintain their program eligibility. Indeed, one of the more important stimuli for upward filtering and new construction that will occur is the drying up of available vacancies; therefore, our baseline estimates of HAP price effects assume complete utilization of the vacant standard stock.

Even under this assumption, nearly 75 percent of the occupants of unrehabilitatable units will not be able to secure replacement housing and will, consequently, lose their program eligibility. As a result, the potential total transfer of \$5.3 million will be reduced to less than \$3.4 million, and

Table 9-5. Housing Allowance Transfer by Housing Need

Housing Need Class	Households		Transfer Cost		R/Y Savings	Consumption Increase	
	Number	Percent of Eligible	Amount[a]	Percent of Total	Amount[a]	Amount[a]	Percent of Total Transfer to Class
Standard Housing	6,878	39.9%	$1,962,900	37.0%	$1,712,000	$ 250,900	12.8%
Not Crowded	6,229	36.1	1,665,800	31.4	1,665,800[b]	—	—
Crowded	649	3.8	297,100	5.6	46,200	250,900	84.4
Substandard Housing	10,382	60.1	3,342,200	63.0	1,136,500	2,205,700	66.0
Not Crowded	1,817	10.5	594,200	11.2	180,500	413,700	69.6
Crowded	259	1.5	148,500	2.8	5,800	142,700	96.1
Unrehabilitatable	8,306	48.1	2,599,500	49.0	950,200	1,649,300	63.4
Potential Total	17,260	100.0	5,305,100	100.0	2,848,500	2,456,600	46.3
Less Unsuccessful House-Seekers	6,216	36.1	1,945,400	36.7[c]	711,100	1,234,300	63.5
Expected Total	11,044	63.9	3,359,700	63.3[c]	2,137,400	1,222,300	36.4[d]

[a] Rounded to nearest $100
[b] Includes $399,800 which will lower rent-income ratios to below .20
[c] % of Potential total
[d] % of Expected total

the actual participation rate will be only 63 percent. Moreover, by eliminating these households, who would devote an above average share of their subsidy to consumption increases, the proportion of the expected transfer that is devoted to R/Y savings increases from 54 to 64 percent. The net consumption effect resulting from the ability of the 2,100 successful house-seekers to access the standard stock is about $415,000. The total direct consumption-related rent increase which the allowance will induce is thus about $1.2 million, which, when averaged over the HAP submarket, represents an average of $48 per year per dwelling (Table 9–6).

In addition to these direct effects, the introduction of an allowance will likely produce indirect, consumption effects that will be borne by higher income, ineligible households. Across the market there are about 3,700 program-ineligible households occupying substandard but rehabilitatable dwellings. Under the pressure of up to 8,300 potential recipient households searching for replacement dwellings, the owners of these salvageable units are likely to upgrade in order to charge the higher rents that the program will support. It is not likely, however, that these units will be released for occupancy by recipient families. If the current income-ineligible occupants of these houses are consuming less than standard quantities of shelter at rents below C^*, we can infer that their relatively

Table 9–6. Rent Effects of a Housing Allowance Program

		Average Annual Rent Increase per Dwelling	
	Aggregate Rent Increase[a]	*HAP Submarket*	*All Standard or Rehabilitatable Dwellings*
Consumption Effects			
Direct	$1,222,300	$ 48	$ 25
Indirect	739,300	29	15
Total	1,961,600	77 (12.6%)[b]	40 (4.4%)
Primary Inflationary Effects			
Direct	399,800	16	8
Indirect	1,823,600	72	38
Total	2,223,400	88 (14.4)	46 (5.0)
Secondary Inflationary Effects	1,737,600	68 (11.1)	36 (3.9)
Total Inflationary Effects	3,961,000	156 (25.5)	82 (8.9)
Total Rent Increase	5,922,600	233 (38.1)	122 (13.3)
Preallowance Average Annual Rent	—	611	917
Number of Rental Dwellings	—	25,474	48,676

[a]Figures rounded to nearest $100.
[b]Figures in parentheses are percent of preallowance annual rent for market sector.

low housing preferences keep them from seeking better accommodations in the higher quality sectors of the stock. If housing across the HAP submarket will rent at C^* once the impact of the program has been felt, these households will not be able to secure cheaper housing than they currently occupy, save in the unrehabilitatable inventory. Consequently, though ineligible to participate in the program, they are likely to remain in their newly upgraded houses now renting at C^*, rather than relinquish their homes to HAP participants.

The consumption-related rent increase that will result from the upgrading of the dwellings occupied by over-income households can best be estimated by assuming an aggregate rent increase equal to the amount HAP participants would spend were the units to be made available to them. Thus, if 3,700 additional recipients in unrehabilitatable housing were to be able to secure these units, they would expend nearly $740,000 of their aggregate transfer to access them. This amount, which averages $29 per dwelling in the HAP submarket annually, is thus attributed to indirect consumption effects.

It is important to note that the consumption effects of a HAP would remain unchanged even if some or all of the ineligibles were to release their rehabilitatable dwellings to HAP recipients. This rent increase is a function only of the number of dwellings that are upgraded, regardless of occupancy by recipients or ineligible households. Assuming that ineligible households would bear the higher postrehab rents improves the efficiency of a HAP program because it induces a three-quarters of a million dollar increase in housing consumption at no direct program cost. Beyond increasing program efficiency, however, the effect of our assumption is to reduce the net participation rate, aggregate transfer costs and the potential for inflationary price increases. Were all 3,700 units to become available to HAP recipients, about $1.2 million would be added to the estimate of the aggregate transfer. Of this amount, $426,000 would be allocated to R/Y savings, which, as we demonstrate below, eventually would feed the inflationary price pressures created by the movement of HAP participants through the market.

In total then, housing consumption will increase by nearly $2 million as a result of the allowance. Across the HAP submarket, this represents an annual increase in rents of about $77 per dwelling, or about 13 percent of the rents currently paid for standard or rehabilitatable housing in this market sector. Among participating households, these consumption-related increases in rent account for about 36 percent of the total transfer, a figure which, in the absence of concomitant inflationary rent increases, would represent the program earmarking ratio. Since inflationary rises are also likely to occur, the earmarking ratio will be considerably higher, although earmarking above this rate will foster the HAP objectives only to the extent that price increases lead to upward filtering and an increased demand for new construction by over-income families. Finally, a significant benefit of the allowance lies in the indirect consumption effect, which produces an expansion of the flow of housing services with no additional transfer cost. Adding these effects to the direct effects increases the expansion of consumption-related rent expenditures to 58 percent of the total transfer costs.

Inflationary Effects: It is unlikely that an allowance program can be implemented without producing inflationary rent increases, particularly in a market in which nearly 30 percent of the households are eligible to participate. The magnitudes of these price rises are difficult to estimate for a number of reasons. They will be a function of all the assumptions we have made regarding market behavior following the introduction of the HAP. Like consumption effects, inflationary price rises are intimately related to participation rates, supply responses, and housing preferences among renters. Beyond these factors, however, the inflationary effects can be moderated by the behavior of nonparticipant households and by administrative actions.

Here we assume that the housing consumption of nonparticipants will not be affected by the HAP. Regardless of their ability to purchase greater levels of housing services and irrespective of the price increases they will have to pay as a result of the HAP, nonparticipants are assumed to remain in their present dwellings. This assumption makes it possible to estimate maximum potential inflationary effects and, therefore, the maximum pressures that could ultimately induce the movement of ineligible households into higher priced submarkets. Administrative procedures that could reduce these effects include, for example, phasing in the HAP or restrictions on the amount of time allowed for the household's search process. We ignore these possibilities and continue to assume universal income eligibility and the effective participation rates derived above.

The source of the inflationary price rise lies in the excess demand for standard housing that will occur at the time the program is implemented. Although the participation rate will be moderated by the unavailability of standard housing for over one-third of all potentially eligible households, this "safety valve" will not attenuate the demand sufficiently to forestall all inflationary price pressures. In fact, the aggregate transactions that will take place among the actual mover households will include about 20 percent of the dwellings in the HAP submarket. Household mobility of this magnitude will undoubtedly lead to extensive price adjustments, even if sufficient program controls exist to spread the transactions over a relatively long time period.

As a result of this HAP-induced mobility, the first observable inflationary effect will be the bidding up to C^* of all standard dwellings which are currently renting at below market rates ($<C^*$). This primary effect is

directly attributable to the disturbance of the existing price equilibrium which the allowance program will cause in the HAP submarket. Subsidized households searching for standard housing will presumably seek out the best bargains, but in order to secure already occupied housing, they will have to outbid the current occupants. Initially, they will be willing to bid up to C^*, thus driving rents up to that level across the market.

There are nearly 11,000 standard quality, occupied rental units in the market which are renting at less than C^*, and it would take over $2.2 million to bring these dwellings up to the market rate.[9] Across the HAP submarket, these price rises would average $88 per year per dwelling unit. More than $1.8 million of this price rise will be borne by nonrecipients, which thus represents an indirect inflationary effect of the program. The remaining $400,000 will be paid by HAP participants residing in uncrowded standard housing which was renting for less than C^*. This direct effect eliminates the pure transfer leakage which would otherwise occur for the small portion of recipients enjoying post-HAP rent-income ratios of less than 20 percent.

The market simulations of de Leeuw et al. [1974:33-35] detected a very similar inflationary phenomenon as a result of a full-scale allowance program. In particular, they found that in cities where the housing supply is inelastic, a large portion of the existing price discount for lower quality housing is eliminated, requiring high earmarking ratios to pay inflated rents. For cities of this type, they estimated earmarking ratios of .94 to .98 and price inflation of 30-40 percent. In the nonmetropolitan cities, the comparable figures are less dramatic, but the price effects of the allowance are, nevertheless, substantial. In the absence of any price inflation, consumption effects alone produce a 36 percent earmarking rate, nearly three times larger than that which would occur under a pure income transfer. The elimination of the price discount enjoyed by HAP participants in standard housing increases the earmarking ratio to 48 percent and produces about a 14 percent price inflation across the HAP submarket. The total price increase resulting from consumption and primary price effects of a HAP would appear to produce an earmarking rate of 125 percent, implying that program participants are forced to allocate to housing expenditures an amount of money exceeding their total transfers, but this is not the case. The misleadingly high earmarking ratio is a function of the fact that some nonparticipating households will expand their housing consumption as their dwellings are upgraded and others will be forced to pay market rents for dwellings they had been renting at bargain rates. When these effects are combined with the direct consumption effects of the HAP, the aggregate increase in rental outlays across the market exceeds the total transfers received by participating families.

Beyond the primary inflationary effect, it becomes an increasingly more speculative analytic exercise to estimate any further demand-induced rent changes that may ultimately appear in the nonmetropolitan rental market. Administrative action, the bumping of nonparticipants and an expansion of the housing supply may retard any further inflationary impact of the program. The potential for secondary inflationary price increases, however, lies in that portion of the aggregate transfer that would otherwise be used to reduce the rent-income ratios of recipient households. Mover households, in an effort to secure standard housing and maintain their program eligibility, would be willing to bid maximum rents equal to their current rent plus the total transfer they receive. This behavioral assumption implies that the transfer would be treated by recipients as a direct payment to rent; the price rise associated with this effect is, therefore, an upper-bound estimate of the result of an intense bidding war for a limited supply of standard quality dwellings. Should this potential secondary price rise materialize, all recipient households would increase their out-of-pocket housing outlays to their preallowance relative rent expense burden.

Consider, for example, a household spending $400 a year for a substandard unit. If it is eligible for a $440 subsidy which would enable it to rent a standard unit at $760 a year, its out-of-pocket expense should fall to $320 to achieve a .20 rent-income ratio. If that household cannot obtain a standard unit at $760, it would be willing to pay for that dwelling a maximum of $840 a year. At this cost, the household will be devoting no more of its income to housing than it did before receiving the subsidy, and it will occupy a standard unit. While the post-allowance optimum for the household is to occupy a standard unit at $760 a year, it would be considerably better off than it was before the program at any rent between $760 and $840. As the bidding war for standard housing expanded and permeated the market, nonmover recipient households would also be willing to allocate their R/Y savings to rent in order to avoid being dislocated by the seekers of replacement dwellings.

In total, therefore, the upper limit on secondary inflationary effects induced by the allowance is equal to the more than $1.7 million in R/Y savings received by all program participants. On an annual basis, this would add an average of an additional $68 per year to the rents of dwellings in the HAP submarket. The maximum inflationary effect is thus in excess of 25 percent of the preallowance rents in this market sector. Were this potential to be realized, the earmarking rate would, of course, be 100 percent, and the aggregate increase in market rents would be 176 percent of the total transfer.

Upward Filtering

In the face of price increases of the above magnitude, it is likely that a significant portion of the ineligible households living in the HAP submarket would be encouraged to move out of their minimum standard dwellings and into the higher priced rental or owner stock. Our model, which assumes no movement of these households, suggests that the induced demand among HAP recipients and the absorption of all standard quality vacancies could lead to a price inflation of more than 25 percent.

One result of the relative decline in the supply of housing in the HAP submarket and the concomitant rise in prices is a narrowing of the gap between post-HAP dwelling rents and rents in adjacent, higher quality submarkets. This adjustment in relative housing prices should encourage some movement out of the HAP submarket by allowance-ineligible families who can secure higher quality housing for less of a rent increase than was possible before the full impacts of the HAP had been transmitted through the market. Grigsby and Rosenburg [1975:256] not only contend that such bumping would be an important market effect of a HAP, but they argue that "allowances would serve as an acceptable substitute for new construction subsidy programs that are intended to maintain housing production at a level adequate to accommodate population growth." While they are concerned that the process of bumping would not ultimately assure that "very much of the increment to home building would occur in the central city where residential investment is vitally needed," such a concern is not relevant to the nonmetropolitan community [Grigsby and Rosenburg, 1975:256].

The potential for bumping is evident in the housing consumption patterns of ineligible households (Table 9–7). Nearly one-third of these families allocate $600 or less to housing expenses at a rent-income ratio of only .08. Since the HAP-induced demand will center on units in the $600-900 rent range, these families, whose housing priorities are obviously very low, will not be affected. In fact, demand in this sector of the market is likely to fall substantially as HAP eligibles search for standard housing, thus producing downward price pressures among the lowest quality units. Included in this low rent sector are standard quality or rehabilitatable dwellings that are renting at below market rates ($<C^*$). These price discounts are likely to be eliminated, but we would not expect this to produce any substantial change in rates of household mobility.

It is among the ineligible households occupying dwellings in the HAP submarket that the primary potential for bumping lies. The nearly one-third of the ineligibles in this sector have average incomes of about $7,200 and allocate less than 13 percent of their incomes to rent. By increasing their average housing expenditures to $120 per month, these families could move into the highest quality sectors of the rental market without exceeding a 20 percent rent-income ratio. As we indicated in Chapter 7, some upward adjustment in the rent structure for higher quality housing is necessary if suppliers are to expand output to any substantial degree.

Table 9-7. Housing Consumption of HAP-Ineligible Households

Annual Rent	Number of Ineligible Households	Percent of Ineligibles	Percent of Rent Class	Average Income	Average Rent	Average Rent-Income Ratio
≤$600	15,370	32.2%	51.8%	$6,940	$ 478	.081
$601–900	15,083	31.6	79.9	7,163	763	.125
901–1,080	8,019	16.8	92.2	8,455	1,013	.149
1,081–1,320	4,344	9.1	91.4	9,169	1,243	.159
>1,320	4,917	10.3	90.0	9,133	1,680	.229
	47,733	100.0	70.8	7,693	851	.129

Rents for newer multifamily dwellings, which currently average around $100 a month, are too low to throw off very much cash after debt service requirements have been met. The same situation exists in the high quality duplex submarket. Should HAP ineligible households who are displaced from the HAP submarket or other higher income families who are eventually bumped by this latter group choose to increase their rental expenditures to around $120 a month, the profitability of higher quality rental dwellings would be enhanced and an incentive provided to suppliers to increase output in this market sector.

While we cannot trace the movement of these families upwards through the rental stock into the new construction and ownership sectors, we can demonstrate that the mobility required to offset much of the HAP-induced price pressure would not be very great. The upward movement of only 14 percent of the ineligibles in the HAP submarket would restore the number of standard vacant units to its preallowance level. Movement in excess of this rate would, of course, make it possible for the HAP participation rate to increase beyond the 64 percent we have estimated. At the extreme, about 55 percent of these families would have to move in order to assure a 100 percent participation rate without intolerable rates of price inflation.

In the absence of any information on the supply elasticity for new construction, we cannot estimate likely HAP-induced rates of mobility across the market. It is highly probable that sufficient movement will occur to return the vacancy rate to preallowance levels and, thereby, to dilute the inflationary price pressures. In fact, if the increased demand is spread across the entire stock of standard and rehabilitatable dwellings via an upward filtering process, the inflationary impact will be considerably lower (Table 9–6). The primary effect, when averaged over the entire market, amounts to only 5 percent, while another 4 percent could be added by secondary effects. Rather than the 26 percent price rise which would occur within the HAP submarket, a 9 percent rate would be observed across the entire rental market.

THE MARKET ENVIRONMENT AND RACIAL DISCRIMINATION

In a perfectly functioning competitive market the role of the public sector should properly be defined in very narrow terms. Consumer and producer sovereignty should prevail, and the price mechanism should be allowed to drive the market toward an optimal position of resource allocation. The public sector should do nothing more than assure a socially acceptable pattern of income distribution via a system of taxation and income transfers. No economy is so neatly structured, however, and as deviations from the simplified ideal increase, so too does the need for public intervention. External effects in production and consumption, lags in supplier responses, the accrual of monopoly powers, market collusion, and indivisibilities all operate to distort and disrupt the operations of the market mechanism.

The housing market is particularly susceptible to various imperfections characteristic of the urban economy where the economic and social well-being of each individual is highly dependent on the activities of others. Traditional housing programs that directly subsidize new construction at least implicitly acknowledge the existence of neighborhood effects on production and consumption, restrictions on the mobility of various population groups, supply inelasticities that lead to unacceptably high prices for shelter services, and monopoly-like powers enjoyed by housing producers in certain market sectors. Demand side assistance programs, on the other hand, either presume that such problems are of no practical significance or, if they are viewed as a matter of serious concern, that they are the long term results of underconsumption of housing by the poor and can be overcome by a HAP. Theoretically, monopoly powers could be undermined by attracting more producers into the market; household mobility rates could be enhanced by expanding housing opportunities of the poor; and the negative effects of neighborhood decline could be lessened by an expansion of upgrading activities and maintenance outlays.

Yet another view of the problem, however, suggests a much less sanguine future for the HAP. Hartman [1975], Weaver [1975] and Grigsby and Rosenburg [1975] are of the opinion that allowances would heighten already existing market instabilities, intensify the pressures on currently stable, though threatened, neighborhoods and foster higher rates of residential abandonment. In the smaller city, however, the most serious barrier to the successful implementation of a HAP is neither market instability nor widespread social disorganization. Rather, the major deterrent is the systematic discrimination against blacks, who constitute a sizable proportion of all renter households.

Severe restrictions on the residential location choices of blacks have led not only to a highly segregated market, but also to substantial price premiums for blacks. Our estimate that black renters living in the ghetto pay 12 percent more for housing indicates that they will remain at a competitive disadvantage relative to whites under any income-conditioned program. It is possible, in fact, that their relative position in the housing market could be made even worse by the infusion of a large aggregate subsidy into a market sector where collusionary-like behavior has produced a highly inelastic supply function. In general, an income transfer in any form "cannot be expected to achieve public objectives which are structural in character [such as] . . . the openness of the market itself" [Mayer et al., 1974:150]. Manifestations of racial discrimination beyond the substantial price differential have been amply documented. The 85 percent rate of housing deprivations suffered by blacks is nearly twice that experienced by white renters. While this difference is in part the result of income differences and, to a lesser extent, of larger family sizes, at every income level blacks are two to three times as likely as whites to occupy substandard housing. Moreover, the substantially lower income elasticity of demand among blacks provides further evidence that increases in black incomes cannot be translated as readily into increased rates of housing consumption.

In the face of this evidence, it is significant that blacks account for over half the HAP participants and for three-fourths of the potential movers. If their participation in the program is unrestrained, save for the discrimination premium they must pay to secure minimally standard housing, then one impact of an allowance program would be the funneling of windfall profits to owners of black-occupied housing. More likely, however, would be a disproportionate rate of forced nonparticipation among blacks whose access to the standard quality stock is severely limited. In this case, lower income whites would be overrepresented among the participants, thus making the program a highly inequitable intervention mechanism which would serve to widen the already broad gap between white and black levels of housing consumption.

The impact of racial prejudice on the equity of an allowance program could be substantial. The program participation rate will be dictated by the availability of standard or rehabilitatable dwellings for potential recipients who must locate replacement housing in order to satisfy the minimum condition requirement. While blacks account for 54 percent of all eligibles, they account for 73 percent of those who reside in unrehabilitatable housing. Were race not a factor in the allocation of the vacant stock, then the forced nonparticipation of 75 percent of the eligible families living in unsalvageable housing would affect blacks and whites equally. Because of the overrepresentation of blacks in this group, however, the proportion of blacks among the total program participants would fall from 54 to 44 percent. To the extent that the inferior housing conditions of blacks are the cumulative results of past discrimination, the equity of the HAP will be diminished even in the absence of any future discrimination. At the other extreme is the possibility that continued discriminatory market practices will contain blacks in existing black areas. Only 39 percent of the vacant units available for HAP movers, however, are in black neighborhoods; if this represents all the housing these families will be able to secure, their representation among HAP participants would fall even further to 37 percent.

The distortion created by discrimination can be viewed in another way. The minimum condition requirement reduces actual program participation to slightly less than two-thirds of the households who are income eligible. Even in the absence of future discrimination, only around half of all black eligibles, compared to 80 percent of the white, would be served. If households searching for replacement housing must conform to the existing pattern of racial segregation in the market, only 44 percent of eligible black households would benefit from the HAP, compared to nearly nine out of ten of eligible whites.

The disproportionately low rate at which the HAP would meet the housing needs of blacks emphasizes a major problem of designing program interventions that are intended to operate through the private market system. The transfer is inherently incapable of alleviating any serious system malfunctions and may actually accentuate existing inequities. In the nonmetropolitan city, the relative position of blacks in the housing market would worsen. Indeed, it is through the elimination of potential black participants in the early stages of the program that the price effects which would be borne by white beneficiaries are dampened, a cruel irony of a program whose benefits are distributed through a distorted private market mechanism. Moreover, this problem is not readily amenable to the enforcement of open occupancy legislation, as we have demonstrated.

One should not necessarily conclude that the surest route to improving the housing welfare of blacks in nonmetropolitan southern cities is through a continued emphasis on traditional supply side assistance programs, although this proposition is not without merit. For the foreseeable future, blacks will be disproportionately represented in the eligibility pools for all low income housing assistance programs, but the likelihood of their being served may vary inversely with the extent to which the respective programs rely strictly upon private market channels to allocate scarce housing resources. Only in the traditional public housing program, which operates outside of the private market context, will poor blacks be served anywhere commensurate with their needs. Indeed, in these communities, blacks account for 48 percent of the renter population which is eligible for public housing, but comprise 82 percent of all current public housing occupants. Though the intensity of racial segregation within the public housing stock may run counter to federal policy, so too does the severely segregated private market. In the small city, at least, it may well be that the clustered development of black-occupied standard housing is to be preferred to none at all. If nothing else, our analysis suggests that a HAP be viewed as one element of a broader housing assistance program that includes a supply side component to drain off some of the potential price pressures generated by blacks who seek to satisfy housing needs that the private market cannot accommodate. With these needs in mind, we turn in the final chapter to an examination of the economics of production strategies in these cities.

NOTES TO CHAPTER 9

1. Heinberg [1971:30-35] estimates the cost of standard housing for metropolitan and nonmetropolitan households using 1969 BLS household budget data. Although his nonmetropolitan figures are 20–30 percent higher than ours, his estimates do not include any adjustments for regional variations. BLS shelter costs for the urban, nonmetropolitan south are very similar to those we have estimated [Sumka and Stegman, 1972:A-27].

2. This figure was obtained by averaging current public housing income limits for the cities in our sample. The estimate required various adjustments to total household income; our income figures include $300 deductions for the income of secondary wage earners. For nonelderly households, net income is 95 percent of adjusted total income; for households headed by a person 62 or older, 90 percent of adjusted income is used. This same procedure is used to estimate Section 236 income limits which are 135 percent of those which apply to public housing [U.S. Department of Housing and Urban Development, 1971].

3. The median income figure we use is the average 1970 median for the four cities inflated to 1972 [U.S. Bureau of the Census, 1970e; U.S. Department of Commerce, 1974:5-8]. Adjustments for family size were made by varying the percentage of the median. The 50 and 80 percent figures were used for a four person family. For one person households, they were 30 and 50 percent, respectively, and they increased to 66 and 100 percent for the largest households [*Housing and Development Reporter,* 1975:30:0055].

4. The minimum condition housing gap design is, of course, only one of many possible program specifications. Since our intent is not to compare various program designs, but to examine the market implications of the allowance approach in general, we provide no analyses of such alternatives as "percent of rent" specifications or hybrid formulations such as the "rent-conditioned housing gap." Economic analyses of a number of designs were performed by Carlton and Ferreira [1975] who found the housing gap design to be among the most efficient and equitable of the alternatives. General descriptions of a number of approaches are also presented by de Leeuw et al. [1970]. The minimum condition housing gap plan, which has a number of attractive features and is the design being employed in HUD's experiments [U.S. Department of Housing and Urban Development, 1975a], is the only design we consider.

5. If the transfer to these households is assumed to be directly applied to rent, then the household's post allowance contribution to rent is:

$$R = C^* - T, \tag{1}$$

where T, the transfer, is:

$$T = C^* - .20Y. \tag{2}$$

Substituting for C^* in (2) yields:

$$R = .20Y, \tag{3}$$

where Y is the household's preallowance income. Thus if the household's preallowance rent, R_0, exceeded 20 percent of its income:

$$R_0 > .20Y \tag{4}$$

it follows that:

$$R_0 > R. \tag{5}$$

If the preallowance rent is less than 20 percent:

$$R_0 < .20Y, \tag{6}$$

and

$$R_0 < R. \tag{7}$$

6. Since the income elasticity for black households was substantially below the market average, disaggregating this analysis by race would reduce our estimate of rent increases. On the other hand, the elasticity for one and two person households, who account for two-thirds of the HAP eligibles, is somewhat higher than the average. Disaggregation of the analysis would be unnecessarily complex and would suggest far more accuracy than we actually can attain.

7. We are assuming that recipient households will treat the transfer as permanent income, which seems likely over the long run. The estimates of permanent household income are derived in Appendix B.

8. Coincidentally, perhaps, this is precisely the proportion of households in one of the HUD experiments that remained in units which were upgraded [U.S. Department of Housing and Urban Development, 1975a:29].

9. This estimate is the number of standard, occupied units for which the current tenants pay less than they would given the HAP definition of C^*. For these dwellings, the aggregate rent deficit was computed as the difference between the current rent and C^* for a family of the same size as the current occupant.

✳ *Chapter 10*

New Construction
Strategies

INTRODUCTION

Weaver [1975:247–55], Schechter [U. S. Senate, 1973], and Downs [1974:144] have argued that the complete abandonment of production programs in favor of income transfers would represent a serious policy mistake in metropolitan centers. In the smaller city such a policy reversal would be particularly intolerable. Despite serious difficulties on a national level, traditional new construction programs seem to work reasonably well in the stable nonmetropolitan market and, although they are by no means inexpensive, they tend to deliver housing services well within the cost ceilings established by the Congress. Though perhaps less efficient than demand side programs because of their higher costs and because they may force some families to overconsume housing, the continuation of production subsidies is warranted on equity grounds. By serving those who would not be served by a market-oriented income transfer program, relatively inefficient supply side programs can contribute to the overall equity of nonmetropolitan housing assistance efforts. Moreover, they remain an important element of an overall housing improvement strategy. No amount of demand side assistance can overcome the market impediments that help perpetuate substandard occupancy, nor are such efforts capable of dealing with serious shortages of standard housing, except at politically unacceptable levels of funding. Accordingly, it is important to the future of these cities that national policy makers not generalize too broadly about the problems with production subsidies and the failures of the low rent public housing program.

While many analysts continue to argue that traditional supply side programs can contribute substantially to inner-city housing improvement efforts, and that serious errors in management rather than program design have been chiefly responsible for current difficulties, we have no empirical basis for supporting or rejecting that proposition [U. S. Senate, 1973:3, 15–20]. This chapter is limited to demonstrating the continued feasibility, competitive advantage, and appropriate role of these production subsidies in the smaller city. It begins with a discussion of the continued need for an active public housing program in the nonmetropolitan city and proceeds to an estimate of required program scale. A comparative cost analysis of public housing in the nation, in metropolitan cities and in our study universe, indicates that, despite serious financial problems nationally, the program remains viable in the smaller community. We define an appropriate role for subsidized, moderate income production programs in the second section. Here we focus on the possible market softening impacts of shallowly subsidized housing and the problem of expanding the supply in a market where, despite production subsidies, assisted families might have to increase their out-of-pocket contributions to rent. The section concludes with a comparative cost analysis of moderate income housing in our study cities and in metropolitan cities. In the final section, we summarize our findings and comment on the potential impact of the recently enacted federal leased housing assistance program.

LOW RENT PUBLIC HOUSING

Throughout most of its nearly 40 years of operation, the public housing program has been the backbone of federal low income housing policy and the main ingredient of central city housing improvement efforts. At the end of 1973, in excess of 60 percent of the nation's 1.3 million low rent dwellings were located in core cities, including 13 percent of the total which were concentrated in six cities with populations of more than a million [Department of Housing and Urban Development, 1973: Tables 145 and 147]. The program's central city image has been further reinforced by the metropolitan orientation of most evaluations of its operations and impacts—be they sociological studies of tenant life styles and behavior, assessments of project location and neighborhood change, or econometric analyses of program costs.[1] In spite of this emphasis, the importance of public housing to nonmetropolitan communities is indicated by the fact that 7 out of every 10 public housing authorities are located outside of SMSA's, as are half of all housing projects and one-quarter of all public housing units. Perhaps partly because of the problems highlighted by some of the above evaluations, a movement away from central city domination of the program is beginning to become evident.

Between 1968 and 1973, for example, around 35 percent of all public housing units placed under annual contributions contracts for the first time were located in nonmetropolitan areas, including 41 percent of all units placed under contract in 1973 [U. S. Department of Housing and Urban Development, 1973: Table 145]. In short, a substantial and growing proportion of the low rent public housing inventory is located in smaller communities.

That the nonmetropolitan community has been an active client of the public housing program is sufficient reason to inquire into the local ramifications of potentially significant program changes or of the curtailment of national public housing activity. Nonmetropolitan program feedback should be considered routinely in national policy decisions, because the smaller city stands to lose relatively more than its metropolitan counterpart should the federal government cease constructing or heavily subsidizing new construction for low income occupancy. The publicly-owned stock of rental housing represents not only a larger portion of the nonmetropolitan city's housing inventory but also a substantially greater share of its rental stock. At the end of 1973, for example, public housing units accounted for almost 6 percent of the nonmetropolitan housing stock, compared to around 4 and 2 percent of the central city and metropolitan inventories, respectively. More importantly, while low rent units represented just 5 and 7 percent, respectively, of metropolitan and central city rental dwellings, fully 15 percent of the rental stock of nonmetropolitan communities across the country was public housing [U. S. Department of Housing and Urban Development, 1974b: Table 160; U. S. Bureau of the Census, 1970b].

That public housing is not a newcomer to the smaller city is important to our ultimate set of nonmetropolitan policy recommendations. National program statistics indicate, for example, that the proportion of the rental stock in our study universe accounted for by public housing (11%) is generally typical of the national, nonmetropolitan experience. That housing deprivations in the smaller city are dominated by physical stock deficiencies suggests that a program of direct construction for the poor may be more important there than in metropolitan cities, where housing problems tend to center more on excessive housing expenses and poor neighborhood environments. Moreover, at least in our study cities, the program disproportionately serves blacks; in the face of racial antagonisms in the private market and the apparent apathy of the local government toward the problems of market discrimination, the program has the potential to accomplish more to improve the housing conditions of racial minorities than does any other government effort yet devised.

The above data indicate that, despite the failure of local communities to allocate tax revenues and discretionary federal funds to improve community housing standards, the use of earmarked federal monies to construct and operate housing for the poor has been institutionalized in more than two thousand nonmetropolitan cities across the country. Finally, the widespread acceptance of public housing in smaller cities implies that the basic philosophical battles over government-owned housing have been fought and won there, and that in each of these communities there exists some minimal housing development and management expertise which can be expanded in the future.

Despite the relatively large share of the nonmetropolitan rental stock already contained in public housing developments, it would still take a substantial increase in program size to house all income-eligible families who would not be served by a market-oriented housing allowance program. The continued need for supply side activity is not a function of the anticipated failures of a demand side assistance effort, but of serious stock shortages that would either result in the forced nonparticipation from a HAP of thousands of needy families, or in substantial price inflation in low and moderate rental submarkets. More specifically, we estimated that some 6,600 low income families, three-quarters of whom are black, would have to drop out of a housing allowance program due to a shortage of physically standard, privately owned rental housing. To rehouse all of these families would require an 80 percent expansion of the public housing stock, and would mean that after demolition of all unrehabilitatable dwellings, almost one-quarter of the nonmetropolitan rental stock would be publicly owned and operated.

Although the magnitude of the required expansion of the public housing inventory may seem unreasonably high, it should be recalled that these production requirements are net of the approximately 11,000 low income families who would receive allowances. That the total number of housing-deficient families is so high is a function of market conditions and not of unrealistic program assumptions. More than likely, the resource requirement of a full-scale program of allowances and public housing construction is too great to implement at once. For example, the HAP could be phased in over a five-year period, and the public housing component of the program could also be phased in after an initial delay. If production of the required 6,600 low rent dwellings were begun in the second year of the HAP and spread over a seven-year period, annual construction goals would not be terribly out of line with past production experience. To achieve the seven-year goal, fewer than 950 public housing units per year would have to be built in nonmetropolitan cities in North Carolina, requiring the construction of around 38 dwellings a year in each of the 25 cities in our universe. This suggests that even with the implementation of a housing allowance program, the level of public housing activity cannot be reduced below previous levels and quite likely should be moderately increased to avoid serious inequities and inflationary effects of a HAP.

Public Housing Client Groups

The coordination of a HAP with a substantial program of deep production subsidies raises two related issues. The first concerns the capacity and willingness of local housing authorities to become housers of last resort as the vast majority of the low risk poor opt for allowances, while the second involves the establishment in the nonmetropolitan city of a racially dichotomized low income housing assistance program. With respect to the first issue, we have no way of assessing the readiness of LHA's to meet the needs of the hypothetical target population which would not benefit from a HAP. An examination of the profile of present public housing occupants, however, suggests that in the past they have taken seriously the responsibility of housing families who have the greatest difficulty obtaining standard housing in the private market: namely, blacks, female-headed households and large families. We have already indicated that over 80 percent of all public housing tenants in our study cities are black, although blacks account for about half of all income eligible renters. Implementation of a HAP would likely increase the black proportion of effective demanders of public housing, because the supply shortfall is concentrated in predominantly black-occupied submarkets, and discriminatory market practices prevent blacks from accessing the standard stock.

Transcending, but not independent of, the issue of race is that of family composition and size, the former relating to the subjective determination of socially acceptable behavior and the latter to the objective reality of construction costs and public subsidies. Typically, private landlords prefer not to rent to families headed by women with young children for reasons which are based partly on actual experience and partly on unfounded conviction, including: the tendency to shy away from renting to welfare recipients, many of whom are female-headed families; the fear that unattached females are more likely than other household types to disturb neighbors; and the related concern that younger children of single women are likely to be poorly supervised and contribute to the rapid deterioration of their housing. For these reasons, low income families headed by women tend to be disproportionately represented on public housing waiting lists. In our study cities, nonelderly, female-headed households account for 41 percent of all eligibles and a higher 47 percent of all tenants. Thus, it is unlikely that implementation of a HAP would require LHA's to alter their admissions policies with respect to female-headed households.

In general, the large poor family is the worst housed family. Not only is the supply of large, standard quality rental dwellings very limited, but most are beyond the large family's financial reach. In efforts to compromise its shelter requirements but still consume standard quality housing, the large family will frequently accept less space per capita than others, only to find landlords unwilling to accept their tenancy for fear that overcrowded conditions will hasten the deterioration of their properties. In the nonmetropolitan city, families with more than five members account for about 16 percent of all renters and a slightly higher 18 percent of all public housing eligibles. To the credit of the local housing authorities in these cities, however, 30 percent of all tenant families have five or more members, which is more than twice the proportion of large families in public housing across the country. The ability of LHA's to house large families in such impressive numbers is likely a function of lower development costs than those prevailing in most metropolitan centers, a matter we discuss in more detail in the following section. The overall profile of public housing seems to parallel rather closely the characteristics of the low income population that we anticipate would not benefit from a program of housing allowances and reflects the willingness of local authorities to serve high risk groups in the nonmetropolitan city.

The public housing programs in these cities will remain predominantly black with or without an allowance program. As long as public housing is the sole low income housing effort in the nonmetropolitan city, few serious problems are posed by the fact that the program is dominated by blacks, who account for just one-third of all renters and less than half of all income eligibles. The introduction of a HAP, which would disproportionately serve lower income whites, raises the specter of a racially based, dual housing assistance program. To oversimplify somewhat, it could be argued that while whites would receive income transfers that would permit them to exercise free choice in the larger market, shop around for bargains, select favored neighborhoods, and negotiate conditions of occupany with landlords as do unsubsidized renters, similarly circumstanced blacks would have to accept housing assistance on a "take it or leave it" basis. Whereas whites could make market decisions, blacks would be told where they must live.

Whether a de facto dual program of low income housing assistance that is entirely federally funded raises legitimate litigable issues we do not know for sure. That it raises serious moral and welfare issues is quite certain. The dilemma simply highlights the fact of longstanding discriminatory market practices that have not been attacked successfully by any level of government. While the underlying problems cannot be solved entirely before efforts are made to improve housing conditions, they are too firmly institutionalized to disappear on their own accord. At minimum, efforts to expand the coverage of federal open occupancy laws must be made, and housing authorities should be encouraged to develop scattered site projects. The dual market system must be eventually dismantled.

The Cost of Public Housing

As we indicated in Chapter 8, public housing program costs in nonmetropolitan cities are substantially below national figures. Indeed, our best estimate is that total development costs in our sample cities average around 30 percent less than in the nation at large, while operating outlays are lower by 41 percent.[2] Because the federal government pays the capital costs of public housing, lower development costs directly translate into lower subsidies. The federal cost of amortizing the typical public housing unit in the nonmetropolitan city is around $102 per month, or 56% lower than the national average.[3] Similarly, because housing authorities traditionally have been responsible for setting rents sufficiently high to pay all operating costs, lower operating outlays translate directly into lower tenant housing expenses. Thus, the average nonmetropolitan public housing rent of $37 is approximately 22 percent less than the national average of $45 (Table 10–1).

Table 10–1. A Comparison of Nonmetropolitan and National Public Housing Operating Experiences, 1972

	Nation Per Unit/Month	Nonmetropolitan Sample Per Unit/Month
Operating Income		
Rental Income	$45.08	$37.06
Other Income	2.23	5.30
Operating Subsidy	13.46	—
Total Operating Income	$60.77	$42.36
Operating Expenses		
Routine		
Administrative	$10.00	$ 9.36
Tenant Services	.83	.87
Utilities	15.52	14.76
Ordinary Maintenance and Operations	21.93	11.01
Payment in Lieu of Taxes (*PILOT*)	2.83	1.95
Collection Losses	.48	.09
Other General Expenses	5.63	2.58
Total Routine Expenses	$57.22	$40.62
Nonroutine Expenses	*4.43*	*3.26*
Total Expenses	$61.65	$43.88
Average Development Cost per Dwelling	$20,967	$14,641

Sources: National program data [HUD, 1973: Table 124]; nonmetropolitan data from forms no. HUD-52599 and 52564 for 1973.

The reason that public housing rents in the smaller city do not reflect the full impact of lower operating costs is because recent legislation has authorized the federal government to contribute to the operations of housing authorities whose rental incomes have not kept pace with rising costs. This has resulted in the typical public housing unit across the country receiving a monthly operating subsidy of $13.46 in 1972 [U. S. Department of Housing and Urban Development, 1973: Table 124]. Because lower operating outlays in the smaller city have enabled local authorities to build up reserve funds out of which operating deficits can be paid, as of 1972 none of the housing authorities in our study cities ever had received any operating subsidies. Consequently, the operating subsidy program has increased the gap between the public costs associated with national and nonmetropolitan public housing programs, with the result that tenants in the smaller city pay a higher portion of direct program costs than do tenants in programs across the country.

While nonmetropolitan administrative program costs are less than ten percent below the national average of $10 per month per dwelling, the major cost saving is in the area of maintenance and operations. Per unit expenditures in the smaller city averaged just $11 per month in 1972, or about half the national average. This cost difference, which is also reflected to a lesser degree in nonroutine maintenance outlays, is likely a function both of lower wage rates for maintenance personnel in the nonmetropolitan city and the lower average age of its public housing stock. Of these two factors, differential wage rates is, by far, the more important.

Since public housing dwellings are not assessed for tax purposes by local governments, housing authorities make payments in lieu of taxes (*PILOT*) to support municipal services received by their tenants. Because *PILOT* payments are a function of public housing rents, these costs are relatively low in the smaller city; in 1972, the nonmetropolitan monthly cost of $1.95 per unit was 45 percent less than nationally. Moreover, since the cost of public housing to the local community is the difference between the *PILOT* and the taxes due were public housing fully taxable, and since tax rates in smaller cities are generally below the national average, the gap widens even further between the full public costs of low rent housing in the nonmetropolitan city and the country at large.

Two additional operating cost items are worth noting, even though neither accounts for any significant cost differences among city classes. The extremely low cost of collection losses in the smaller city implies the absence of high and sustained levels of rent delinquency and a high level of management capability. The second item, the cost of tenant services, is of interest not because it is low, but because it exceeds the national average. While we cannot comment on the quality of services rendered public housing tenants, nor on the kinds of services that they can be provided at an annual cost of less than ten dollars per household, the fact that average expenditures in nonmetropolitan programs are above national levels implies that concern for tenant welfare is no less important there than in public housing programs elsewhere in the country.

The national program data summarized above reflect the operating characteristics of all public housing programs in the nation. Although comparably rich data are not available for only central city programs, de Leeuw [1970b:27] found average operating costs in 23 large central city authorities in 1968 that were around 20 percent higher than the 1972 costs in our sample cities. If his estimates are adjusted to 1972 by the 7 percent annual rate of inflation prevailing between 1965 and 1968, then per unit operating costs in these large authorities were around 60 percent higher than in our smaller sample cities, and around half again as large as in the nation as a whole.

Although none of the above analyses reflects the full revenue impact of the several Brooke Amendments which redefined tenant incomes for rent-paying purposes and established rent ceilings at one-quarter of income, more recent data would not be likely to alter our major conclusions. In 1973 the combined effect of the Brooke Amendments was to reduce monthly rental income by an average $13 per dwelling for the nation as a whole.[4] In 1972, the comparable revenue decline in our study cities was less than half the national loss, or $6.20 per dwelling. Clearly, the loss of any rental income impairs the capacity of local authorities to deliver housing services, and unless the revenue loss is offset by operating subsidies, smaller city programs like those in metropolitan centers are likely to suffer. Nevertheless, despite the general financial problems confronting the nation's low-rent housing effort, the program remains viable in the nonmetropolitan city.

The Relative Costs of Public Housing and Income Transfers

We have not estimated the costs of a full-scale combined HAP-public housing assistance program since, on the face of it, the required magnitude of an effort to eliminate all low income housing deprivations would be so great as to make such a program financially infeasible. Regardless of eventual program scale, however, relative cost differences between the two program components are important. In the previous chapter, we estimated the average HAP transfer payment to be $23 per month, excluding federal and local administrative costs. Measurement of the federal costs of supporting a single public housing unit is more troublesome, and involves the translation of capital costs to carrying charges, estimates of taxes foregone, and discount rates. Our best estimate, however, is that the average nonmetropolitan public housing unit costs the federal government approximately $102 per month, or almost five times the cost of the average housing allowance payment. Thus, for each public housing eligible family who is served by a HAP instead of public housing, taxpayers will save around $950 a year. Since a full-scale allowance program could conceivably meet the needs of around two-thirds of all public housing eligibles, or around 11,000 families, long run savings would amount to some $10.5 million a year over the costs required to house the HAP participants in public housing.

The fact that a large scale program is not likely to materialize in no way minimizes the importance of these substantial cost differences. Market and housing conditions are such in the smaller city that a substantial portion of low income families could improve their housing circumstances with very moderate restricted income transfers. Clearly, federal housing resources are not great enough to make a substantial dent in the low income housing problem through deep production subsidies. Despite the fact that financial conditions of nonmetropolitan local housing authorities remain sound, new construction programs will always be costly relative to existing stock oriented efforts.

MODERATE INCOME HOUSING

The appropriate role for a shallow subsidy production program in the nonmetropolitan city is much less obvious than it is for public housing. For one thing, we were able to estimate public housing needs in conjunction with the simultaneous implementation of a housing allowance program. Because production requirements were defined in terms of the forced nonparticipation rate under a HAP, maximum production requirements were scaled down by more than two-thirds of what they would be in the absence of a demand side program. No clear-out guidelines are available with respect to moderate income production needs. Under present program criteria, which define income eligibility in terms of a multiple of maximum public housing income limits, fully one-quarter of all nonmetropolitan renters are eligible for moderate income housing assistance. The income limits range from $4,600 for single individuals to $9,200 for households with 7 or more members. These income limits correspond to rent-paying abilities that bracket the broad, middle range of the nonmetropolitan rent structure, suggesting that subsidized moderate income housing might well compete for tenants with the private stock. This hypothesis is supported by the fact that the average rent for existing, subsidized, moderate income housing in these cities ($73) is slightly lower than the marketwide mean rent for standard housing ($81).

While an increasing rate of public housing construction could weaken the market for the worst quality housing, lower prices would benefit the poor families locked into this stock. Moreover, market operations at the bottom are relatively independent of activities in other sectors, since the occupants of seriously substandard housing typically cannot afford standard quality dwellings. The market implications of higher rates of moderate income housing are much less clear. We have indicated previously that the nonmetropolitan rent structure is already relatively depressed; consequently, any substantial level of new production in the moderate reaches of the market could depress rents even further, discourage capital investment and contribute to a long-run decline in maintenance and housing quality. Alternatively, an expansion of supply in this market sector could eventually drive vacancies down to the bottom of the market by permitting the upward filtering of families into the better quality stock. Precisely what market outcomes would accompany a moderate income program cannot be determined without knowing more about the kinds of dwellings released by families moving into the new stock and the resultant chains of moves induced by this initial round of mobility. We will return to this matter in our later discussion of the relationships among the components of a nonmetropolitan housing assistance program.

A major problem inherent in defining the role of moderate income programs in the smaller city relates to the housing tastes and market behavior of income-eligible families. Almost two-thirds of all moderate income eligibles suffer from one or more housing deficiencies, including 44 percent who occupy physically inadequate shelter (Table 9–2). The high incidence of substandard occupancy is consistent with our earlier determination that the nonmetropolitan rental market is characterized by serious stock constraints and inadequate supplies of good quality housing. A high deficiency rate for nonpoor families is also consistent with generally low levels of housing preferences. To some extent, the latter proposition is supported by the fact that the mean rent of all eligibles is only $63, with the typical family allocating only 17 percent of its income to rent. Even though the rent-income ratios are calculated using gross incomes, while existing moderate income programs allow substantial deductions from income when computing household rent-paying ability, a large proportion of eligibles would have to increase their out-of-pocket contributions to rent in order to occupy subsidized moderate income dwellings. In other words, for many eligibles, subsidized project rents, which are typically calculated at one-quarter of adjusted household income, would exceed the current rents these families are now paying in the private market.

We have no way of estimating the proportion of all eligibles who would elect to increase their housing consumption by moving into moderate income dwellings at higher rents than they currently pay. To the extent that the market is functioning relatively smoothly, the low consumption levels will reflect low housing preferences, and relatively few eligibles are likely to be attracted to subsidized housing at the cost of increased rent expenditures. On the other hand, in Chapter 7 we indicated that vacancy rates in the relatively small high quality black-occupied submarket were under 2 percent, which suggests that moderate income blacks may be forced to under-consume housing because of supply shortages (Table 7–6). Even in the high quality white-occupied submarket, the 3 percent vacancy rate is too low to provide full freedom of movement and choice for those who have both the resources and desire to improve their housing conditions.

To pursue the matter of identifying a pool of effective demanders for shallowly subsidized new construction, we separate all eligibles into three groups. The first is comprised of the 16 percent of all families whose current rent-income ratios exceed one-quarter of their incomes; though it includes occupants of both substandard and standard housing, the latter account for an overwhelming 95 percent of all renters in this cohort. The remaining two groups consist of families who are not burdened by excessive housing costs, with one occupying standard and the other substandard housing. The standardly-housed families, who enjoy a mean relative housing expense level of just 16 percent of their incomes, account for 41 percent of all eligibles. Occupants of substandard dwellings, including a small number of overcrowded families, comprise the remaining 43 percent of all potential program participants.

Of the three groups, only the first, the 16 percent who currently allocate more than one-quarter of their incomes to rent, would indisputably benefit by occupying new subsidized housing. By moving, they would obtain housing of equal or superior quality to that which they currently occupy at lower rents than they currently pay. The most serious reservation we have with defining this group as effective demanders for subsidized housing, however, is that solving these families' excessive housing cost problems through a production program would be grossly inefficient. Since most of these eligibles are already standardly housed, their problems could be most efficiently dealt with through housing allowances. Since their incomes are sufficiently high to pay for minimally standard housing, however, they are not eligible to participate in a HAP according to the program design standards elaborated in the last chapter. Were we to broaden eligibility criteria sufficiently to include these moderate income families in a HAP, overall eligibility rates would soar, as would average and aggregate transfer costs. Transfer leakage, or the proportion of all allowances used by participants to lower rent-income ratios, would also rise and potential inflationary effects of the HAP would, likewise, increase. In short, families in this group fall between programs and would not likely benefit directly by any potential public sector effort.

Nor do we choose to define as effective demanders of moderate income housing a significant proportion of standardly-housed families who are not spending disproportionate shares of their incomes for rent. While technically eligible for participation in shallow subsidy programs on income grounds, none of these families suffers from any measurable housing deficiency. This 41 percent of all eligibles represents the mainstream moderate income population which the unassisted rental market serves very well. Of the three cohorts, only a portion of the third, the 43 percent of all eligibles who occupy substandard housing at rents less than one-quarter of their incomes, represent potential demanders of subsidized moderate income housing to whom the public sector should be responsive.

For most of this last group of families, the move into higher quality housing would be at the cost of higher rents than they currently pay. Given the tight market conditions in the better quality multifamily stock, those eligibles whose current housing expenses are equal to or exceed the prevailing rents in subsidized housing are defined as the target population for the nonmetropolitan moderate income rental program. In effect, we judge the housing preferences of the others in this cohort to be sufficiently low that they would not elect to increase their out-of-pocket rent payments by the necessary amount in order to move from substandard to standard subsidized housing.

More specifically, the target population is comprised of the ten percent of all families in the third cohort who occupy substandard housing at rents competitive with those charged in moderate income programs. An important implication of this decision rule is that the nonmetropolitan need for moderate income housing is reduced to 4 percent for all eligibles, representing 1 percent of the total renter population, or just 650 dwellings. Moreover, 90 percent of all moderate income eligibles who occupy substandard housing at relatively low rents were judged to be unlikely candidates for assisted housing on the basis of their current consumption patterns. When this latter group is combined with the 16 percent of all eligibles who are standardly housed at excessive rent-income ratios, around one-half of all potential program participants, all of whom are housing deficient in one way or another, will not be served by any housing assistance effort.

While it could be argued that the criteria for defining the effective demand for moderate income construction in the smaller city are too rigid, a conservative approach to estimating demand is warranted by virtue of the potential destabilizing effects that an excess supply of housing can have in the moderate reaches of the market. Should more inadequately housed families than we anticipate indicate a willingness to increase their housing expenditures in exchange for obtaining high quality housing, production could be expanded without any adverse market effects since the dwellings vacated by these renters would all be substandard. What must be avoided, however, is the cumulation of vacancies in the rent range above HAP submarket levels.

The Cost of Moderate Income Housing

Public housing is developed by local housing authorities with the proceeds of government-backed securities that are fully amortized by federal annual contributions. Consequently, public housing rents are about one-half of what they would be without the deep subsidy [Taggart, 1970:22–3]. Existing moderate income programs, under which some 550,000 dwellings have been produced nationally, require private sponsorship and involve different financing and subsidy systems. The Section 221(d)(3) program, under which 188,000 housing units were produced, provided nonprofit or limited profit sponsors with direct federally-insured loans at below market interest rates (BMIR). In 1968, the direct federal loan approach was replaced by one requiring the participation of private lenders. Under the Section 236 program, more than 370,000 moderate income dwellings have been developed by limited and nonprofit sponsors with the proceeds of private FHA-insured mortgages on which interest payments are subsidized by the federal government [U. S. Department of Housing and Urban Development, 1974b: Table 176]. The subsidy is sufficient to reduce the sponsor's effective mortgage interest rate to one percent. In contrast to public housing rents, which traditionally were pegged to cover only operating costs, moderate income dwelling rents must cover all operating and capital costs in addition to nominal interest payments. Consequently, rather than the 50 percent rent discount prevailing in the public housing program, moderate income rents are proportionately higher, but still substantially below the rents for otherwise comparable housing in the private market.

We cannot say for sure whether the nonmetropolitan community lacks the professional packaging expertise upon which nonprofit sponsors must rely to realize their sponsorship objectives; whether smaller city developers lack the necessary program information and experience with government housing efforts that is necessary for their efficient utilization of available subsidy funds; or whether the private sector has little interest in developing limited-profit housing developments which would compete with their unassisted stock. Whatever the reasons, however, subsidized moderate income programs have not gained a foothold in the nonmetropolitan city comparable to that of the public housing program. At the end of 1973, 86 percent of all moderate income dwellings were located in metropolitan cities [U.S. Department of Housing and Urban Development, 1974b: Table 176]. While we cannot account fully for the relatively low level of moderate income program activity in nonmetropolitan cities, it is likely that the reasons are not merely capital and operating cost constraints.

The development costs for the fewer than 200 moderate income dwellings in our sampling universe averaged around 35 percent less than in the nation at large [U.S. Department of Housing and Urban Development, 1974b: Table 264]. In 1973, nonmetropolitan vacancy rates were less than one percent, operating costs were maintained at their 1971 levels and cash flow was positive, averaging $100 a dwelling (Table 10–2). Although comparable operating data are not available for moderate income dwellings across the country, in Chapter 8 we indicated the general need for operating subsidies, as rental incomes have not kept pace with rising costs. Inasmuch as mean rents for Section 236 housing across the country in 1972 were $132, or almost twice the nonmetropolitan level, and substantial numbers of metropolitan project mortgages have been foreclosed recently or assigned to FHA because project operating incomes fell below debt service requirements [U.S. Department of Housing and Urban Development, 1974b: Table 266], it is reasonable to infer that nonmetropolitan operating costs are substantially lower than those in metropolitan areas. Thus, the competitive advantage of smaller cities in developing and maintaining viable moderate income projects is about as great as it is with respect to public housing.

More important, perhaps, than the comparative cost advantage enjoyed by nonmetropolitan developments is their stability of operations over a period of generally rising prices. Between 1971 and 1973, for example, statewide vacancy rates were maintained at just 1 percent, while monthly average operating outlays increased by only 4 percent, or by around $1 a unit (Table 10–2). Offsetting the cost increase was a moderate 4 percent increase in average rentals. On a relative basis, there were no dramatic shifts in expenditure categories for the state's subsidized housing between 1971 and 1973. Maintenance and repair outlays grew from around 9 percent of gross collectibles to 13 percent, while the combined costs of taxes and insurance declined from around 18 percent to 15 percent of collectibles. In both 1971 and 1973, after debt service, net cash flow per dwelling amounted to 11 percent of collectibles or to around $100 a year.

Despite these figures, we cannot conclude that the revenue cost squeeze affecting moderate income projects across the country will not

Table 10–2. Operating Statement for Subsidized Moderate Income Housing in Nonmetropolitan Universe, 1971 and 1973

	1971		1973	
	Per Unit per Month	*% of Gross Collectibles*	*Per Unit per Month*	*% of Gross Collectibles*
Gross Collectibles	$72.22		$75.43	
Less:				
Vacancy/Bad Debt	.22	.3%	.83	1.1%
Effective Rental Income	72.00		74.60	
Less:				
Property Taxes and Insurance	13.13	18.2	11.31	15.0
Maintenance and Repair	6.58	9.1	10.14	13.4
Operating Expenditures	.88	1.2	1.08	1.4
Utilities	.06	*	—	*
Administrative	8.68	12.0	7.50	9.9
Replacement Reserve	3.37	4.7	3.93	5.2
Total Expenses	32.69	45.3	33.96	45.0
Net Cash Flow Before Debt Service	39.30	54.4	40.64	53.9
Debt Service	31.16	43.2	32.18	42.7
Net Cash Flow After Debt Service	8.14	11.2	8.46	11.2
Average Development Cost Per Dwelling	$11,663			

* Less than .1%

Source: FHA Form No. 2558 for projects for 1971 and 1973. Development Cost is average of development costs for all moderate income dwellings in study cities.

eventually catch up with projects located in large and small communities in North Carolina. Development costs in smaller cities are, however, likely to remain substantially below metropolitan levels for some time to come. In addition, the smaller community typically is characterized by lower tax rates than central cities, where recent increases have been partly responsible for the financial problems burdening project sponsors. In nonmetropolitan projects, utilities are paid for by the tenants, so the recent steep rise in fuel and electricity costs is not reflected in the project operating statements. Even though these costs remain the responsibility of tenants, the higher rates reduce rent-paying abilities. In small cities in North Carolina, as elsewhere, there is an upper limit to what moderate income families are willing and able to pay for housing. However, the relationships among tenant incomes, project rents, and operating expenditures are much more stable than they are across the country.

The Relationships Between Production
Subsidies and Housing Allowances

The production of moderate income housing should not be considered in isolation from public housing construction, and neither production program is independent of a HAP. Since we estimate the direct federal cost of subsidizing a moderate income dwelling in the smaller city to be around $47 per month, or less than half the cost of supporting a public housing unit, there is an obvious incentive to produce more of the former and less of the latter if such a tradeoff would not impede the achievement of low income housing objectives.[5] Obviously, for such a program tradeoff to be successful, higher levels of moderate income production must induce families out of standard or rehabilitatable dwellings that can be occupied by lower income households who are living in unsalvageable units. Every moderate income dwelling that induces such a chain of moves saves the federal government $32 a month. This savings is the difference between the direct federal cost of public and moderate income housing ($102–$47) less the cost of the income transfer ($23) to which the low income occupant is entitled.

For the nonmetropolitan city, potential savings to the federal government are not likely to be substantial given the estimated demand for moderate income housing of only around 650 dwellings, and the tradeoff of moderate for low income construction is only possible if the new occupants of subsidized housing vacate rehabilitatable units. Since 80 percent of all substandard housing occupied by demanders of moderate income housing is not salvageable, the construction of the full supply of 650 subsidized dwellings would release only 130 houses that could be occupied by lower income families. At maximum then, replacing 130 public housing units with moderate income housing would save the federal government some $4,200 a month. With implementation of the subsidized housing program, including the moderate for low income tradeoff, the nonmetropolitan housing assistance program mix would be as follows: of the 90 percent of eligibles who would participate in low income programs, around 11,000 families or 62 percent would be receiving housing allowances, and another 38 percent would occupy new public housing units; 650 moderate income families, or 4 percent of all eligibles, would occupy new moderate income housing. Alternatively, all housing deficient low income families would be served, while just 8 percent of all housing-deficient moderate income eligibles would benefit from the program mix and scale we propose.

THE FUTURE OF SUPPLY SIDE PROGRAMS

Housing conditions in nonmetropolitan cities cannot be materially improved without substantial levels of subsidized supply-side activity. Because of inadequate incomes, large quantities of rental housing that cannot be feasibly rehabilitated, and serious racial barriers that restrict residential mobility, there is a strong and continuing need for an active public housing program. The required public housing effort is partly a function of the eventual scale of a housing allowance program and the extent to which a moderate increase in shallow subsidy program activity would eventually loosen supply in the lower market reaches.

The integration of component programs in the smaller city, while important, is not as delicate an issue as it is in metropolitan centers where so many neighborhoods are in an advanced state of deterioration or could be destabilized inadvertently by program activity of the wrong kind or magnitude. In the nonmetropolitan community, program level and mix have important client and cost implications, but less serious implications for community development. For example, the more public housing and the less housing allowance activity, the more blacks will be served, the greater the potential number of unrehabilitatable dwellings that will be forced off the market, and the more costly the housing assistance program. In the reverse case, proportionately more whites would be served, bigger reductions in excess housing expenses would result, fewer substandard houses would be withdrawn from the market, and total program costs would be lower. Neither of these program extremes has serious neighborhood stabilization implications in the smaller city.

The nonmetropolitan experience with both deep and shallow subsidy production programs has been more favorable than in the core city, and no serious changes are required to maintain their continued viability. It is the case, however, that these programs are being phased out in favor of a new federal program of leased housing assistance. Enacted into law as Section 8 of the Housing and Community Development Act of 1974, the program has both existing housing and new construction components. Under the former, private owners of standard or rehabilitated housing who will rent to income eligible families can receive federal housing assistance payments equal to the difference between fair market dwelling rents and tenant rent payments that are based on either 15 or 25 percent of adjusted income.[6]

Although private landlords in our study cities evidenced little support for federal housing programs in general, Section 8 may eventually obtain a reasonable level of investor support. For one thing, the program assures landlords a greater stability of rental income than they currently enjoy, since they may enter into a five year housing assistance agreement with the administering agency. If vacancies occur during the lease period and good faith efforts are made by the owner to attract eligible tenants, the housing assistance payment contract calls for the government to pay 80 percent of the market rent for the first 60 days the dwelling is unoccupied. More importantly, even though the average rent for standard housing across our universe is $81, the average federally approved fair market rent for existing housing under the program is $123.[7] Although the fair market rent includes utilities while our rent estimate does not, and despite the fact that our survey data are for 1972 costs while the approved fair market rents ostensibly reflect 1975 prices, the average nonmetropolitan landlord would substantially enhance his cash flow position by participating in the program. This is particularly the case for owners of rehabilitatable houses which tend to be larger than average and currently rent at below market rates. Indeed, since our estimates of rehab feasibility were based upon potential increments to rental income that would be generated by bringing the rents of renovated dwellings up to market levels, a larger proportion of the substandard stock than we estimated would be salvageable under the higher rent structure of the new leased housing assistance program. This would probably be true despite the fact that regulations provide for the first-year tenant sharing of subsidy savings resulting from their obtaining standard dwellings at less than federally approved fair market rents.

Despite the fact that private owners of standard housing would receive subsidy payments directly from the government rather than from the tenant, the Section 8 existing housing program closely resembles a program of housing allowances. Just as under a HAP, families are certified as eligible to participate in Section 8 and are required to shop around for housing that meets the program's quality and rent standards. Under federal guidelines, the local housing authority certifies household eligibility, while actual program scale is a function of fund reservations funneled to the LHA. Thus, the period over which the program is phased in is also a function of aggregate federal appropriations and local allocations. However, should the program ever grow to the scale envisioned for a full-scale HAP, we would anticipate the same problems we discussed with respect to housing allowances. As the program gains momentum, a large portion of the eligible blacks would find it difficult to access the standard stock and would obtain no program benefits. Nothing in the regulations enhances the equity features of Section 8 over a program of direct cash assistance. Indeed, it is even possible that if fair market rent levels are as out of line with the prevailing rent structure as we believe them to be, even more serious market dislocations can accompany a large-scale Section 8 program than a HAP. The rent differential available under the program could be substantial enough to encourage landlords who do not rent to low or moderate income families to force current tenants out of their dwellings because going rents for subsidized tenants are higher than those which higher income, unsubsidized families are willing to pay.

In concept, the new construction component of Section 8 is elegant in its simplicity and overcomes some serious limitations of the conventional public housing program. Essentially, the subsidy arrangement for new Section 8 housing differs little from that governing the existing house program with the exception that for each new dwelling there will be established a federally-capitalized reserve fund, the proceeds of which can be used to cover unavoidable rental increases caused by rises in necessary operating expenses over the lease period. This reserve fund represents the federal effort to avoid both the operating subsidy problem now plaguing the public housing program and the foreclosure crisis that characterizes the moderate income programs which Section 8 is intended to replace. While local housing authorities are charged with the responsibility of administering the used house program, private developers are eligible to receive direct housing assistance payments for new developments built to Section 8 regulations. Private sector competition with public housing authorities is intended to enhance efficiency of operations in both sectors and to encourage greater variety in project design and location than is characteristic of public housing generally. Moreover, federal guidelines require more economic mixing in Section 8 projects and encourage project proposals which seek to mix subsidized and unsubsidized families in the same multifamily developments.

Project rentals are limited to fair market rents established by HUD for each market area across the country. The level of the approved rents, in conjunction with prevailing land and construction costs and going interest rates, determines project feasibility and potential investor interest in the program. Private developers of Section 8 housing are responsible for securing interim and permanent financing from nonfederal sources so that the direct federal subsidy is limited to housing assistance payments plus operating reserves established to cover cost increases. Since tenant rent payments are independent of the fair market rentals, federal cost is a direct function of fair market rents. Although the program's designers expect the federal subsidy per dwelling under Section 8 to be substantially below the cost of supporting an otherwise comparable public housing unit, this might not be the case. Based on preliminary program guidelines and subsidy formulae, Welfeld [1975:1110–1111] has concluded that, by almost any standard, Section 8 will be inordinately costly. He estimates annual dwelling subsidies would average more than $2,500 and those for modal income-eligible families would be as high as $7,000 in some market areas. In part, he attributes these high costs to HUD's overreaction to the current financial plight of subsidized housing sponsors and LHA's nationally and suggests that by taking all of the risks out of subsidized housing ownership, the federal government has unnecessarily increased program costs.

Possible high costs notwithstanding, the major problems we envision with the new construction component of Section 8 relate to the program's heavy reliance on the private sector in markets characterized either by sluggish supply conditions or discriminatory market practices. With respect to the former, we indicated previously that low demand elasticities were due, in part, to supply inadequacies at the top of the market and that prevailing rents for high quality housing are too low to support new construction at prevailing interest rates. Although approved fair market rents for Section 8 housing in nonmetropolitan cities far exceed prevailing rents for high quality multifamily housing, federal regulations require most new developments for which Section 8 subsidies are requested to be marketable to unsubsidized families at market rental rates. That is, proposed developments that are not feasible without subsidies will not be approved for Section 8 assistance. This suggests that new multifamily developments proposed under Section 8 in the smaller city must be brought in at rent levels substantially below approved fair market rates if they are to be potentially marketable in the private sector. If actual rents are below Section 8 maxima, the incentive is reduced for private participation in the program in rental markets characterized by investor indifference or apathy towards government housing programs. Coupled with the unwillingness of nonmetropolitan landlords to rent to blacks who dominate the eligibility rolls, it could be that the transition from public housing to Section 8 would materially reduce the level of deep subsidy production activity in the smaller city. Alternatively, if investor disinterest in the program enhanced the opportunity of LHA's to sponsor and develop new Section 8 housing, then our earlier analyses of supply side requirements would stand. The transition to Section 8 would have little overall effect on the shape of the nonmetropolitan housing assistance program.

NOTES TO CHAPTER 10

1. See, for example: Rainwater [1970]; Starr [1971]; de Leeuw [1970b].
2. Program operating data and development cost data for the nation were

obtained from U.S. Department of Housing and Urban Development [1973: Tables 124 and 153]. Operating data for nonmetropolitan cities are from a survey of local housing authorities in our survey cities. Nonmetropolitan construction costs are estimated from a weighted average of prototype construction costs for various dwelling unit sizes. Total development cost, including land, is estimated by dividing the prototype costs by the ratio of construction to development cost (.65) for the nation [U.S. Department of Housing and Urban Development, 1973: Table 154].

3. Amortization costs were computed on the basis of a 40-year payback period and an 8 percent interest rate. The 40-year term is consistent with the term of local housing authority bonds that are issued to finance public housing developments. The 8 percent discount rate, which is higher than the face interest rate of tax-exempt, government guaranteed authority bonds is an approximation of the real resource cost to the government of financing public housing. The accuracy of the 8 percent figure is not relevant to the analysis.

4. "Myths/Realities of Public Housing," *Journal of Housing*, no.4 (April 1973), 186.

5. Direct federal subsidy costs for the average nonmetropolitan subsidized, moderate income dwelling were estimated as follows. Average replacement cost per dwelling is $11,663. Limited profit project sponsors can obtain FHA insured mortgages equal to 90 percent of replacement cost under the Section 236 program, or in this case $10,497. Assuming a 40-year mortgage term and an 8 percent interest rate, annual debt service requirements would be $880.28. The annual payment on a 40-year 1 percent mortgage is $318.51. The direct federal interest subsidy is the difference between these debt service requirements, which amounts to $561.77 a year, or $46.81 a month.

6. Discussion of the existing housing component of Section 8 is based upon the Code of Federal Regulations of the U.S. Department of Housing and Urban Development, Title 24, Chapter VIII, Low Income Housing, Part 882, Docket No. R-75-308, 1975c. References to the new construction component of Section 8 are from Part 880, Docket No. R-75-304.

7. Fair Market Rent for nonmetropolitan cities was computed as average Fair Market Rent for a 2 bedroom nonelevator apartment in our four study cities. Source: *Federal Register*, 40, no.6, Pt. IV (January 9, 1975), 1971, 1975, 1977; 39, no.245, Pt. III (December 19, 1974), 43955.

Appendix A

Data Collection and Preparation Procedures

SAMPLING PLAN

A sample of 589 rental housing units was selected from the 25 eligible nonmetropolitan cities in North Carolina using a multistage stratified cluster sample. This approach was intended to minimize sampling error by assuring that the sample was drawn from four cities which contain the full range of housing types present in nonmetropolitan cities. At the second stage, six census enumeration districts (ED) were selected from each city, and from each a systematic random sample of rental dwellings was drawn from prepared lists. At each stage, sampling probabilities were computed to assure that the sample was self-weighting.

City Selection

The universe of eligible cities was defined by the successive application of decision rules which served to eliminate cities that, for one or more reasons, were not appropriate for the study. In all cases the census urban place definition which was employed to delineate cities excluded suburban and rural fringe areas. City-wide data were obtained from: U.S. Bureau of the Census, 1970e. Although we attempted to use rigorous, quantifiable criteria for deciding whether to exclude particular types of cities, some elements of judgment were required. Nonmetropolitan cities were defined to include all cities with populations from 10,000 to 40,000. The lower limit, which assured that each city would contain a well-developed housing market with a substantial proportion of rental units, eliminated rural-based communities whose primary function is providing supporting services to agricultural economies. At the upper bound, we eliminated all central cities of SMSA's, including all places with 50,000 or more persons and two cities which were classified as SMSA's by the census but whose populations were slightly below 50,000.

A total of eight places within the specified size ranges were ineligible. These included three military bases, two unincorporated places, one place that is in an SMSA urbanized area, and two "impacted cities." This last category was defined to include places which have been subjected to unusual economic forces that are likely to distort the housing market. One city in the group contains a large military population, the other, a large university-related population. Both have experienced unusually high growth rates and unusually high rent levels. The elimination of the city proximate to a military base was partially based on the amount of the impact funds available to the local school board under Public Law 874 using information that was provided to us by the Division of School Planning, North Carolina Department of Public Instruction.

The cities were stratified into four categories and one was selected from each with probability proportionate to size. Thirteen housing indicators available from the 1970 Census were investigated as potential stratification variables. Ultimately, a two-dimensional, four cell matrix was constructed using, as the two axes, a composite housing condition indicator and the percent of rental units in single family structures. This construct allowed us to encompass a number of features of the market within the stratification structure, and it produced a maximum difference between the intercell populations (i.e., number of rental units) of less than 20 percent. The structural condition index is a linear combination of: the percent of the units built before 1940; the percent with incomplete plumbing facilities; and the percent estimated to be dilapidated using a procedure suggested by the census [U.S. Bureau of the Census, 1972]. The rank correlation between the index and single family rental units is .342, indicating only a weak relationship between the rankings produced by the two dimensions of the matrix.

The four cities selected for inclusion in the study contained, on average, 22,500 persons and 3,200 renter households in 1970. Analysis of variance tests were performed to examine the "representativeness" of the study cities and the effectiveness of the stratification process. For none of the 10 rental housing characteristics presented in Table A–1 was the difference in the mean value between the entire universe and the study cities statistically significant, indicating that the latter encompass a representative distribution not only of the stratification variables but also of other rental housing indicators.

Table A-1.   Selected Rental Housing Characteristics for Nonmetropolitan North Carolina Cities

Indicator	Universe (N = 25)	Sampled Cities (N = 4)
Rental Occupied Units as a Percent of Total	42.4	46.1
Rental Vacancy Rate	6.3	6.5
Percent of Vacant Rental Units Vacant for Six Months or More	15.6	13.6
Percent of Rental Units in Single Family Units	63.8	61.2
Percent of Rental Units Renting for Less Than $30 per Month	6.7	5.5
Percent of Rental Units Occupied by Black Households	30.5	36.5
Percent of Rental Units Containing 1.01 or More Persons per Room	14.2	14.9
Percent of Units Built Before 1940	47.3	42.8
Percent of Units Lacking Complete Plumbing	14.1	15.2
Percent of Units Dilapidated with Full Plumbing*	1.2	1.3

Source: U.S. Bureau of the Census, 1970e.
* Estimated from percent of units lacking central heat [U.S. Bureau of the Census, 1972].

Enumeration District Selection

To assure an adequate spread of housing and household variables in the sample, enumeration districts were selected from each of two strata within each city. After examining rankings based on a number of ED characteristics [U.S. Bureau of the Census, 1970g], race was selected as the stratification variable. The high rank order correlation between race and mean rent assured an adequate representation not only of black households, but also of housing costs and quality. In order to produce approximately equal stratum populations, ED's containing 10 percent or fewer black rental households were classified as "low black," those with more than 10 percent, "high black." Any ED which contained no rental housing units and which, according to the most recent official city maps, had no publicly designated streets, was excluded; ED's containing fewer rental units than were required for the minimum cluster size were combined into a single cluster with an ED adjacent to it in the ranking. Three clusters were selected with replacement from each stratum; the selection probabilities were proportionate to size, where cluster size was defined as the number of rental units as reported by the 1970 Census, less any public housing units. Adjustments for new construction and demolitions were not made since available data were not disaggregated by neighborhood and since construction and demolition activities were not extensive during the three years following the publication of the census.

Listing the Households

Once the clusters were selected, a list of all housing units within each was compiled from city directories and utility and building inspection records in order to provide a complete count from which the rental unit sample could be drawn directly. Field checks were made to establish the boundaries of each ED in terms of street addresses and to resolve problems that arose during the listing process. Using the address guide section of each city directory, all dwellings were listed on a block by block basis, and tenure and occupancy status were recorded. On the average, the directory counted 7.3 percent fewer dwellings than did the Census and 15.9 percent fewer rental units. In the predominantly white ED's, the deviations were, respectively, 6.1 percent and 18.5 percent; although we had been cautioned that the directory would undercount by up to 40 percent in low-income areas, in only three clusters were the counts of total units as much as 20 percent lower than the Census.

The directory lists were checked and updated using building inspection files, meter books or computer lists of utility customers which the cities made available to us. The accuracy of these lists was expected to be nearly perfect in counting households. As a general rule, units not found in the utilities records were assumed to be demolished; those added were assumed to have been either omitted from the directory or constructed after its publication. In a number of instances, however, field checks were made to confirm that units not on the utilities records were actually nonexistent. Units added by the utilities were not assigned any tenure unless they were in multifamily structures, in which case they were assumed to be renter-occupied. As a rule, the utilities records did not alter the total counts substantially, although significant numbers of units were added and subtracted. The net result of the validation of the lists and the final field checks was to reduce the deviation between our count and the Census to 6 percent for all units and 11 percent for rental units.

Once the listing process was completed, two systematic random samples were drawn from each cluster. The first sampled "known" renters based on the city directory and utility information, and the second sampled units for which no tenure information was available. The latter group represented, on the average, seven percent of the total sample.

DATA COLLECTION AND PREPARATION

Four sets of primary data were collected. For each rental unit, we interviewed the occupant household and the landlord and obtained the tax appraisal card. In addition, we photographed each structure for preliminary classification purposes. Approximately 18 percent of the 731 units originally selected were found to be ineligible or nonexistent, with nearly 90 percent of the losses being owner-occupied dwellings. Of the 589 remaining units, 548 were occupied at the time of the survey, and interviews were completed with over 90 percent of the households. The sampled units were owned by 392 landlords, of whom 88 percent were interviewed.

The landlord schedule consisted of two parts: a series of questions related to the owner's background, market experience and perceptions (Part I), and a separate schedule (Part II) designed to elicit dwelling and tenant-specific information related to each unit sampled from the owner's portfolio. In many cases managers were interviewed to obtain the latter information, and a 90 percent completion rate was obtained for the Part II interviews. Tax appraisal cards were obtained in all but two cases. Both household and landlord Part II interviews were completed for 84 percent of the dwellings; neither was obtained for only two percent.

In order to minimize any potential nonrespondent bias, incomplete household interviews were replaced with a completed schedule from the same second stage cluster on the assumption that the important characteristics of a nonrespondent household are likely to be more similar to those of respondents from the same sampling cluster than they are to other respondents. For each noncompletion, the address of the unit unambiguously defined the race of the occupant. Additional information obtained from the owners, tax cards, and photographs enabled us to specify for virtually all nonrespondents the following information, in order of importance: race; type of structure occupied; sex of head; number of persons in household. Since the first two items were available for each case, they represent the minimum information specified for each replacement. The additional items were specified wherever available to generate from each ED a list of potential replacement households, from which a random selection was made. If none was available, the specified items were deleted one at a time until at least one household was generated. In this manner an unbiased replacement was obtained for each of the 52 nonrespondents.

Landlord Part II replacements were made in a similar manner by selecting a dwelling from the same ED using information contained on the tax card for each nonrespondent. The data used, in order of priority, were: units in structure; size of structure; value of structure. Landlord Part I non-completions were replaced on a city rather than an ED basis since owner portfolios often transcended ED boundaries. For every landlord, the number of units owned in the city, current residence and the form of ownership used were determined from tax records. For many, we also knew the race and sex of the owner. Random replacements were thus made using the following specification, in order of importance: current residence; form of ownership; scale of ownership; race; sex.

Since tax cards were obtained for all but two DU's, the replacement problem was minimal. Selections were made using the photographs to match exterior characteristics and using the following landlord Part II data items: number of units in structure; age of structure; rent.

We did not attempt to replace all data on a question-by-question basis, and, as a result, response rates vary to some extent among analyses which rely on various data items. A number of tests which were performed on basic information revealed that no serious biases are caused by this problem. Although complete household income information is available for only about 90 percent of the sample, the rent distribution is virtually identical between this subset and the full sample. Similarly, the distribution of important variables, such as rent, indicated no bias between the landlord and household samples.

Each rental unit had an equal probability of selection; however, the probability of selecting landlords was a function of portfolio size and, therefore, unknown and variant. From the Part I schedule or from tax records, we obtained the number of rental dwelling units each landlord owned (a_i). For the purposes of the analyses in Chapter 4, in which we generalized to all landlords, each response was weighted by ($1/a_i$). This enabled us to develop a random sample of landlords as if the probability of selection was known a priori. For dwelling-specific analyses, Part I responses were appended to the dwelling unit record and were effectively weighted by the number of dwellings sampled from an owner's portfolio. Part II responses were dwelling-specific and, therefore, self-weighting.

Certain critical pieces of data that were available from more than one source were replaced on an item basis. If rent was only available from either the owner or household file, the obtained response was utilized in lieu of the missing item. Similar adjustments were made for household size and length of tenure, for example, and structure age was taken from either the landlord Part II or the tax file, depending on its availability. In the few instances in which owners responded that rents were reduced for any reason or if there was no cash rent, the rent was adjusted to the owner's estimate of market rent or the case was eliminated. If a household reported an income that appeared unreasonably low given its rent, the case was deleted for income analyses on the assumption that either the information was wrong or the household was drawing heavily on accumulated wealth.

Some modifications to the appraisal records had to be made to produce dwelling unit-specific data. Each tax record contained one land appraisal, regardless of the number of structures on the parcel, and a separate appraisal for each building. In general, proportional allocations of the areas and tax values of both the land and the building were made. The assumption that all dwellings in a single structure are of the same size and have the same features is reasonable. In the cases of units contained in owner-occupied single family conversions, allocations were not made because of the radical differences between the owner's living area and that of the renter, and these structures are deleted from many analyses. This problem did not occur for resident landlord buildings which were originally intended for multiple-occupancy. Another small portion of the units are in structures containing commercial uses. For these, only data relevant to the rental living area were used, but again these units are not included in a number of analyses. Finally, it should be noted that the dwelling unit square footage data are for gross interior area, and not just useable living space, and, in some cases, small exterior areas such as porches are included in the figure. Neither of these problems, however, is likely to cause a serious overstatement of dwelling unit size.

Appendix B

Estimate of Permanent Income

Since the current consumption of housing is based on a relatively long-term commitment, a household will purchase an amount of housing which has a cost consonant with its expected ability to pay for that housing over a finite time horizon. Those elements of the household's income which are perceived as being transitory will not affect the amount spent on housing; thus, the larger the transitory component, the lower will be the estimate of the elasticity based on current income data. When only cross-sectional information is available, the transitory elements of income can be eliminated through an averaging process in which household incomes are replaced by the average incomes for homogeneous socioeconomic cohorts. In effect, the group mean represents the permanent income of each member of the group under the assumption that the mean transitory income approaches zero within each household cohort.

As Ramanathan [1971:170] notes, there are two sources of error in this cohort-averaging technique. First, between-group differences in expected future earnings are not reflected in the averages. For example, if cohorts are defined according to the age and education of the household head, younger and better-educated heads may have average incomes similar to older, less well-educated heads, but the expectations of the two groups about future earnings may be very different. To use the mean incomes of the cohorts, therefore, may not reflect accurately their permanent incomes. A second weakness of this technique is that "the permanent income of two households belonging to the same group may differ because of factors other than those used in forming the group" [Ramanathan, 1971:178]. The income of secondary wage earners may affect household consumption patterns differently than would an increase of the same amount in the head's earnings. Similarly, nonwage income and differences in wealth will impact on expenditure patterns.

FUTURE EARNINGS EXPECTATIONS

Ramanathan [1971] developed a methodology which attempts to overcome these weaknesses of the cohort-averaging process. We have modified his general approach and applied it to our data in an effort to remove the downward bias from our estimates of income elasticity. The procedure requires that household cohorts be defined according to characteristics relevant to income-earning potential. We defined 24 household cohorts according to the age of the head and the head's educational attainment. Although occupational status was examined as a possible dimension, we found educational groups to be far more homogeneous with respect to earnings. Future earning expectations were calculated by estimating the annual growth rate in income for each educational class. The estimates of permanent income were then obtained by deriving a weighted average of current and estimated future earnings.

More specifically, the expected earnings of household heads in the (ij)th class t years in the future can be estimated from:

$$Z_{ij}(t) = y_{ij} (1 + h_{ij})^t (1 + g_i)^t \qquad (B-1)$$

where: y_{ij} is the mean earnings of the group; h_{ij} is the annual growth rate in mean earnings between the jth and ($j+1$)th age group; and g_i is the annual growth rate of earnings for the ith education group. The growth rate in the mean earnings between adjacent age groups in the same education classes was estimated directly from our survey data by assuming all household heads are at the middle of their age class. Thus:

$$(1 + h_{ij})^{10} = y_{i,j+1}/y_{i,j} \qquad (B-2)$$

The earnings growth rate for each educational group was obtained from census data [U.S. Bureau of the Census, 1970(f), 1960] for all persons living in urban places in North Carolina over the decade 1960–70. Using these data we derived g_i from:

$$(1 + g_i)^{10} = y_{i,70}/y_{i,60} \qquad (B-3)$$

Both of these growth rates enable us to adjust for future earnings expectations which are likely to vary both with the age and education of the household head. On the one hand, h_{ij} represents the expectations of persons whose earnings potential will grow as a result of their occupational mobility, which is partially determined by their educational background. For each educational class, the average earnings potential peaks in either the 35–44 or the 45–54 age group (Table B–1). Persons with eight years or less of schooling average a maximum of $4,200 in the 35–44 age group; for persons with at least some post-high school education, the peak of $8,400 is attained in the same age class. With only minor exceptions, the mean earnings for every age class increases monotonically with the level of education.

The value of g_i, on the other hand, accounts for the possibility that the earnings of various educational classes increase at different rates as the general economy expands. The census data indicate that the major difference is for persons who have or have not finished high school. For persons with eight years or less of school, g_i equals .037, and for those with some high school, it is .035. High school graduates as a group experienced an increase in earnings of .025 per year, while for those with at least some post-high school education, the annual growth rate was .027.

Once values for h_{ij} and g_i were derived and substituted into the expression for Z_{ij}, the estimate of permanent income was obtained by taking the weighted average of the discounted stream of present and expected future earnings:

$$Y_{ij}^* = \frac{\sum_{t=0}^{9} [Z_{ij}(t)/(1 + r)^t] + \sum_{t=0}^{10} [Z_{i,j+1}(t)/(1 + r)^{t+10}]}{\sum_{t=0}^{20} (1 + r)^t} \qquad (B-4)$$

Table B–1. Estimated Permanent Income by Age and Education of Household Head*

| | Years of Schooling | | | |
Age of Head	<8	8–11	12	>12
<25	$4,225 (2,340)	$5,425 (4,275)	$5,995 (4,601)	$6,931 (4,244)
25–34	$5,318 (4,146)	$6,461 (5,172)	$7,466 (5,105)	$8,788 (5,751)
35–44	$4,791 (5,016)	$6,193 (5,534)	$7,304 (6,409)	$7,834 (8,370)
45–54	$2,799 (3,822)	$4,306 (5,467)	$5,180 (7,569)	$6,276 (7,093)
55–64	$3,982 (2,666)	$5,545 (4,111)	$6,084 (3,371)	$8,808 (7,263)
65+	$1,908 ($4,920)	$2,000 ($4,326)	(1,908) (4,920)	(2,000) (4,326)

* Figures are sum of nonwage income plus average, discounted earnings of head. Figures in parentheses are sum of nonwage income plus average current earnings of the head.

This formulation assumes a 20-year horizon over which expected earnings are estimated. The first summation in the numerator is the aggregate expected earnings of a head in the (ij)th class over the next ten years, including his current year earnings. The second summation represents his aggregate expected earnings for the second ten-year period, and it accounts for the fact that the head has moved from the jth to the ($j + 1$)th age group. The denominator is the amount of a 20-year annuity with a present value of one. From Equation (B–4), therefore, we obtain a weighted average of present and estimated future income. The discount rate, r, reflects both the time rate of preference for future earnings and the uncertainty of future income. Our estimates of permanent income employ a four percent discount rate.

For heads in the 55–64 age group only a ten-year horizon is assumed, and the second summation in the numerator, therefore, is eliminated. For heads over 65, their current earnings are assumed to be their permanent earnings, and the means for the group are used. Thus:

$$Y_{i6}^* = \bar{y}_{i6}, \qquad i = 1,4 \tag{B–5}$$

NONWAGE INCOME AND SECONDARY WAGE EARNERS

Ramanathan [1971] eliminates the effects of wealth and the number of wage earners in the household by estimating their impact on transitory income. As he notes, his technique is similar to that used to remove a trend effect in time series data. Unlike the technique for estimating the permanent earnings of the head, which assumes that all members of a given cohort have the same current earnings and future expectations, this adjustment varies from household to household. We also made adjustments based on each household's particular circumstances, although our approach is somewhat different from that of Ramanathan.

Although we have no data relating to wealth, we do have information on the sources and amounts of nonwage income. About 48 percent of the renter households receive income from at least one nonwage source; over one-third of these families have multiple nonwage income sources. Of the total number of these sources, 76 percent are payments that can be considered to be relatively invariant and, therefore, can be treated as permanent income sources. Included in this group are all forms of retirement benefits (pensions, social security, and public welfare old age benefits) and disability payments. For those who receive less permanent forms of nonwage income (unemployment insurance, gifts, public welfare payments to families with dependent children, etc.) there is no way to estimate the transitory components. Since these payments represent a relatively small portion of all nonwage income sources and since they are not very large in dollar terms, all nonwage income was assumed to be viewed as permanent income by the household. As a result, we added to our estimate of the head's permanent earnings the total nonwage income the household receives to obtain the estimated permanent income of the household. For most cohorts, nonwage income constitutes a relatively small portion of the total; for households headed by persons over 65, however, the head's earnings provide from 6 to 30 percent of the total.

The second factor that affects household income, but which is not taken into account in our estimate of permanent income, is the income of the secondary wage earners. Over 37 percent of the renter households contain multiple wage earners, and one-fifth of these families contain three or four working adults. Rather than adjust our estimates of permanent income, we treated the income of secondary wage earners as a pure transitory component, which seems reasonable—particularly for lower-income families. In the generalized demand model, secondary income is entered as an independent variable, which enables us to estimate the rate at which it is allocated to housing.

Table B–2 contains the elasticity estimates based on current income and on two estimates of permanent income. Defining the latter using the mean earnings of the head for each age-education group yields an elasticity which is more than double that obtained using current earnings. Projecting future income and using the weighted average of current and expected

Table B–2.   Comparative Estimates of Income Elasticities of Demand for Rental Housing*

		*Income Definition***	
	Current	*Cohort Average*	*Average Discounted Permanent*
Elasticity (b)	.112	.344	.370
(Std. Error b)	(.027)	(.043)	(.036)
Constant	5.660	3.707	3.432
R^2	.052	.117	.179
SEE	.437	.422	.407
C_v	.067	.064	.062
Mean Income ($\bar{Y}$)	$4,514	$4,537	$5,481
(Std. Dev. Y)	(2,833)	(1,875)	(2,336)
$N = 482$			

* Based on model: $R = aY^b$
  where R = annual contract rent
  Y = annual income
** Includes only earnings of head and nonwage income.

earnings produces an elasticity which is only about 8.5 percent greater than that obtained using the simple group average. Although the two permanent income elasticities are not statistically different, using the latter estimate gives a somewhat better prediction in terms of accuracy and explanatory power. It appears from these results that the transitory component of the earnings of household heads is substantially reduced by using the group average method of estimating permanent income and by eliminating the income of secondary wage earners. Accounting for differences in expected earnings over a relatively long but finite time frame improves on this method only marginally.

Bibliography

American Public Health Association. *An Appraisal Method for Measuring the Quality of Housing, Part I: Nature and Uses of the Method.* New York: 1945.
———. *An Appraisal Method for Measuring the Quality of Housing, Part II: Appraisal of Dwelling Conditions.* New York: 1946.
———. *Basic Principles of Healthful Housing*, 2nd ed. New York: 1939.
Bailey, Martin J. "Effects of Race and Other Demographic Factors on the Values of Single-Family Homes," *Land Economics*, 42, (1966), 215–20; reprinted in *Urban Analysis*, ed. by Alfred N. Page and Warren R. Seyfried. Glenview, Ill.: Scott, Foresman, 1970; 320–25.
———. "Note on the Economics of Residential Zoning and Urban Renewal," *Land Economics*, 35 (1959), 288–92; reprinted in *Urban Analysis*, ed. by Alfred N. Page and Warren R. Seyfried. Glenview, Ill.: Scott, Foresman, 1970; 316–20.
Baldwin's Kinston, N.C. City Directory. Charleston, S.C.: Baldwin Directory Company, 1936.
Baldwin's Lexington, N.C. City Directory. Charleston, S.C.: Baldwin Directory Company, 1937.
Becker, Gary S. *The Economics of Discrimination*, 2nd ed. Chicago: University of Chicago Press, 1971.
Berry, Brian J.L., and Bednarz, Robert S. "A Hedonic Model of Prices and Assessments for Single-Family Homes: Does the Assessor Follow the Market or the Market Follow the Assessor?" *Land Economics*, 51 (February, 1975), 21–40.
Blalock, Hubert M., Jr. *Social Statistics*. New York: McGraw-Hill, 1960.
Blank, David M. and Winnick, Louis. "The Structure of the Housing Market," *Quarterly Journal of Economics*, 67 (1953), 181–208.
Bonham, Gordon Scott. "Discrimination and Housing Quality," *Growth and Change*, 3 (1972), 26–34.

Carliner, Geoffrey. "Income Elasticity of Housing Demand," *Review of Economics and Statistics*, 55 (1973), 528–32.

Carlton, Dennis W., and Ferreira, Joseph, Jr. *The Market Effects of Housing Allowance Payment Formulas*. Cambridge: Joint Center for Urban Studies of MIT and Harvard, Working Paper No. 32, 1975.

Cole, Layer, Trumble Co. *Field Appraiser's Manual for Use in Davidson County, North Carolina*, 1972.

de Leeuw, Frank. "The Demand for Housing: A Review of Cross-Section Evidence," *Review of Economics and Statistics*, 53 (1971), 1–10.

———. "Discussion of: A Hedonic Approach to Rent Determination," *Proceedings*, American Statistical Association, Business and Economic Statistics Section (1970a), 193–4.

———. *Operating Costs and Public Housing*. Washington, D.C.: The Urban Institute, 1970b.

de Leeuw, Frank; Marshall, Sue; Ozanne, Larry; Schnare, Ann; Struik, Andrew; and Struyk, Raymond. *The Market Effects of Housing Policies*. Washington, D.C.: The Urban Institute, 1974.

de Leeuw, Frank; Leaman, Sam H.; and Blank, Helen. *The Design of a Housing Allowance*. Washington, D.C.: The Urban Institute, 1970.

Donnison, David V. "The Housing Problem," in *The Right to Housing*, ed. by Michael Wheeler. Montreal: Harvest House, 1969.

Downs, Anthony. "The Successes and Failures of Federal Housing Policy," *The Public Interest*, 34 (Winter, 1974), 124–45.

Eisenlauer, Jack F. "Mass Versus Individual Appraisals," *The Appraisal Journal*, 36 (October, 1968), 532–40.

Eisenstadt, Karen M. *Factors Affecting Maintenance and Operating Costs in Private Rental Housing*. New York: The New York City Rand Institute, R-1055-NYC, 1972.

Emerson, Frank C. "Valuation of Residential Amenities: An Econometric Approach," *The Appraisal Journal*, 40 (April, 1972), 268–78.

Farrar, Donald E. and Glauber, Robert R. "Multicollinearity in Regression Analysis: The Problem Revisited," *Review of Economics and Statistics*, 49 (1967), 92–107.

Federal Register, 40, no.6, Pt. IV, January 9, 1975.

Federal Register, 39, no.245, Pt. III, December 19, 1974.

Foley, Donald L. "Institutional and Contextual Factors Affecting the Housing Choices of Minority Residents," in *Segregation in Residential Areas*, ed. by Amos H. Hawley and Vincent P. Rock. Washington, D.C.: National Academy of Sciences, 1973, 85–147.

Frieden, Bernard J., and Atkinson, Reilly. *Forecasting the Nation's Housing Needs: Assessing the Joint Center's First Efforts*. Working Paper No.30. Cambridge: Joint Center for Urban Studies, 1975.

Fuguitt, Glenn V. "Population Trends of Nonmetropolitan Cities and Villages," in *Population Distribution and Policy*, The Commission on Population Growth and the American Future, Vol. V, ed. by Sara Mills Mazie. Washington, D.C.: USGPO, 1972.

Gillingham, Robert, and Lund, David C. "A Hedonic Approach to Rent

Determination," *Proceedings*, American Statistical Association, Business and Economic Statistics Section (1970), 184–92.

Grebler, Leo; Blank, David M.; and Winnick, Louis. *Capital Formation in Residential Real Estate*. Princeton, N.J.: Princeton University Press, 1956.

Grigsby, William G. *Housing Markets and Public Policy*. Philadelphia: University of Pennsylvania Press, 1963.

Grigsby, William G. and Rosenburg, Louis. *Urban Housing Policy*. New York: APS Publications, 1975.

Hartman, Chester W. *Housing and Social Policy*. Englewood Cliffs, N.J.: Prentice-Hall, Inc., 1975.

Harvey, David. *Social Justice and the City*. Baltimore: The Johns Hopkins Press, 1973.

Haugen, Robert A. and Heins, A. James. "A Market Separation Theory of Rent Differentials in Metropolitan Areas," *Quarterly Journal of Economics*, 83 (1969), 660–72.

Heinberg, John D. *The Transfer Cost of a Housing Allowance: Conceptual Issues and Benefit Patterns*. Washington, D.C.: The Urban Institute, 1971.

Henderson, James M., and Quandt, Richard E. *Microeconomic Theory: A Mathematical Approach*. New York: McGraw-Hill, 1958.

Hill's Kinston, N.C. City Directory. Richmond, Va.: Hill Directory Company, 1928, 1951.

Housing Affairs Letter. Washington, D.C.: Community Development Services, Inc., April 18, 1975a.

————. April 4, 1975b.

————. March 7, 1975c.

————. February 28, 1975d.

————. February 7, 1975e.

————. January 31, 1975f.

————. January 17, 1975g.

————. January 3, 1975h.

————. October 11, 1975a.

————. September 27, 1974b.

————. September 20, 1974c.

Housing and Community Development Act of 1974, P.L. 93-383.

Housing and Development Reporter, "Section 8 Leased Housing Assistance Payments Program" (24 March 1975), 30:0055-0070.

Housing and Development Reporter. Washington, D.C.: Bureau of National Affairs, 2, no.5 (July 29, 1974), 193.

Housing and Urban Development Act of 1969, P.L. 91-152.

Housing and Urban Development Act of 1968, P.L. 90-448.

Hu, Tei-Weh. *Econometrics: An Introductory Analysis*. Baltimore: University Park Press, 1973.

Ingram, Gregory K.; Kain, John F.; and Ginn, J. Royce. *The Detroit Prototype of the NBER Urban Simulation Model*. New York: National Bureau of Economic Research, 1972.

Johnston, J. *Econometric Methods*. New York: McGraw-Hill, Inc., 1963.

Kain, John F. "Effect of Housing Market Segregation on Urban Develop-

ment," *Savings and Residential Financing: 1969 Conference Proceedings.*
Chicago: United States Savings and Loan Association, 1969; reprinted in *Housing Urban America*, ed. by Jon Pynoos, Robert Schafer, and Chester W. Hartman. Chicago: Aldine, 1973, 251–66.

Kain, John F., and Quigley, John M. "Note on Owner's Estimate of Housing Value," *Journal of the American Statistical Association*, 67 (1972), 803–6.

———. "Measuring the Value of Housing Quality," *Journal of the American Statistical Association*, 65 (June, 1970), 532–48.

King, A. Thomas. *Property Taxes, Amenities, and Residential Land Values.* Cambridge: Ballinger, 1973.

King, A. Thomas, and Mieszcowski, Peter. "Racial Discrimination, Segregation, and the Price of Housing," *Journal of Political Economy*, 81 (1973), 590–606.

Kish, Leslie, and Lansing, John B. "Response Errors in Estimating the Value of Homes," *Journal of the American Statistical Association*, 49 (1954) 520–32.

Kornai, Janos. *Anti-Equilibrium.* Amsterdam: North Holland Publishing Company, 1971.

Krohn, Roger G. and Fleming, E. Berkeley. *The Other Economy and the Urban Housing Problem: A Study of Older Residential Neighborhoods in Montreal.* Cambridge: Joint Center for Urban Studies, Working Paper No. 11, 1972.

Krohn, Roger G., and Tiller, Ralph. "Landlord Tenant Relations in a Declining Montreal Neighborhood," in *The Sociological Review Monograph*, #14, ed. by Paul Halmos. Great Britain: University of Keele, 1969.

Lancaster, Kelvin J. "A New Approach to Consumer Theory," *Journal of Political Economics*, 74 (1966), 132–57.

Lapham, Victoria. "Do Blacks Pay More For Housing?" *Journal of Political Economics*, 79 (1971), 1244–57.

Lee, T.H. "Housing and Permanent Income: Test Based on a Three-Year Re-interview Survey," *Review of Economics and Statistics*, 50 (1968), 480–90.

Lowry, Ira S. *Housing Assistance for Low-Income Urban Families: A Fresh Approach.* New York: NYC RAND Institute, May, 1971.

Maisel, Sherman J., and Winnick, Louis. "Family Housing Expenditures: Elusive Laws and Intrusive Variances," *Proceedings*, the Conference on Consumption and Savings, University of Pennsylvania, Vol. 1, 1960; reprinted in *Urban Housing*, ed. by William L.C. Wheaton *et al.* New York: The Free Press, 1966, 139–53.

Mayer, Robert; Moroney, Robert; and Morris, Robert. *Centrally Planned Change: A Reexamination of Theory and Experience.* Urbana: University of Illinois Press, 1974.

Mercer, Norman A. "Discrimination in Rental Housing: A Study of Resistance of Landlords to Non-White Tenants," *Phylon*, 23 (1962), 47–54.

Message from the President of the United States Recommending Improvements in Federal Housing Policy, 93rd Cong., 1st Sess. Washington, D.C.: USGPO, Doc. No. 93–152, Sept. 19, 1973.

Mollenkopf, John, and Pynoos, Jon. "Boardwalk and Park Place: Property

Ownership, Political Structure and Housing Policy at the Local Level," in *Housing Urban America*, ed. by Jon Pynoos, Robert Schafer and Chester W. Hartman. Chicago: Aldine, 1973, 55–74.

Morris, Earl W.; Woods, Margaret E.; and Jacobson, Alvin L. "The Measurement of Housing Quality," *Journal of Land Economics*, 48 (Nov., 1972), 383–7.

Morrison, Peter A. "Population Distribution Trends and Projections," in *Population Distribution and Policy*, The Commission on Population Growth and the American Future, Vol. V, ed. by Sara Mills Mazie. Washington, D.C.: USGPO, 1972.

Muth, Richard F. *Cities and Housing*. Chicago: University of Chicago Press, 1969.

———. "The Spatial Structure of the Housing Market," *Papers of the Regional Science Association*, 7 (1961); reprinted in *Urban Analysis*, ed. by Alfred N. Page and Warren R. Seyfried. Glenview, Ill.: Scott, Foresman and Co., 1970, 197–206.

———. "The Demand for Non-Farm Housing," in *The Demand for Durable Goods*, ed. by Arnold C. Harberger. Chicago: The University of Chicago Press, 1960; reprinted in *Urban Analysis*, ed. by Alfred N. Page and Warren R. Seyfried. Glenview, Ill.: Scott, Foresman and Co., 1970, 146–55.

"Myths/Realities of Public Housing," *Journal of Housing*, no.4 (April, 1973), 179–191.

Nevitt, Adela Adam. "Some Economic and Social Aspects of Twilight Area Housing," in *The Sociological Review Monograph*, #14. Great Britain: University of Keele, 1969.

Nourse, Hugh O. *The Effect of Public Policy on Housing Markets*. Lexington: Heath, Lexington Books, 1973.

Olsen, Edgar O. "A Competitive Theory of the Housing Market," *American Economic Review*, 59 (1969), 612–21.

Pascal, Anthony H. *The Economics of Housing Segregation*. Santa Monica: The RAND Corp.; March, 1965.

Rainwater, Lee. *Behind Ghetto Walls*. Chicago: Aldine, 1970.

Ramanathan, R. "Measuring the Permanent Income of a Household: An Experiment in Methodology," *Journal of Political Economy*, 79 (1971), 177–85.

Rapkin, Chester. "Price Discrimination Against Negroes in the Rental Housing Market," in *Essays in Urban Land Economics*. Los Angeles: Real Estate Research Program, University of California, 1966.

———. *The Real Estate Market in an Urban Renewal Area*. New York: The New York City Planning Commission, 1959.

Ratcliff, Richard. *Current Practices in Income Property Appraisal: A Critique*. Berkeley: University of California, Center for Real Estate and Urban Economics, 1967.

Reid, Margaret G. *Housing and Income*. Chicago: University of Chicago Press, 1962.

Ridker, Ronald G., and Henning, John A. "The Determinants of Residential Property Values with Special Reference to Air Pollution," *Review of Economics and Statistics*, 49 (1967), 246–57.

Rosen, Sherwin. "Hedonic Prices and Implicit Markets: Product Differentiation in Pure Competition," *Journal of Political Economics*, 82 (1974), 34–55.

Rothenberg, Jerome. *Economic Evaluation of Urban Renewal.* Washington, D.C.: The Brookings Institute, 1967.

Sanborn Map Company. *Insurance Maps of Greenville, N.C.* New York: Sanborn Map Co., 1929.

————. *Insurance Maps of Kinston, N.C.* New York: Sanborn Map Co., 1930.

————. *Insurance Maps of Lexington, N.C.* New York: Sanborn Map Co., 1929.

————. *Insurance Maps of Statesville, N.C.* New York: Sanborn Map Co., 1930.

Schnore, Leo F. and Evenson, Phillip C. "Segregation in Southern Cities," *American Journal of Sociology*, 72 (1966), 58–67.

"Sixth Annual Report on the National Housing Goal," House Document No. 94-18, 94th Cong., 1st Sess. Washington, D.C.: USGPO, January 14, 1975.

Smolensky, Eugene. "Public Housing or Income Supplements: The Economics of Housing for the Poor," *Journal of the American Institute of Planners*, 34 (1968), 94–101; reprinted in *Housing and Economics*, ed. by Michael A. Stegman. Cambridge: The MIT Press, 1970, 252–72.

Solomon, Arthur P. *Housing the Urban Poor.* Cambridge: MIT Press, 1974.

Solomon, Arthur P., and Fenton, Chester G. "The Nation's First Experience with Housing Allowances: The Kansas City Demonstration," *Land Economics*, 50 (1974), 213–23.

Southern Building Code Congress. *Southern Standard Housing Code.* Birmingham, Ala.: 1969.

Southern Directory Company. *Miller's Greenville, N.C. City Directory.* Asheville: Southern Directory Company, 1926–27, 1936–37, 1947–48, 1956–57.

————. *Miller's Lexington, N.C. City Directory.* Asheville: Southern Directory Company, 1925–26, 1947–48, 1955–56.

————. *Miller's Statesville, N.C. City Directory.* Asheville: Southern Directory Company, 1925–26, 1938–39, 1948–49, 1958–59.

Starr, Roger. "Which of the Poor Shall Live in Public Housing?" *Public Interest* (Spring, 1974), 116–24.

Stegman, Michael A. "Housing Finance Agencies: Are They Crucial Instruments of State Government?" *Journal of the American Institute of Planners* (September, 1974), 307–20.

————. *Housing Investment in the Inner City: The Dynamics of Decline.* Cambridge, MIT Press, 1972.

Stegman, Michael A., and Sumka, Howard J. "The Economics of Landlord/Tenant Reform in Smaller Cities," *Popular Government*, 40 (Winter, 1975), 1–14.

Sternlieb, George. "Slum Housing: The Economics of Reality," *Proceedings*, the American Real Estate and Urban Economics Association, 4 (1969), 103–12.

————. *The Tenement Landlord.* New Brunswick: Rutgers University Press, 1966.

————. *The Urban Housing Dilemma: The Dynamics of New York City's Rent Controlled Housing.* New York: Department of Rent and Housing Maintenance, Housing and Development Administration, 1970.

Sternlieb, George, and Burchell, Robert W. *Residential Abandonment: The*

Tenement Landlord Revisited. New Brunswick: Center for Urban Policy Research, Rutgers, 1973.

Sternlieb, George, and Indik, Bernard P. *The Ecology of Welfare: Housing and the Welfare Crisis in New York City.* New Brunswick: Transaction Books, 1973.

Straszheim, Mahlon R. "Hedonic Estimation of Housing Market Prices: A Further Comment," *Review of Economics and Statistics,* 56 (1974), 404–6.

Sumka, Howard J. "Racial Discrimination in Urban Rental Housing." Unpublished Ph.D. dissertation, University of North Carolina at Chapel Hill, 1976.

Sumka, Howard J., and Stegman, Michael A. *The Housing Outlook in North Carolina: Projections to 1980,* State Planning Report 146.04. Raleigh, N.C.: Dept. of Administration, Office of State Planning, 1972.

Taeuber, Karl E., and Taeuber, Alma F. *Negroes in Cities.* Chicago: Aldine, 1965.

Taggert, Robert III. *Low Income Housing: A Critique of Federal Aid.* Baltimore: Johns Hopkins Press, 1970.

Thompson, Robert A.; Lewis, Hylan; and McEntire, Davis. "Atlanta and Birmingham: A Comparative Study in Negro Housing," in *Studies in Housing and Minority Groups,* ed. by Nathan Glazer and Davis McEntire. Berkeley: University of California Press, 1960, 13–83.

Triplett, Jack E. *The Theory of Hedonic Quality Measurement and Its Use in Price Indexes,* BLS Staff Paper 6. Washington, D.C.: USGPO, 1971.

Turvey, Ralph. *Economics of Real Property.* London: George Allen and Unwin, 1957.

U.S. Bureau of the Census. Census of Housing: 1970a. *Detailed Housing Characteristics.* Final Report HC(1)-B1. United States Summary.

———. Census of Housing: 1970b. *General Housing Characteristics.* Final Report HC(1)-A1. United States Summary.

———. Census of Population: 1970c. *General Social and Economic Characteristics.* Final Report PC(1)-C1. United States Summary.

———. Census of Population: 1970d. *General Population Characteristics.* Final Report PC(1)-B1. United States Summary.

———. *Census of Housing and Population:* 1970e. Fourth Count Summary Tapes, North Carolina.

———. *Census of Housing and Population:* 1970f. First Count Summary Tapes, North Carolina.

———. Census of Population: 1960a. *Characteristics of the Population.* United States Summary, Vol. I, Pt. 1.

———. Census of the Population: 1960b. *Characteristics of the Population.* North Carolina, Vol. I, Pt. 35.

———. Census of Housing: 1960c. *General Housing Characteristics.* North Carolina, Vol. I, Pt. 35.

———. *Measuring the Quality of Housing: An Appraisal of Census Statistics and Methods,* Working Paper No. 25. Washington, D.C.: 1967.

———. *Proposed Procedure for Estimating Substandard Housing in 1970.* Washington, D.C.: February, 1972.

U.S. Department of Commerce, Bureau of Economic Analysis. *Survey of Current Business,* 54, no.12 (Dec. 1974).

U.S. Department of Health, Education, and Welfare. *APHA-PHS Recom-*

mended Housing Maintenance and Occupancy Ordinance. Washington, D.C.: Public Health Service Publication No.1935, 1969.

U.S. Department of Housing and Urban Development, Office of Policy Development and Research. *Experimental Housing Allowance Program: Interim Report.* Washington, D.C.: USGPO, April, 1975a.

————. *Section 8 Housing Assistance Payments Program Existing Housing Processing Handbook.* Washington, D.C.: Transmittal No. 7420.3, April, 1975b.

————. *Code of Federal Regulations*, Title 24, Ch. VIII, "Low Income Housing," Pt.882, Docket No. R-75-308; Pt.880, Docket No. R-75-304, 1975c.

————. *Housing in the Seventies.* Washington, D.C.: USGPO, 1974a.

————. *1973 HUD Statistical Yearbook.* Washington, D.C.: USGPO, 1974b.

————. *1972 HUD Statistical Yearbook.* Washington, D.C.: USGPO, 1973.

————. "Family Income Limits for FHA Sections 235 and 236 Housing [North Carolina]," Washington, D.C.: HUD, HPMC-FHA, April 1, 1971.

U.S. Senate. *An Analysis of the Section 235 and 236 Programs*, prepared by Henry B. Schechter for the Congressional Research Service, Library of Congress, for the Subcommittee on Housing and Urban Affairs of the Committee on Banking, Housing and Urban Affairs (May 24, 1973).

Vaughn, Ted R. "Landlord-Tenant Relations in a Low-Income Area," in *Tenants and the Urban Housing Crisis*, ed. by Stephen Burghardt. Dexter, Michigan: The New Press, 1972.

Weaver, Robert C. "Housing Allowances," *Land Economics*, 51, no.3 (August, 1975), 247–57.

————. "Housing and Associated Problems of Minorities," in *Modernizing Urban Land Policy*, ed. by Marion Clawson. Baltimore: Johns Hopkins Press, 1972.

Weicher, John C., and Simonson, John C. "Recent Trends in Housing Costs," *Journal of Economics and Business*, 27 (Winter, 1975), 177–85.

Welfeld, Irving H. *America's Housing Problem: An Approach to Its Solution.* Washington, D.C.: American Enterprise Institute for Public Policy Research, 1973.

————. "The Section 8 Leasing Program: A New Program in an Old Rut," *Housing and Development Reporter*, 2, no.22 (24 March 1975), 1106–11.

Wendt, Paul F., and Cerf, Alan R. *Real Estate Investment Analysis and Taxation.* New York: McGraw-Hill, 1969.

Wihry, David. "Price Discrimination in Metropolitan Housing Markets," *Proceedings*, the American Real Estate and Urban Economics Association, 4 (1969), 69–101.

Winnick, Louis. "Long Term Changes in Evaluation of Residential Real Estate by Gross Rent," *The Appraisal Journal* (October, 1952).

Index

About the Authors

Michael A. Stegman is a professor in the Department of City and Regional Planning, University of North Carolina at Chapel Hill. He has overall responsibility for the Department's housing curriculum and teaches courses in housing market operations, public policy and real estate investment analysis. His recent research activities have focused on lower income housing market dynamics, with the analysis contained in the present book having been supported by a grant from the RANN Division of the National Science Foundation. Professor Stegman has written extensively on a wide range of housing issues and is the author of *Housing Investment in the Inner City: The Dynamics of Decline*.

Howard J. Sumka is an assistant professor in the Graduate Program in Urban Planning and a research associate at the Institute for Social and Environmental Studies at the University of Kansas. He was formerly a research associate at the Center for Urban and Regional Studies at the University of North Carolina and was Deputy Project Director of the NSF study upon which this book is based. He received his Ph.D. in Urban and Regional Planning from the University of North Carolina and holds degrees from Stevens Institute of Technology and Northwestern University. In addition to a number of articles in professional journals, he is coauthor of a series of reports on state housing policy which were prepared for the North Carolina Department of Administration.